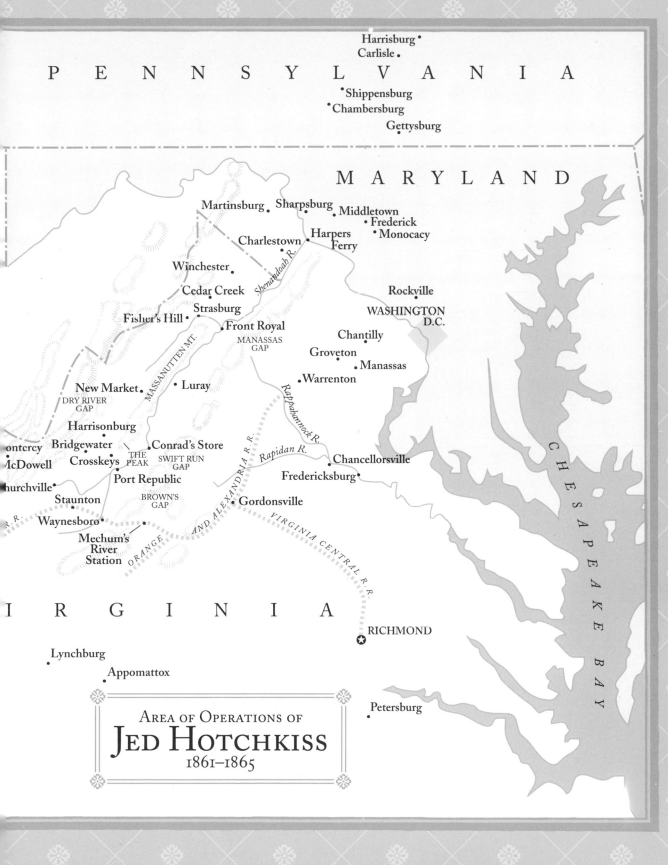

PENNSYLVANIA

Harrisburg
Carlisle

Shippensburg
Chambersburg
Gettysburg

MARYLAND

Martinsburg · Sharpsburg · Middletown
· Frederick
Charlestown · Harpers · Monocacy
Ferry

Winchester

Cedar Creek
Strasburg
Fisher's Hill · Front Royal
MANASSAS
GAP

Rockville

WASHINGTON
D.C.

Chantilly

Groveton
Manassas

New Market · Luray
DRY RIVER
GAP

Warrenton

Harrisonburg

ontcrcy · Bridgewater · Conrad's Store
THE · SWIFT RUN
McDowell · Crosskeys · PEAK · GAP
hurchville · Port Republic

Chancellorsville

Fredericksburg

Staunton · BROWN'S · Gordonsville
GAP

Waynesboro

Mechum's
River
Station

VIRGINIA

RICHMOND

Lynchburg

Appomattox

Petersburg

CHESAPEAKE BAY

MASSANUTTEN MT.

Shenandoah R.

Rappahannock R.

Rapidan R.

ORANGE AND ALEXANDRIA R.R.

VIRGINIA CENTRAL R.R.

AREA OF OPERATIONS OF
JED HOTCHKISS
1861–1865

Mapping for Stonewall

The Civil War Service
of Jed Hotchkiss

For Susan

"A kind heart is a fountain of gladness,

making everything in its vicinity to freshen into smiles"

—Washington Irving

Designed by Gibson Parsons Design
Edited by Owen Andrews

Photography credits: page 10: Mary Baldwin College Archives; page 13: Library of Congress (LC), Hotchkiss Collection, Box #1; page 15: LC, Hotchkiss Collection, Box #1; page 17: Mary Baldwin College Archives; page 20: Mary Baldwin College Archives; page 22: Virginia State Library & Archives; page 25: LC H71; page 28: LC BK.1/cover; page 32: LC BK.1/#42; page 38–39: LC G3880 1859 B6 no.5; page 44: LC B8151–10163; page 47: Virginia State Library & Archives; page 50–51: Massachusetts Commandery/ Military Order of the Loyal Legion and the U.S. Army Military History Institute; page 56: LC B8184–10117; page 61: LC BK.1/#96; page 65: LC H89; page 70: LC BK.1/#26; page 76: LC USZ62–8240; page 80: LC BK.5/#32–33; page 84–85: United States Military Academy, West Point; page 86–87: LC BK. 8/#12; page 88: LC B8184–7964; page 90: LC B8184–10528; page 95: LC H129; page 96–97: Massachusetts Commandery/ Military Order of the Loyal Legion and the U.S. Army Military History Institute; page 102: Virginia State Library & Archives; page 104: LC H31; page 108: U.S. Military History Institute; page 114: Katherine Wetzel, Eleanor S. Brockenbrough Library, The Museum of the Confederacy, Richmond, Virginia; page 116–117: LC BK.1/#72; page 120: LC B813–6585; page 122: LC B8184–10551; page 127: LC H159; page 128: LC, The Papers of Jedediah Hotchkiss, Container 7, Family Correspondence folder; page 134–135: LC BK.8/#2A; page 136–137: LC BK.8/#4; page 138: LC B8184–6408; page 141: LC BK.8/#15/755; page 143: Valentine Museum, Richmond, Virgina; page 144: Valentine Museum, Richmond, Virginia; page 147: Massachusetts Commandery/ Military Order of the Loyal Legion and the U.S. Army Military History Institute; page 148: LC H195; page 150: Valentine Museum, Richmond, Virginia; page 157: OR map plate 82/#9; page 160: Civil War Times Illustrated.

Library of Congress Cataloging-in-Publication Data
Miller, William J., 1959–
        Mapping for Stonewall : the Civil War service of Jed Hotchkiss /
    William J. Miller.
            p.   cm.
        Includes bibliographical references and index.
        ISBN 1-880216-11-6 (hardcover)
        1. Hotchkiss, Jedediah, 1828–1899. 2. Cartographers—United
    States—Biography. 3. United States—History—Civil War, 1861–1865—
    Cartography. I. Title.
    GA407.H67M55 1993
    526'.092—dc20
    [B]   93-18611
                                                               CIP

Mapping for Stonewall

THE CIVIL WAR SERVICE OF JED HOTCHKISS

By William J. Miller

Elliott & Clark Publishing
Washington, D.C.

ACKNOWLEDGMENTS

I am grateful to many people for their interest in and cooperation on this book. Mr. Ben Ritter of the Handley Library in Winchester, Virginia, is an invaluable resource for anyone researching the Civil War in the Shenandoah Valley, and he was helpful in directing me to people and books that could answer my questions; Mr. Robert Lee Haddon of the U. S. Geological Society library in Reston, Virginia, patiently searched the catalogues of his institution's holdings and led me to several extremely valuable volumes.

I am indebted to Mr. Robert K. Krick who generously shared of his limited time and expansive knowledge to help me understand Hotchkiss's role at the Battle of Chancellorsville. He also provided a detailed and well-reasoned identification of the photograph on page 108. Mr. Edwin C. Bearss offered many suggestions on and corrections to the manuscript, and he has my gratitude. Among those who took time to respond to my questions are Dr. James I. Robertson, Jr., of Virginia Polytechnic Institute; Richard W. Stephenson, former head of the Geography and Map Division of the Library of Congress; Ronald Grim, Head, Reference and Bibliography Section, Geography and Map Division of the Library of Congress; and Harry Katz, Curator of Popular and Applied Graphic Arts, Prints and Photographs Division of the Library of Congress. Especially generous of his time was Mr. Sam Liggett, Jr., of Jed Hotchkiss's hometown of Churchville, Virginia. I visited Churchville in March 1992 in search of information about Hotchkiss and Loch Willow Academy. After seeking help of several residents, I was directed to Mr. Liggett's farmhouse. Though I arrived unexpected, unannounced, and unknown to him, he immediately invited me into his home and listened to my questions. He then took me in his car to the site of Loch Willow Academy, to Loch Willow Presbyterian Church, and to the site of Hotchkiss's Sunday school. I saw in his cordial manner and his sincere desire to help a stranger something of the same honesty and forthrightness of character I had seen in Hotchkiss's letters. Somehow Mr. Liggett helped me understand Hotchkiss and the people of the Valley better.

Ms. Mary Ann Harrell made many astute comments on the manuscript, and the book is better for her attentions. I am grateful to Dr. Kevin C. Ruffner, of Washington, D.C., for his encouragement and his comments on the manuscript. The Reverend Dr. Charles K. Norville of Edinburg, Virginia, answered questions about Hotchkiss's faith and helped me identify and locate an old hymn admired by Hotchkiss. He and his son Charles R. Norville of Alexandria, Virginia, read the manuscript and offered many valuable suggestions. Both of these gentlemen not only showed great interest in this project, but gave me their companionship on a long, arduous, and wet climb in Hotchkiss's footsteps to the top of Massanutten Mountain above Strasburg, Virginia. I am grateful to them.

I am thankful as well for the hard work of Mr. Owen Andrews of Carlisle, Massachusetts, whose skills as an editor made this a better book than it was a manuscript. Mr. Jim Gibson of Charlottesville, Virginia, lent his experienced eye for design to the process of selecting the maps reproduced herein, and then executed the handsome layout and design of the book. Ms. Marilyn Fennell of Bluegrass Data Services in Nokesville, Virginia, quickly and accurately typed portions of the manuscript. I thank Doug Elliott and Carolyn Clark for giving me the chance to do this book in the first place. I am especially grateful to Carolyn for her patience and friendly support as deadlines came and went and still I failed to deliver the manuscript. Her forbearance made this a better book. Finally, and as always, I thank my parents, who are a part of everything I do.

Table of Contents

Preface   7

Chapter One: "Live for Some Purpose"   10

Chapter Two: Seventy-Nine Days at War   22

Chapter Three: "And Ye Shall Chase Your Enemies"   44

Chapter Four: Campaigning with Lee   76

Chapter Five: "This Winter of Our Sorrow"   90

Chapter Six: "Death Will Hold High Carnival"   108

Chapter Seven: "Judge Not the Lord By Feeble Sense"   120

Chapter Eight: "All Things Work Together for Good"   138

Epilogue: "Glorying in Even Sad Memories"   155

Endnotes   163

Bibliographic Essay   169

Index   173

PREFACE

For more than three years during the American Civil War, Jedediah Hotchkiss served as topographical engineer to some of the great leaders of the Confederacy. He worked closely with Thomas J. "Stonewall" Jackson, Robert E. Lee, Richard Ewell, Jubal Early, John B. Gordon, and others. His job as topographer was to learn as much as possible about the terrain in the army's area of operations and transmit that knowledge to his generals. In a war in which maps were scarce and commanders often moved blindly, an effective topographer like Hotchkiss was an indispensable asset to his generals. He was a candle in their darkness.

Hotchkiss had little to assist him in his task. With few maps as guides, he had to ride over the country personally, conducting his own surveys and sketching maps from horseback. He measured distances himself, checked the height of hills, followed streams and cow paths to their sources, evaluated fords, estimated the load capacities of roads and bridges, recorded the name of the resident of every house he passed, and noted sources of wood and water. Later, he turned those sketches and notes into maps and presented them with his report to his general.

This book began in the minds of its publishers when they saw several of the many Hotchkiss maps now in the Library of Congress. They envisioned a book that would at last bring these beautiful maps before the public. I undertook the research and writing of the text intending to investigate Hotchkiss's professional abilities and define his contribution to the Confederacy as a topographer and map maker. The text was to merely provide a context in which to appreciate the maps. Soon after I began research in the Hotchkiss papers at the Library of Congress, I realized this book would be a much larger undertaking than we had expected.

I have learned that Jed Hotchkiss was not merely an intelligent and energetic engineer with artistic abilities, and I was surprised to realize that his service with Stonewall Jackson and the other luminaries in the Confederate gallery was not even the most interesting part of his story. It became clear as I worked through the huge collection of his papers—more than 20,000 items occupying thirty-two feet of shelf space—that I had a rare opportunity to get to know a man who had lived through some of the more interesting and exciting times in our history. I could read his journals, kept through most of his life beginning at age sixteen. I could study hundreds of his letters, including scores written to his wife that included his most personal thoughts and concerns. And I could come to see him through the eyes of his friends, who wrote long, affectionate letters full of camaraderie and esteem. Rarely does an historian or biographer have such an opportunity to enter the mind and heart of a subject, but this was my good fortune—though I often thought the plethora of source material a curse, for I could not possibly include it all. The most difficult problems I faced were over what to cut out, and my decisions will surely not please everyone.

Getting to know Jed Hotchkiss has been exceptionally pleasant, for he is fine company on paper. He was a serious man—in the thousands of pages I read of his writing, only two or three original witticisms come to mind—but he was a good audience and enjoyed humor, often favoring his wife with a somewhat dulled retelling of a joke he had heard. He was extremely observant and wrote with intelligence and sincerity and an endearing sense of compassion for those around him. A devoted husband and father who neither drank nor smoked, a devout Presbyterian who worked long hours and enjoyed doing so, he sought above all else to be steady and reliable. He enjoyed the company of his family and friends and the tranquillity of his home, and became bland in the wholesome way of all responsible people. He had faults, of course. He talked too much, he was sometimes too quick to judge others, and he could be cliquish. But he rarely expressed anger, and although he occasionally voiced his disapproval of others' conduct, his criticisms were reproofs, not malicious attacks. There was no venom in Hotchkiss, and scarcely any egotism. Preparing his memoirs (which he never finished) after the war, he proofread typed copies of his wartime letters and diaries. Many other men had taken similar opportunities to alter the evidence, making themselves appear more important or successful. Hotchkiss changed nothing but typographical errors.

But the most enjoyable part of coming to know Jed Hotchkiss was learning from him. He lived through a difficult period in our history, and as we get farther from that time, it becomes harder for us to understand the thoughts and motivations of the people of that era. How could they have been so filled with hate and anger that they went to war with their countrymen? How could they have looked upon the truly unimaginable horrors of the battlefields and not have lost their taste for war? How could they have endured the loss of children and spouses and friends and retained their faith in other men and God? How could young men advance toward almost certain death or maiming and feel no fear? Jed Hotchkiss provides answers, and, in doing so, provides an inspiring illustration of character and faith.

As for Hotchkiss's work during the war, it was uniformly excellent. Jackson, who was always careful with a compliment, said Hotchkiss's abilities as a topographer exceeded those of any man he had ever known. Lee praised Hotchkiss's industry and recommended him for promotion. Jeb Stuart also recommended him for higher rank, writing that his was "an extraordinary case of merit," and added for good measure, "and [he] is a fine fellow." General Ewell said, "His services could not, to my knowledge, be performed by anyone else, & I take pleasure in adding my testimony to that of Generals Lee, Jackson, & Stuart."

Hotchkiss was one of those accomplished, talented people who are sometimes mistaken for geniuses. He was exceptionally bright, with a sharp, agile mind that could quickly grasp concepts and principles, but there was nothing phenomenal about his intelligence, and his many abilities seem more like acquired abilities than gifts from God. He could write well and draw with great skill, but nothing he ever made bore that certain spirit—the inspiration—that would elevate it from the category of outstanding workmanship to that of masterwork of genius.

If there ever was any genius in Jed Hotchkiss, it was in his ability to accept what the majority of men never do.

He saw that there was but one thing between him and the life he wanted: himself. He became master of his mind, his spirit, and his body. He knew all he had to do to achieve what he wanted was to work for it and God would eventually give it to him. And so he worked—constantly and tirelessly. There is genius in hard work. It is perhaps the most common and least-wished-for form of genius, but it serves its owner faithfully, and so it served Jed Hotchkiss.

Many students of the war recognize his name because his wartime journal has been published. *Make Me A Map Of The Valley*, thanks to the able editing of Archie P. McDonald, provides a clear view through Hotchkiss's eyes of life at various headquarters in Lee's army between 1862 and 1865. Other historians writing on Lee's army, his battles, or the men who fought them have quoted from Hotchkiss's letters, making him a well-known and reliable witness. But Hotchkiss the man has remained much in the shadows. Historians have treated Hotchkiss primarily as an ocular through which to view Lee's army. I have tried to not look through Hotchkiss, but to turn the lens around and look at him. Here he is not an observer, but a participant and survivor.

This book is not a biography in the usual sense. It is not a study of a man's lifetime, for I give only cursory treatment to a large portion of his life while examining another, much smaller portion in minute detail. The final thirty-four years of Jed Hotchkiss's life, during which he worked to rebuild Virginia, are important to the history of that state and of the Shenandoah Valley in particular, but any detailed account of that period of his life would have come at the expense of examining his experiences at war—the years that provide the best opportunities to observe the character and quality of the man.

Ultimately, this is a portrait of a man who left his home, went to war, became utterly disgusted with what he saw, endured to the end purely out of a sense of duty, returned to his home, and began life anew, almost from scratch. It is the story of millions of men who marched off to that war. That this man was a cartographer who produced handsome work, who served with some of the great figures in military history, and who played a crucial part in a campaign that is considered a masterpiece of military art adds much to the story of Jed Hotchkiss. But the element with the most value to history, I think, is of how one man bore the hardships and horrors of a long and terrible war. The story is timeless and universal. The story of Jed Hotchkiss's contribution to the Confedcracy is a peculiarly American story in which an obscure, unheralded, largely self-taught man plays a central role in one of the nation's great dramas. But more than that, it is a story of survival and the tremendous power of faith, a force that held lives, families, and communities together when virtually everything else was lost. This narrative may shed light on General Jackson, his relationship with and use of his staff, and the conduct of some of his campaigns, but those are not my principal goals. The focus here is on Hotchkiss, and men like him, and how they found strength to endure.

— W. J. M.
Manassas, Virginia

This photograph of Jedediah Hotchkiss in his mid-thirties dates from about the end of the Civil War.

CHAPTER ONE
"LIVE FOR SOME PURPOSE"

On a cold day in March 1862, just north of the village of Tom's Brook, Virginia, Maj. Gen. Thomas J. Jackson, CSA, sat stoically on his small red horse and watched panic break out among his men. The soldiers, 380 recruits in only their third day in the army, were exhausted after laboring with packs and muskets over eighteen miles of dusty highway. For the last hour or more, they had been unnerved by the sight of bloody men in ambulances retreating southward from yesterday's battle at Kernstown. At least some of the newcomers were uneasy, too, about what they were marching into as reinforcements. They knew that the Confederate soldiers whipped at Kernstown were not novices like themselves, but veterans, and those veterans had been overwhelmed by large numbers of Federals—who now lurked someplace up ahead, over the horizon, or perhaps just over the next hill.

Suddenly the column of recruits came upon General Jackson by the road. He sat alone—no staff or troops anywhere in sight. In a few crisp, quiet words, he told them what to do: turn around, march back several miles, and then stop. He offered no elaboration.

Perhaps the unexpected orders rasped their already raw nerves, or perhaps the fatigue and tension of the long march at last caught up to them, but, whatever the reason, the recruits had about reached the limit of their psychological endurance. Somewhere in the ranks, a man lost his tenuous grip on self-control and began shouting. The army had been routed, he yelled, and the Federals were descending upon them right that very minute and would cut them to pieces. The wild words found ready listeners and panic swept through the column.

The officers of the little battalion scrambled to regain control. One officer, a tall, bearded man in civilian dress, seemed especially energetic, and his vigor caught Jackson's eye. Shouting commands and cajoling men back into line, the officer had a serious manner; he seemed to give orders easily and confidently, as though he were accustomed to controlling situations. Very soon, he and the others in charge had quelled the panic and restored order.

The silent general realized he knew this man. He had met him years ago and had renewed the acquaintance just in the last few days. His name was Jedediah Hotchkiss; he was a teacher from near Staunton, Virginia. The general recalled that Hotchkiss had abilities as an engineer and cartographer and that he knew the Shenandoah Valley inside and out. A mutual acquaintance, Col. William Baylor—a man whose opinion Jackson respected—spoke well of Hotchkiss, suggesting to the general that he would be a valuable addition to the headquarters staff. But the general had not been quick to appoint Hotchkiss. He did not invite just any man to join his staff. It was not enough that a man have knowledge and abilities. He needed energy, character, and a cool head. The safety of the army and the success of the cause depended on the quality of the men in positions of responsibility, and the general did not have enough personal knowledge of Mr. Hotchkiss to trust him with a portion of that great burden. Until now. The general liked what he saw in the teacher that day on the turnpike—the sureness and self-possession—and he began thinking about how he might put Mr. Hotchkiss's gifts to use.

The incident on the highway would surely have passed into obscurity had not Hotchkiss thought it one of the key moments in his life. Two days later, Jackson hired Jed Hotchkiss as his topographical engineer, and in the next fourteen months, Jackson built a reputation for achievement unparalleled in American military history. The general himself acknowledged that much of his success was due to the efforts of Jed Hotchkiss. Theirs was an extremely productive partnership, each man complementing and enhancing the abilities of the other. To know the brilliance of Jackson, one must know the work of Hotchkiss.[1]

Jedediah Hotchkiss was born in a stone house near Windsor, New York, not far north of the Pennsylvania border, on November 30, 1828. His ancestors had founded the town, and his father, Stiles, had been in business there his whole life, dealing first in lumber and turning later to farming. Lydia Hotchkiss, mother of the boy, was a member of the venerable Beecher family of Connecticut. Like many of their neighbors, the Hotchkisses were of Scottish descent and devout in faith. Jedediah grew up under the influence of his parents, his pastors, and the land. He was curious by nature and was fortunate enough to be nurtured by intelligent adults who put a high value on knowledge. From the outset, Jed, as he preferred to be called, loved books and reveled in study. He pursued learning with a determina-

tion that approached desperation. His chief fascinations were botany and geology, and when he was not reading books at home or in school, he roamed the fields and forests with a notebook, identifying trees, plants, and minerals and writing copious observations. According to one fellow student, Jed was renowned for the way he applied himself to study. He was remembered as "a little ragged boy" who impressed teachers and classmates alike with his determination to learn. As a teenager, he ignored the ridicule of his male schoolmates and entered a botany class composed entirely of girls, and he later graduated to membership in a botanical club of which almost all the other members were adults.[2] He was an inveterate record keeper, and his large collections of plants and minerals were all meticulously identified. He kept a journal, at first not much more than a record of events of each day, but later a chronicle of his thoughts and accomplishments.

Jed often walked to an old apple orchard on his father's farm, the site of a long-abandoned Indian village and burial ground. Tuscaroras had lived there, a branch of the Iroquois nation, and as Jed later wrote, "the remains of these people, in the shape of arrow heads, tomahawks, pestals, stone knives, beads, and other trinkets were washed out and exposed by the annual freshets of the river or by the plow-share."[3]

Jed remembered these solitary visits to that long-gone and almost forgotten village for the rest of his life. He maintained a deep fascination with artifacts, historical documents, and oral history and seemed keenly aware of his own life as part of a continuum.

But reality did not allow him the luxury of uninterrupted study. His father grew corn and other cash crops, and Jed and his two brothers worked on the farm throughout the year. That scholarly inquiry had to be fitted around chores apparently did not bother the youngest Hotchkiss son, for he understood that his responsibility, his duty, was

Jedadiah Hotchkiss.

Weather & Flower

Table

Kept

at

Mossy Creek

Augusta Co. Va.

A. 1850

Lat. 38° 35' N. Long: 2° W.

to his father and family. It was that simple. He accepted this, and he went to work in the fields cheerfully. Thus instilled in him early in his youth, duty became a dominant theme in his life.

The boy's habitual cheerfulness was due in a large part to the strength of his faith. He was taught early that he must love and obey God, and his devotion to this simple edict brought him peace of spirit. Methodism and Presbyterianism both had strong roots in his community, but in the tenets of the latter faith he found the formula for personal happiness. He would remain active in his church until his death. It was, in fact, Jed's love of God and His creations that enabled him to enjoy the hard work in the field. Each page of his journal rang with exaltations of life and the benevolence of his Heavenly Father. "Beautiful day," he would write, "to the Lord should be given praise for the mercies of the day and for the blessings of our nation," and "Great is the mercy of God," and "Blessings come from the Lord only." [4] As he grew, the exuberance of his rhetoric would fade, but his faith would never dim, and he would forever remain in love with the beauty of God's creation.

A typical day for Jed at age sixteen began about 4:30 a.m. After washing with cold water, he tended the family's kitchen garden. In the predawn darkness, he would have worked on his knees, weeding, thinning, and harvesting until daylight allowed him to finish quickly and turn to his books. For two hours, he studied Latin, Greek, or Italian and then snatched some breakfast before heading for

HOTCHKISS HAD A PASSION FOR PRECISE DATA. IN THIS HOMEMADE PAMPHLET, HE CHARTED THE WEATHER AND THE GROWTH OF PLANTS DURING THE EARLY PART OF THE GROWING SEASON. NONE OF HIS JOURNALS INDICATE THAT HE COLLECTED THIS DATA FOR ANY REASON OTHER THAN THE PLEASURE OF DOING SO.

school, four hours after rising. At school he studied algebra and rhetoric, practiced declamation and continued his work in languages. In the afternoon, he resumed his chores in his father's fields until dinner, after which he again turned to his books: writing, reading, and pressing flower and plant specimens that he had managed to collect and identify during the day. Around 10 p.m., he would at last retire.[5]

By the time he was seventeen, Jed Hotchkiss's curiosity had outgrown Broome County. In the autumn of 1846, with the blessing of his mother and father, he bade his family good-bye and headed south into Pennsylvania, traveling by canal boat and on foot. Soon he came face to face with reality: though the hours of labor in his father's fields were over, gone too were the meals at his father's table and the bed in his father's house. And so he went to work. He found work as a teacher in a small community of German immigrants not far from Harrisburg. He must have impressed his employers with his knowledge and demeanor, for they hired him despite his age and his inability to speak German. Undaunted, he found a tutor and learned the language.

The next spring, emboldened by his success, he again struck off southward. He walked down the Cumberland Valley, stopping to see some of the sights, including the capitol in Harrisburg and the U.S. Army barracks at Carlisle, which he would see again in his lifetime under quite different circumstances. Later that spring, he crossed the Potomac River and entered Virginia at Harpers Ferry. From the day when Jed Hotchkiss first walked into the Shenandoah Valley, he would never have a home anywhere else. The boy who strode into the Valley that summer with little more than a few clothes, a journal, a light heart, and a hungry mind would become one of the more important men in the history of the region.

For a budding geologist with time to wander, the Shenandoah Valley was paradise. Everywhere Jed looked, mountains, rivers, streams, and caverns offered an opportunity for study. Hotchkiss frequently stopped to make notes or sketches of an especially interesting ridge or rock formation. He was not concerned with capturing the beauty or the essence of things. He wanted the details. He was at heart a scientist, not an artist, so he sketched to record data, taking great care to accurately portray the details of terrain and the indentations of ridges and ravines. In Rockbridge County he made a point of going to see the famous natural bridge, a 200-foot-high stone span formed by millions of years of wind and water erosion. He was fascinated not only by the beauty of the natural wonder but by the physical principles that had formed it through the ages. He sat down and executed a clean and attractive sketch, capturing much of the bridge's beauty, but concentrating on the details that revealed clues to its formation. After finishing the sketch, he moved a few yards, looked again at his subject, noticed some aspect that he had missed the first time, and sat down and drew it again in the same depth of detail.[6]

Hotchkiss was a creature of precision. He had not seen something unless he had studied it, examined it from several angles, and even measured it. Near Port Republic, he visited Weyer's Cave, one of the Valley's many caverns, and explored it with a guide. His journal contains a precise, almost clinical description of the size of the cave: "We went through a narrow passage 66 feet descending 13 feet and came to … a fine and spacious hall at right angles to the main passage. 3 feet in length and 45 in breadth." Another time, in the town of Staunton (pronounced Stanton), he visited "Van Amburgh's Traveling Menagerie." For the first and perhaps only time in his life, he saw some of the rare and exotic creatures that shared the earth with him: an elephant, a camel, a "white bear," and many more. But rather than dwelling upon the amazing physiological features of these curious beasts, young Hotchkiss simply catalogued them—all of them. The list of animals took up an entire page in his journal as he named each animal and how many of each he saw. His concern was enumeration, quantification, not abstractions.[7]

In the summer, his wanderings in the Valley suddenly took on a purpose. He met Henry Forrer, who operated an ironworks. Forrer took a great interest in the eighteen-year-old Hotchkiss and was impressed enough by the boy's intelligence and manners that he offered him a job as a private teacher. Forrer's brother, Daniel, operated Mossy Creek Ironworks in Augusta County and had a household full of children needing instruction.[8] Hotchkiss took the

job, and in the autumn of 1847 began teaching at the home of Daniel Forrer in the village of Mossy Creek.

Thus ended the most important eighteen months of Hotchkiss's life. His journey from New York to Augusta County defined him. The journey had whetted rather than sated his hunger for knowledge, and he redoubled his efforts to learn. He was, and would ever remain, a student.

HOTCHKISS'S POCKET JOURNAL FOR 1847 REVEALS THAT THE EIGHTEEN YEAR OLD ALREADY HAD A TALENT FOR GATHERING TOPOGRAPHICAL INFORMATION. HIS ENTRY ABOUT A VISIT TO WEYER'S CAVE CONTAINS A SKETCH OF THE PASSAGES AND GALLERIES.

He took up his tasks at Forrer's with zeal and found that he liked teaching very much. "It is, indeed, a pleasant task, most of the time," he confided in his journal, "to nurse the tender thought, to expand the germs of mind, more, and more, until they assimilate nearer and nearer to perfection." [9] But the engagement at Mossy Creek was not without turmoil. The custom in Virginia at the time was for school to continue through the entire day, "from morning to night." The young schoolmaster, by then all of nineteen years old, thought this was detrimental to the students, who were denied the benefits of fresh air and sunshine. Hotchkiss sought to change his hours of instruction but encountered opposition. He believed he was right, however, and went ahead with his plan, beginning school early and letting out early. The students liked the policy, and when the parents saw that it could work, the critics eventually fell silent. [10]

Daniel Forrer was greatly pleased with his young teacher, so pleased that he and several other local men invested in the construction of a building in which Hotchkiss could teach. The school was called Mossy Creek Academy, and Hotchkiss was installed as principal. Under his direction, the enterprise grew in size and reputation until it was considered one of the finer primary schools in Virginia. For Hotchkiss, however, the best thing about teaching was that he was able to surround himself with books and ideas and other hungry minds. In this atmosphere, his intellect flourished. His days began early as he prepared for and then conducted classes, but the evenings were his own. "I study at this time from dusk to midnight," he wrote in his journal, "delving among the treasures of knowledge." [11] The years at Mossy Creek were Hotchkiss's university years. He was his own master, made his own lesson plans and reading lists, and judged his own progress. He learned what he wanted to know, and few actual university students could have gotten a more thorough, more practical education.

Life at Forrer's was happy and productive, but as Hotchkiss entered his mid-twenties, he began to look to the future. His thoughts were filled increasingly with a young woman, Sara Ann Comfort, a Pennsylvanian he had met half a decade before while he was teaching in the German school. Four years his junior, she was a bright student who excelled in languages. The details of the courtship and engagement are not clear. Hotchkiss lived in Virginia in the years after their first meeting, and whether the two saw much of each other is not known. No correspondence remains, but they somehow managed to keep their affection for one another growing, and Jed came to think of Sara as the woman with whom he wished to spend the rest of his life.

He knew, though, that he was not yet prepared for marriage. He was not yet respectable, for he had no means. His trade was teaching, by which he could earn an adequate living for himself, but supporting a wife and family might be difficult on his salary. So he began to consider other sources of income, and almost at once, his lifelong pursuit of knowledge took a sharp and very practical turn. The poetry and meditative essays that he had begun writing at Forrer's ceased, and the language books were set aside. He borrowed books on geology, surveying, and engineering. His long-standing interest in geology drew him naturally toward the related field of topography—the observation and recording of the physical features of the landscape. The practical application of topography was surveying and mapping, so Jed Hotchkiss began drawing maps.

Predictably, he threw himself into the new endeavor completely, riding over the countryside, taking notes and measurements, and making rough sketches in a notebook. Soon he began doing surveys for landowners. The entries in his diary in the winter of 1850 spoke of his new passion: "A fine, clear, cold day—spent it mapping" and "Have been mapping all day." [12] The beginning of Hotchkiss's work as

THE HOTCHKISS BROTHERS' SCHOOL, LOCH WILLOW ACADEMY IN CHURCHVILLE, VIRGINIA, WAS ALSO THEIR HOME. NELSON'S FAMILY SHARED THE "MANSION" ON THE HILL WITH BOARDERS. JED AND SARA LIVED AND HELD CLASSES IN THE WHITE HOUSE ON THE LEFT, WHICH STILL STANDS.

---

a surveyor and cartographer marked the end of the first phase of his life at Mossy Creek. In his first five years there, between 1847 and 1853, he was single, relatively free of responsibility, and in every way a student. The work ethic that had sprouted and been fostered in his youth reached full flower. The second phase began in December 1853 when he married Sara Ann Comfort just a month past his twenty-fifth birthday.

After the couple returned to Mossy Creek, they immediately began planning for a family. In January 1855, less than thirteen months after the wedding, Sara gave birth to Ellen May (Nelly).[13] Less than two years later, in October 1857, Sara delivered Anne Lydia, but this second birth was difficult, and the slightly built Sara needed a long time to recover. In 1858, Hotchkiss resigned from Mossy Creek and moved the family to nearby Stribling Springs, where Sara could regain her strength with the help of the mineral waters. She improved rapidly, but at the age of twenty-five, her child-bearing years were over.

In the meantime, the young father saw his reputation as an educator grow. He served as a visiting examiner at Washington College in Lexington, Virginia, one of the finest schools in the region. On one visit to Lexington, Hotchkiss was a guest at the home of the college president, Dr. George Junkin, and met the president's son-in-law, a professor of natural philosophy from the nearby Virginia Military Institute. His name was Thomas J. Jackson.[14]

In 1859, with Sara's health much improved, Hotchkiss considered moving the family again. This time, however, the move would mark the beginning of a major business venture. Hotchkiss and his older brother Nelson laid plans for a self-supporting boarding school. The property would include not only the school building and the dormitory, but also a farm that would provide all or most of what was needed to feed the scholars, the teachers, and their families. Jed and Sara would handle administration and instruction at the school, while Nelson and his wife, Harriet, ran the farm. The brothers had found an ideal location, a farm on a knoll just outside of the village of Churchville in southern Augusta County. Churchville was on a stage route eight miles from the railroad at Staunton, the county seat, so students from around the region would have no difficulty with transportation, and, given Hotchkiss's strong reputation as an educator, students would undoubtedly come from beyond the immediate area. The spot was also beautiful and serene, rising up above a mill pond named Loch Willow (like the Hotchkisses, many of the residents were of Scottish extraction, hence the Scottish influence on the pond's name).

They named their school Loch Willow Academy. As principal of the school, Hotchkiss hired teachers to help him present a balanced curriculum. Mr. O. M. Grinnan was made a professor and taught several subjects; Miss Emily Griggs, only eighteen years old, taught music; and Miss L. V. Allen presented instruction in art. Hotchkiss himself taught a course in surveying and topographical drawing. Interestingly, none of these teachers were Virginians. Hotchkiss found them in the fount of his own intellectualism, Broome County, New York. Loch Willow Academy, then, was a colony of Northerners—New Yorkers and a Pennsylvanian—in the heart of Virginia. In the months to come, the irony would grow acute.[15]

The Hotchkiss clan thus entered into a period that promised great contentment. Jed Hotchkiss had, at the age of twenty-nine, created a life very much to his liking. At Loch Willow, everything he desired for happiness was near at hand. He was surrounded by his family, not just his own wife and two daughters, but his nephews and nieces in his brother's large household. He had interesting employment and intellectual stimulation at the academy and at home in his topographic pursuits. He had a fulfilling place of worship in Union Presbyterian Church, where he immediately took an active role, teaching Sunday school regularly. And he had the earth. From his boyhood when he toiled in the garden to his young manhood when he explored caves and collected rock and plant specimens, Hotchkiss had always been tied to the earth. He loved nature in all its variety and manifestations, and in Churchville, in the heart of the rich Shenandoah Valley, he could enjoy God's gifts fully.

On a Sabbath morning in October 1860, he was able to articulate for his Sunday school class the philosophical basis of his happiness, making clear that he and all his listeners were the authors of their own tranquillity. In a lecture he called "Live for Some Purpose," he told them that God had given life to them so that they might use it to good advantage. Life, the great gift, was short, and must not be wasted. He spoke of the passing of the seasons and of how none of the trees or plants of the earth lived in vain, each giving life and sustenance to other living things, leaving the earth richer, stronger, more beautiful. "Can as much be said for man?" he asked. "For the churchyard and its inmates?"

"The majority of men lead aimless lives," he said, "eat, drink, sleep—darkness and light—tread-mill of habit, turn mill of wealth." For most men, reason was overseer to thoughts, the mere tools of a trade. Life for many was "the mere running down of a handless clock," while "the holy things," those worth living for, went unfelt. "Such is not life," he announced. "Knowledge, truth, love, beauty, goodness, faith … to awaken joy in human bosoms; to shed tears of sympathy; to refresh dry and thirsty hearts … to obey the dictates of conscience … to be alive to the realities of childhood's years, to prayers that bind us to the future, to the mysteries of death, to the hardships of life, and then to mould from these a mortal life that has a purpose, that, accomplished, shall [be] fit for putting on an immortal being. That," he declared, "is life." [16]

But hardly had the venture at Loch Willow Academy begun when events far away from Augusta County threatened the life the Hotchkisses were building. Throughout 1860, Hotchkiss, a great lover of newspapers, had been reading of the national debate over the limits of the U. S. Constitution. Slavery, and its extension to new states and territories, was at the heart of the debate. Hotchkiss did not own slaves, though he did lease a black man named William Gearing from a slaveowner to help with the chores around the academy. Hotchkiss was not opposed to slavery on principle, but seemed lukewarm on the idea of owning slaves. He obviously thought the institution could be justified morally, for he continued to lease Gearing through the war, until January 2, 1865, and then bought him. [17] Hotchkiss suffered no such ambivalence on the issue of states' rights. He felt that the people of a state or a region knew what was best for them, and that God had given every citizen the right to determine his own government. Still, he loved his country, having lived in both the North and the South, and thought secession would be a mistake. In feeling this way, Hotchkiss was squarely in the mainstream of opinion in Augusta County.

Augusta County was a agricultural region with a hardworking, extremely religious population. Only two counties in all of Virginia had more churches in 1860 than Augusta, and both of those contained major urban areas. [18] In the face of the coming crisis, the Presbyterians and Methodists of Augusta, far and away the county's two largest denominations, prayed ardently for peace and the preservation of the Union. In the 1860 presidential election,

John C. Breckinridge, who was viewed as the secession candidate, received little support. Abraham Lincoln, who was for preserving the Union, was detested by the Deep South states, and many Virginians felt his election would surely have lead to secession. So Augusta County supported a compromise candidate, John Bell. Lincoln won the election, and as promised, South Carolina began the process of seceding from the Union. Virginians in Augusta were alarmed and immediately called a mass meeting to decide what to do. At the courthouse in Staunton on November 28, 1860, two days before Jed Hotchkiss's thirty-second birthday, a committee adopted resolutions expressing sympathy with their fellows in South Carolina and urging them to moderate their anger. The Virginians declared that the Constitution of the United States was "the easiest yoke of government a free people ever bore, and yet the strongest protector of rights the wisdom of man ever contrived." The committee also urged Augusta's representatives in the state legislature at Richmond to "bend all their energies to keep Virginia to her moorings as 'Flag Ship of the Union.' " [19]

In December, South Carolina seceded, and several other Southern states followed. Pro-Union sentiment was not as strong in all parts of Virginia as it was in Augusta County, and the state legislature called a special convention to consider Virginia's withdrawal from the Union. Augusta sent three Union men to be her representatives. The convention debated for weeks, but finally, in mid-April, events brought the Virginians to the point of decision. Confederate troops fired on U. S. troops at Fort Sumter in Charleston Harbor on April 12, 1861. In Augusta County, citizens were stunned and saddened and wondered what would happen next. Within days, their sadness turned to shock and anger.

On April 15, President Abraham Lincoln called for 75,000 volunteers to subdue the rebellion. Lincoln wrote

to the governor of each state still in the Union asking that he raise a quota of troops. Most of the Northern states responded with alacrity, but Virginia's Governor John Letcher was outraged and answered Lincoln curtly: "I have only to say that the militia of Virginia will not be furnished to the powers at Washington for any such use or purpose as they have in view.... Your object is to subjugate the Southern States, and a requisition made upon me for such a purpose … will not be complied with."[20]

Lincoln's call on April 15 pushed many Southerners over the edge in support of secession. "Lincoln's call for troops to invade and coerce the newborn Confederacy," wrote Hotchkiss later, "and Letcher's reply to that call, wrought an immediate change in the current of public opinion in Virginia, from the mountains to the sea."[21] On April 17, the Virginia Convention passed an ordinance of secession, which would be approved by a vote of the people in May. The collective conscience of the people of Augusta was clear; they felt they were not responsible for the war.[22]

Hotchkiss was angry over what he saw as a violation of his right to self-government. "All we ask of the North is to be left alone in the enjoyment of our inherited rights," he would write a few months later. But war was not a step to be taken lightly, and there could be no doubt that Virginia's secession meant the state would have to fight. War meant that everything Hotchkiss valued—his home, his family, and his friends—was at risk. As a state bordering on the North, Virginia would probably be the scene of fighting, though no one knew how much. Most Americans felt that the war would not last very long. They envisioned a few clashes after which the other side would relent

---

JED AND SARA HOTCHKISS SIT IN FRONT OF THEIR TEENAGE DAUGHTERS IN A FAMILY PORTRAIT DATED 1870, WHEN JED WAS FORTY-ONE.

and retreat and peace would return. Both sides badly misjudged the other's resolve.

Personally, ideologically, war was a catastrophe for Hotchkiss. He was not a businessman who might somehow grow rich on war profits. Nor was he a lawyer or a politician who might rise in power and influence on the wings of a glorious military career. He was a teacher—an architect of social growth and prosperity whose professional life was given over to developing the intellectual and moral strength of his pupils. Hotchkiss was a purveyor of knowledge, and his entire life was a paradigm for productivity. Ignorance and its children—war, violence, destruction, and hatred—were his avowed enemies.

The arrival of war and the subsequent calls to arms had an intoxicating effect on young men throughout the land. Thousands of men and boys across Virginia formed companies and rushed to recruiting offices, fearful that the war might somehow end before they could strike the enemy. In Churchville, students fled Loch Willow Academy and joined companies with other young men in the area. Professor Grinnan resigned from the academy and took the lead in recruiting. The tuition from students that remained was too meager to keep the school afloat, and Hotchkiss regretfully suspended classes. Loch Willow Academy was among the first casualties of the war.

For the time being, Hotchkiss was reduced to hoping that hostilities would not last long and that all would soon be well. The family could not endure a long war without income, and this fact, along with his conviction that the Federal government was wrong, played a part in Hotchkiss's decision to enter the army. "I have urged resistance [against the Federal government]," he would write to Sara some time later, "and cannot but use my feeble efforts to resist, trusting to a kind overruling God to bring all things to a happy conclusion and to reward all those that do their duty."[23]

WILLIAM W. LORING'S MILITARY EXPERIENCE BROUGHT HIM A GENERAL'S COMMISSION IN THE CONFEDERATE STATES ARMY, BUT HIS CLEAREST CONTRIBUTION TO THE WAR WAS RECOGNIZING HOTCHKISS'S POTENTIAL VALUE IN 1861 AND PUTTING THE TOPOGRAPHER TO WORK. THROUGH THIS ASSIGNMENT HOTCHKISS CAME TO KNOW ROBERT E. LEE.

CHAPTER TWO
SEVENTY-NINE DAYS AT WAR

For hours, the caravan of heavily laden wagons labored up the steep road in the mountains of western Virginia. Deep ravines choked with laurel and honeysuckle fell away from one side of the narrow byway and faces of granite rose up from the other. The lead wagon was far ahead of the others in the train, so when the driver's straining horses leaned into their harness and at last dragged their burden onto the crest, the teamster reined them in and gave them a rest. He paused for a few moments to admire the view, then went to work.

The respite was a chance for Jed Hotchkiss to exercise his travel-weary mind. He took up some of his engineering tools—compass, aneroid barometer, record book—and began making notes. He took the elevation of the summit, as he had on all the mountains he had crossed in the last two days, and recorded it in his notebook, along with his estimate of the number of miles from his starting place. He recorded the condition of the road surface and the type and size of the trees growing nearby and jotted casual observations on rock formations, soil, and wildflowers and other plant life, noting how green the still-young grass looked and how immature the wheat was at that altitude. After Hotchkiss had scribbled for a few minutes in his book, hearing that the labored breathing of his team had

subsided and seeing that the other wagons had closed the distance behind him, he set aside his instruments, took up the reins, and resumed his journey.[1]

The measurements and observations Jed Hotchkiss made on that drive over the mountains were unlike any he had ever taken. The countless elevations and triangulations and notations of his years surveying portions of the Shenandoah Valley had all been done in the name of pleasure and professional growth. Topography and cartography had been hobbies that had grown into a useful occupation when school was not in session. Now, however, Hotchkiss was taking readings with no such peaceful and commercial ends in mind. He had left his home and entered the war at last, and all the topographical data he gathered now might have a military purpose.

His role in the army was undefined. In fact, he was not even officially in the army. In the large and chaotic military hierarchy forming throughout Virginia, he was just a teamster trundling supplies to a depot somewhere in the vast mountain country. He had no rank, no uniform, and no pay. But Hotchkiss, ever the optimist, had hope. He was driving a supply wagon only because that was the contribution to the war effort he could make at the moment. He had much more to offer Virginia and the Confederacy and hoped for the opportunity to show what he could do.

He was driving a team, but he was something more than a mere teamster: he was a wagon driver with a bag full of engineering instruments.

But Hotchkiss's plan of obtaining a position as a military engineer had no real basis. He had no influential friends in the army and no military experience, while scores, perhaps hundreds, of other surveyors and engineers had both. The United States Military Academy had been producing military engineers every year for decades, and plenty of other working engineers had learned their profession in state military academies. In the contest for highly prized engineering posts, Hotchkiss, despite his abilities, was at a great disadvantage. He entered the military realm with an overabundance of optimism, just as he had eagerly walked into the Shenandoah Valley thirteen years earlier, with only the assets he carried with him.

The road over which Hotchkiss guided his wagon was the Parkersburg-Staunton Turnpike, a macadamized[2] stage route through some of the more rugged and beautiful country in America. The pike wound up and down mountain after mountain, through close valleys and gorges, and in and out of dense forests of pine, chestnut, laurel, and magnolia. It was a main route between Virginia and Ohio, which made control of it essential for both the Federal and Confederate armies.

By June 3, the Federals were moving aggressively through the mountains, and the only Confederate troops on the scene were unable to stop them. From their foothold in the mountains, the Federals could move southward and eastward toward the Shenandoah Valley and the farms and railroads in the Virginia Piedmont east of the Blue Ridge Mountains, areas that were vital to the Confederate war effort. Gen. Robert E. Lee, commander of Virginia's military forces and advisor to President Jefferson Davis, quickly acted to stem the Federal advance by directing reinforcements into the mountains, assigning a much-

respected aide, Brig. Gen. Robert S. Garnett, to take command. It was as a small part of this wave of reinforcements that Jed Hotchkiss went to war as a teamster.

By June 15, Garnett had marched most of his small army north to Beverly, Virginia. Two roads converged at Beverly, and one was the turnpike down which the next Federal attack would probably come. Beverly therefore became a crucial gateway, and Garnett made it a key point in his defense. Garnett divided his men into two groups. One small infantry force, under Lt. Col. Jonathan Heck, marched with some cavalry and artillery to the western foot of nearby Rich Mountain and there established Camp Garnett on the turnpike about seven miles forward of Beverly. Garnett took the remainder of the force and moved farther north to strong natural positions on Laurel Hill, an extension of Rich Mountain. Beverly became the Confederate supply base.

The supplies in Hotchkiss's wagon were intended for a company of cavalry with Heck at Rich Mountain. The outfit, known as the Churchville Cavalry, had been raised in and around Churchville and was commanded by a local man, Capt. Franklin F. Sterrett, so Hotchkiss knew many of the men as friends, neighbors, and former students. Professor Hotchkiss, as many of the men called him, arrived at Sterrett's camp on July 1 in high spirits, which, ironically, seemed to result from the arduousness of his five-day journey over the mountains. Each night he had ended his drive stiff-fingered and sore-armed from managing the team's reins all day, but weary as he was, he still had hours

HOTCHKISS DREW THIS SKETCH OF THE ENGAGEMENT AT RICH MOUNTAIN, VIRGINIA, JULY 11, 1861, FROM MEMORY AND WITHOUT HAVING SURVEYED MOST OF THE AREA. HE MARKED THE APPROXIMATE ROUTES TAKEN BY FLANKING PARTIES, INCLUDING HIS OWN. THE MOUNDS ON THE MAP'S UPPER THIRD REPRESENT CAMP GARNETT.

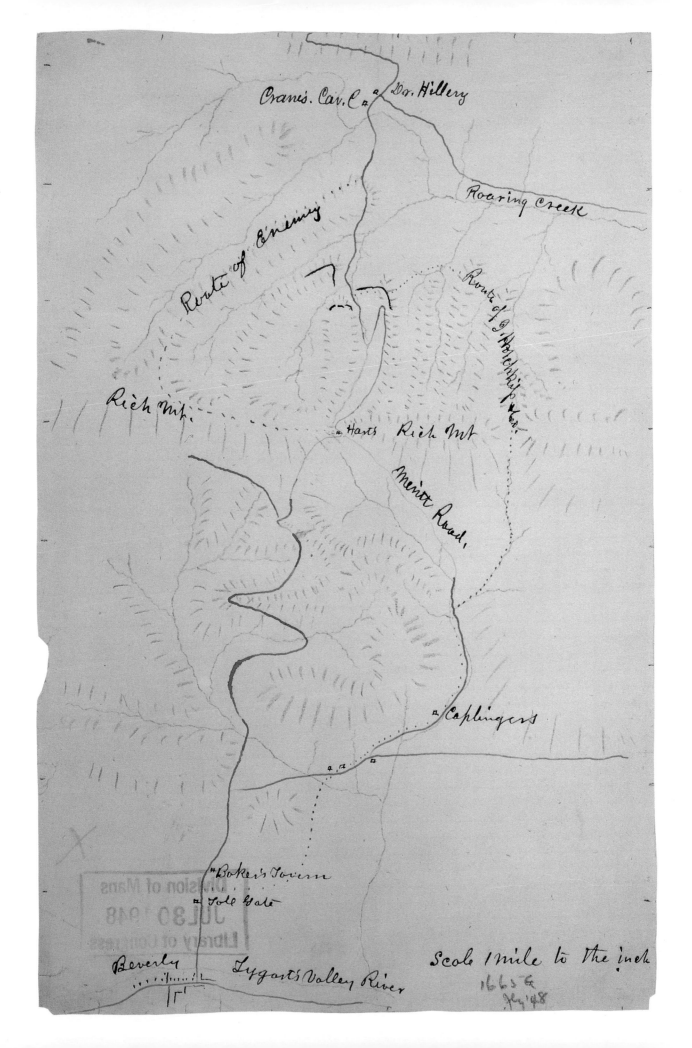

Crane's. Cav. C.   Dr. Hillery

Roaring creek

Route of Enemy

Route of Reinforcements

Rich Mt.

Harts   Rich Mt

Meritt Road,

Caplingers

Baker's Tavern

Toll Gate

Beverly   Tygart's Valley River

Scale 1 mile to the inch

of work before him in caring for his horses. And even then sleep was less than restful. One night he slept wrapped in his cloak on the hard, plank floor of an abandoned mountain cabin and awakened with a bruised hip and dozens of gnat bites. Another night he could find no bed more suitable than the tops of the boxes piled in his wagon. He awoke abruptly when one of his companions, who was sleeping beneath the wagon, began screaming: he had dreamed that a snake had coiled itself around his neck. The hard work, fatigue, and exposure to hot sun and cold rains kept Hotchkiss and his fellow teamsters on edge, but for Hotchkiss at least, the excitement of being at war, the companionship strengthened by sharing hardships with his fellows, and the belief that he was making sacrifices for the cause kept his spirits soaring.[3]

Once Hotchkiss had delivered his cargo and visited with friends, he got down to the real business of his journey. He told Sterrett of his desire to obtain an engineering position. Sterrett, a mere captain of volunteer cavalry, could do nothing more for Hotchkiss than to write a short letter of introduction to Lieutenant Colonel Heck. Hotchkiss, of course, accepted the offer and was soon off on a borrowed horse en route to Heck's headquarters at Camp Garnett.

Jonathan McGee Heck, just past his thirtieth birthday, was a lawyer from Monongalia County, Virginia. He was in temporary command of a regiment of infantry, soon to be designated the 25th Virginia. Heck did not know the Professor personally but might have by reputation since many of his men were from Augusta County and the surrounding area, and he showed keen interest when Hotchkiss told him he could provide maps of the area. The two men immediately liked each other, and Heck declared that he wanted Hotchkiss to serve on his staff as engineer. But such appointments had to go through channels, so Heck wrote a note for Hotchkiss to carry to General Garnett requesting that Hotchkiss be assigned to engineer duty with the regiment at Rich Mountain.

Garnett's camp was some miles distant from Camp Garnett, and there Hotchkiss got his first look at the destructiveness of war. "We got there just at dark," he wrote to Sara, "and found the camp at the foot of the mountain with long lines of trenches dug around the sides of the mountain for men to fire from, for more than a mile, and hundreds of acres of trees cut down by the soldiers to enable them to have a fair field for a fight." Exploring this raw wound on the landscape, Hotchkiss found Garnett's tent and presented Heck's note.[4]

Robert Selden Garnett was a Virginian and a professional soldier from a family notable for military men. His grandfather had been a French general and a cousin would rise to prominence as a Confederate general. Trim and erect, Garnett received Hotchkiss and promptly referred Heck's request to his chief engineer, who thanked Professor Hotchkiss and made it clear that he did not need any assistance. Hotchkiss was stunned.

The engineer's refusal of Hotchkiss's services reflected the intense elitism within the military engineer corps. The top graduates of each class at the U. S. Military Academy were given their choice of service in the cavalry, artillery, infantry, or engineer corps, and, with rare exceptions, the class leaders chose the engineering branch. As in all exclusive societies, there was a degree of snobbishness among the members of the corps. Even considering the great amount of labor Garnett's engineer had in preparing for operations in a largely unknown region, and given the scarcity of qualified topographers immediately available, he was too proud to accept help from a self-educated civilian. Throughout the war, the closed ranks of the Engineer Corps would frustrate Hotchkiss. Time and time again his superiors sought to reward him with promotion or appointment in the corps, but each effort met with defeat and disappointment. Hotchkiss would persevere, however, and succeed despite official prejudice. He would become the most recognized and valuable topographic engineer in the Confederate army, but he would never officially be a part of the Confederate Engineer Corps.

Hotchkiss returned to Heck with the disappointing news, apparently resigned to resuming his role as teamster. But Heck would have none of that and insisted Hotchkiss serve as his topographer. If the Confederate States Army would not put Hotchkiss on its payroll, Heck would put him on his. With no authorization, Heck hired Hotchkiss, apparently as an independent contractor, and ordered him to begin a survey of Camp Garnett and Rich Mountain at once.

Thus Jonathan Heck made his one great contribution to the Confederate war effort. In giving Hotchkiss his first job as a military engineer, Heck helped the amateur cartographer establish professional credentials. This addition to his resume would assist him in acquiring another, far more important position several months later, a position in which he would play a key role in one of the great dramas of the war. The next day, July 3, Hotchkiss began surveying Rich Mountain.

As a military topographer, Hotchkiss's job was to explore and report on the region assigned to him by his chief. He had to learn the physical features of the terrain, broadly broken down into elevations and depressions (or drainage), and he had to identify and mark the artificial features of the landscape, anything made or introduced by man. Together these categories embraced everything in the army's environment—from hills and streams to houses, bridges, roads, and cornfields. Hotchkiss's interest in geology and botany was not crucial to his role as a topographer, but it added another dimension to his understanding of the terrain, and therefore to his success in the profession.

Hotchkiss found Rich Mountain and the surrounding area rugged and wild. Huge trees covered steep and rocky slopes, growing so close together that the forests were dense and dark. Daunting as the task of surveying the region was, he went to it with a will.

His first step in creating a map was to establish the dimensions of the area to be drawn. He could measure distance a number of ways. Small distances, up to several hundred yards, could be measured with a rope or chain of a given length used to count and mark off distances in small increments that would be added together. Longer distances, from a thousand yards to several miles, were either estimated by eye or measured in paces. A talented topographer with an experienced eye, like Hotchkiss, could estimate distances to within 250 yards at a distance of a mile—but terrain and certain weather conditions made estimation less accurate. For example, full sunlight could make objects seem nearer, especially when the sun was at the topographer's back, and hazy air and steep inclines could make objects seem farther away. Because of such optical illusions, estimating distances by eye was not always reliable. The most accurate way to measure long distances was by pacing. A topographer preparing to measure a distance by pacing first had to measure the length of his stride (technically a stride equals two paces; the size varies with each individual). Once the topographer knows how many inches of ground he covers with each stride he needs only to count strides and perform a bit of mathematics to determine the length of his journey in yards or miles. The surveyor could guard against losing count of his strides by picking up a pebble and dropping it in a pocket every 100 strides. Once he knew the length of his stride, and how many paces fell per minute, he could measure long distances with a pocket watch. Naturally, a topographer traveling over great distances could measure more ground in less time by simply measuring his horse's gait. Pacing was

This volume is my field sketch book that I used during the Civil War. Most of the sketches were made on horseback just as they now appear. The colored pencils used were kept in the places fixed on the outside of the other cover.

These topographical sketches were often used in conferences with Generals Jackson, Ewell and Early.

The cover of this book is a blank Federal Commission found in Gen. Milroy's quarters at Winchester.

Jed. Hotchkiss

by far the most accurate method Hotchkiss could have used, with a range of error of about three percent. But measuring distances by pacing had a severe drawback: the length of the surveyor's stride was shortened by sloping ground, and the degree of the slope determined the amount of change in the stride. This fact was especially important in hilly country like the Rich Mountain area or the Shenandoah Valley. Hotchkiss might have gotten around this problem by using the chain or rope method on the slopes, or he might have used a formula by which he could calculate the changed length of his stride by the degree of slope. Either way, the process was laborious and complicated.[5]

Longer distances of several miles or more were somewhat easier to determine, though with a significant drop in accuracy. Hotchkiss often plotted points using triangulation, a geometric process that required a compass and some known distances and angles to compute unknown distances.

The most expensive instrument in Hotchkiss's kit was his aneroid barometer, a large, round, highly sensitive instrument about the size of a dinner plate, which measured atmospheric pressure. Since the pressure of the atmosphere increases with elevation above sea level, a surveyor could use the barometer to measure the heights of mountains. The device was generally accurate, but the user had to pay close attention to the fluctuations of the dial to note the influence of other factors, such as changes in the weather, that affect atmospheric pressure and sometimes render the barometer useless for taking elevations. For that reason, Hotchkiss often had to plan his work around the weather.

Certainly the surveyor's most important tool was his

HOTCHKISS TREATED THE COVER OF THIS BATTERED FIELD BOOK WITH VARNISH OR SOME OTHER WATER-PROOFING SUBSTANCE TO PROTECT IT FROM THE WEATHER.

lensatic compass. Small enough to be carried in his pocket, it included collapsible sights that allowed him to find bearings and set courses. While surveying an area, Hotchkiss referred to his compass constantly, and, if time permitted and an extremely accurate map was wanted, he would stop at each bend in the road and take a new heading, marking the changes on his sketch to be later incorporated into the final map.

Hotchkiss needed all this equipment with him as he rode about on a survey. The barometer was encased in leather with a long shoulder sling. The other items, the compass, field book, and reference maps, if any, had to be carried in pockets. Later in the war, Hotchkiss had a captured Federal overcoat altered for the purpose. His wife dyed the coat black, and a local seamstress reinforced the lining and added large, deep cargo pockets inside under the arms.[6]

After he had gathered his survey data, Hotchkiss was ready to prepare a map. He had taught himself well, for his military maps are model illustrations of the basic principles of cartography: they are accurate, they are legible even in poor light, and they use easily understood symbols to denote landscape features. The lettering is clear and uniform; Hotchkiss favored the roman and italic typefaces, which were popular with cartographers of the time. And whenever possible, he used durable, high-quality drawing paper, often requesting that Sara send him some from his personal stock at home.

The finished product was something to be proud of. His maps were admired not only for the wealth of information they conveyed, but also for their style and clarity, and Hotchkiss, not unduly modest, did take pride in his work. After presenting one map at headquarters, he wrote Sara with obvious delight that it had been the theme of much praise.[7]

Hotchkiss excelled as a cartographer at least partly because he possessed in abundance a mapmaker's greatest asset: patience. He was a craftsman who, despite frequent calls from headquarters for assigned maps, took his time in creating each drawing, often working through the night and for days on end. Each map had to be drawn at least twice, first in pencil, so survey errors could be corrected, then in ink. The drawing board had to be dry and protected from the weather, for a few drops of water could ruin hours of inking. Hotchkiss also had to plan which parts of the map he would draw first—not an arbitrary decision. A right-handed draughtsman, for example, would begin inking in the upper left-hand corner of the paper and work diagonally to the lower right to keep his hand moving ahead of the wet ink, reducing the possibility of smudges and smears. The colors of the inks used also determined which should be applied first.

And even after the map was completed, Hotchkiss's job continued. Armies actively alter the topography of every landscape they occupy, by building or destroying bridges, leveling forests, or erecting fortifications, for example, so maps are outdated literally as soon as the ink dries. A cartographer simply draws the map, but the topographer must continue documenting the changes in the landscape until the army moves on. Or as was often the case with Hotchkiss, his commander would order him to precede the army to its new area of operations, scout and survey, and begin preparing new maps. And if there was no surveying to be done, Hotchkiss would continue to work each day in his tent, updating maps, making copies for other officers, or preparing finished maps from sketches to accompany official reports of army operations.

Hotchkiss was happy at headquarters and enjoyed roughing it among the other men. He and another member of the regimental staff "built a bark tent and stretched a piece of cotton over it and got two boards to fasten up in one corner for a table." They had "two stools made by driv-

ing a post into the ground and nailing on a board and two beds made by a pole to fence off a space and bark laid down and then straw filled in." [8] He thought Heck "a No. 1 good fellow," and liked all the aides and clerks as well. [9] He wrote Sara cheerfully about the "tough" fare at headquarters, noting that the staples were "greasy cakes of dough made into the shape of biscuits and hardened on the outside and part way through … coffee and meat, sometimes hard crackers, now and then a taste of butter, sometimes a loaf of bread from somewhere as a present, or a piece of cake procured in the same way." [10]

But Hotchkiss also found army life difficult and physically demanding. He missed the comfortable working conditions of home, where he could choose where and when to conduct a survey. Soldiers worked in all kinds of weather. After getting caught in a downpour he wrote to Sara, "Yesterday I was out in the woods finding a line of picket and got wet through and through.… I came back after the rain and never washed off as much dirt in my life. It made me almost sick through the night." [11]

And there was more unpleasantness to field service. Disease was everywhere, and with it came death. Each day, Hotchkiss saw wagons filled with sick men set out eastward for the long trek over the mountains to the hospitals in the Shenandoah Valley and beyond. And in the first week of July, after a clash of scouts, he saw his first battle casualties. "Three of our men were badly wounded, one shot through and through the lungs, another in the head and shoulder and another in the leg I think," he wrote to Sara. The Federal casualties were left on the field, but the Confederates brought the personal effects of one of them back to camp, where Hotchkiss got a good look at the human side of the awful business in which he was engaged. "Our men took the pistols, gun and money of one of the men and two letters that were on him. His name was Johns, from Ohio. One letter was from a young sister, full of love for him, wishing he would come home, not caring whether promoted or not if the war would only end so that he could come back to them.… The other letter was from a cousin who seemed to think everything of the young man and prayed that he might get back, but alas the poor fellow was destined never to see them again. The scouts said his body was the fairest of any they had ever seen."[12] Like most front-line soldiers, Hotchkiss would soon become inured to the sight of the dead, but he struggled constantly against revulsion over the horrible waste of young lives and the destruction of families, lamenting to Sara, "Oh! how many precious lives must be lost, and how many homes made desolate before the end shall come." The lament was not a question, but a statement.[13]

Hotchkiss kept up his spirits by writing long, detailed letters to Sara. He established a routine of writing home every Sunday, and usually sent off shorter notes during the week. For an hour or so each Sabbath, he would allow his mind to return home and dwell in thoughts of the peace and joy he had left in Churchville. His musings were bittersweet, for he was homesick and anxious about Sara and the children. "I got your sweet letter of Sunday," he wrote to Sara, "how I longed to be with you—it was so kind in you to write me a long, cheering and kindly letter—it did me such an amount of good that I would not like to tell how much lest you might doubt it."[14] Sara was having trouble adjusting as well, and he tried hard to brace her up. "I know your fond heart will always find the hours weary and home desolate when I am not there, but Providence wills it that I must be away, it seems, for the path of duty is to me the path to be trodden, and I can only despise those who in this hour of their country's danger keep back any assistance they can render." Duty took priority for Hotchkiss; he weighed his sense of obligation to Virginia against his responsibility to his family, and saw in the end that the two were tied together. "I hope you will be of good

cheer and not repine or complain because I do not come," he wrote to her from the mountains, "for I want to come badly enough, Heaven well knows, but then I owe a duty to my country that I must discharge that she may be enabled to put the shield of protection over my family and enable me and them to spend some portion of our days in peace and at least transmit to our posterity freedom—of thought and action."[15]

And his daughters were in his thoughts as well. He especially worried about their growth and behavior. Knowing that Sara would read portions of the letters to them, he inserted small greetings, expressions of affection, and admonitions intended for their ears. "Kiss my babies for me many times," he wrote in one typical closing. "How I want to see their sweet faces. Pa wants them to be good, very good. Good-bye my sweet little wife.—Write to me often."[16]

Hotchkiss's concern for Sara and the children sometimes led him to act outside the spirit of the law. After drawing supplies on the commissariat, he sent them home to Churchville. "I have also sent you 4 lbs. of sugar, 3 lbs. of rice and 1 lb. of coffee, and am sorry that I cannot send you more, but I can only get these things by certifying that they are for 'my own use,' and as such I send them to you, and you can use them and say nothing about it to any one, not even telling the children where they came from, though I prefer that you should have them as part and parcel of myself."[17]

Given the extraordinary depth of Hotchkiss's devotion to his family, his decision to leave home and enter the service might seem puzzling. Even accepting his rationale that serving his country was the surest way to protect his family in time of war, one suspects that his dedication to the cause was not as strong as the bonds that tied him to his family. In fact, his motivation for entering the service was not entirely patriotic—it was partly economic. The family had

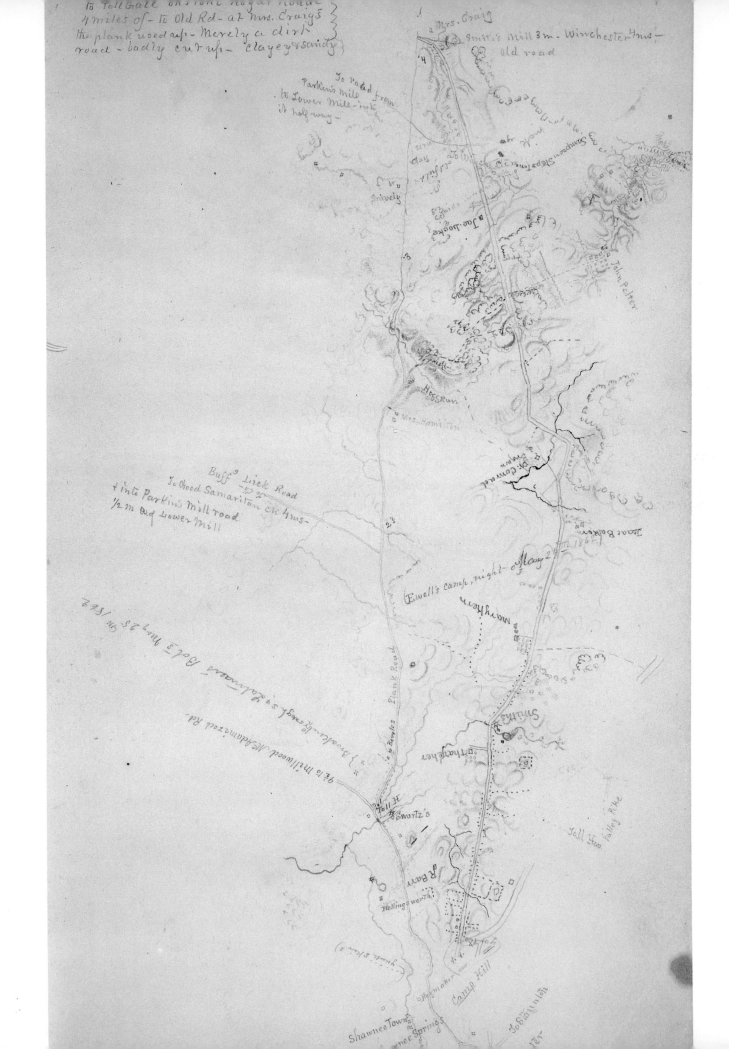

begun a major business venture—the academy—less than two years earlier. Once all the young men left for war, shutting down the school, money became a problem in the Hotchkiss household. After April, the academy property was a tax liability, and the farm, run by brother Nelson, was intended to support the school, not to make money in its own right. Deprived of his principal means of livelihood, Hotchkiss was almost completely without money to provide for his family. Like tens of thousands of other men, he sought work with the country's largest employer: the army. Hotchkiss's letters home were filled with talk of money and finances. After he had secured an official position as a topographer, he wrote to Sara "I get 100 dollars a month … I cannot afford to lose my place in such hard times as these, when a few months service will enable me to get money enough to keep us comfortable for some time, and I shall certainly spend the winter at home, teaching a short 3-month-or-so session, leaving the army as soon as it goes into winter quarters."[18] Throughout his army service, even through the hectic and stirring weeks of the great campaigns, Hotchkiss would earn extra money by drawing maps for those willing to pay for them. He began this extra duty during his first campaign in western Virginia. "I have agreed to do an extra job," he told Sara, "for a Lieut. Humphreys of Miss. and make him a map…. He wants to send it home, and I shall get pay for that, eight or ten dollars, and if I can only get the rest that is due me I shall be able to get along very well."[19] Most of the money Hotchkiss earned in this way he sent home.

While Hotchkiss worked on his survey of Camp Garnett, the command situation changed with the arrival of Lt. Col. John Pegram of the 20th Virginia Infantry. Young, clear-eyed, strikingly handsome, Pegram was a native of Petersburg, Virginia, and a professional soldier. Though he was a lieutenant colonel, he outranked Heck by virtue of having been in the service longer, and when he arrived at Camp Garnett, he took command. Hotchkiss, who was apparently present when Pegram arrived, disliked the new commander from the start, thinking him "arrogant" as well as "arbitrary and selfish."[20] Pegram, it seems, was especially rude to Hotchkiss's friend and sponsor Heck, which rankled the surveyor deeply. Despite Hotchkiss's views, Pegram's resume was impressive—he had been graduated in the top ten in his class at West Point, served as cavalry instructor there, and was a veteran of cavalry service on the western plains. But he was just twenty-nine years old and had little experience commanding troops—and no experience leading volunteer soldiers, many of whom disliked West Point professionals. Pegram apparently made little effort to strengthen his relationship with Heck and his men and seemed not to care whether he had their respect or support. Many of the rank and file, and the officers for that matter, willingly withheld both. Hotchkiss would never forget or forgive Pegram's haughtiness at Camp Garnett, and his dislike of Pegram would be plain more than three years later, when the war brought the two men together again.

Hotchkiss had begun his survey of Rich Mountain area none too soon. Just days later, the Federals began their move toward Beverly. The Federal commander, Maj. Gen. George B. McClellan, planned a two-pronged advance against Garnett. While a small column moved from the north toward Garnett's position at Laurel Hill, a second, stronger column would approach Camp Garnett from the west on the turnpike. McClellan would lead this column in the hope of cutting off Garnett's lines of supply and communication at Beverly.

As McClellan's force drew near, the Confederates at Camp Garnett grew more vigilant. Heck and Pegram knew they would need every one of their men in action if they were to defend the camp. Heck gave Hotchkiss a musket and ordered him into the breastworks. There the engineer passed most of July 10 and all of the 11th as an infantryman waiting for the Federals to attack. But the Federals would never attack Camp Garnett.

Before dawn on July 11, Brig. Gen. William S. Rosecrans led a portion of McClellan's force, just under 2,000 men, on a silent march through thick forests around the southern flank of the defensive positions occupied by Heck's and Pegram's men at Camp Garnett. The Federals moved past the Confederate camp and up the western face of Rich Mountain, intent on seizing the crest at the point where the turnpike crossed. By 3 p.m., Rosecrans's men were in position to attack, but they found the road more heavily defended than they had expected. The Confederates had learned of the imminent attack just in time and had rushed reinforcements to the mountain crest. The Southerners offered stiff resistance in the yard of a farmer named Hart, but the Federals persisted, and by concentrating sharpshooter fire on Confederate artillery horses, they created enough confusion among the Confederates to finally dislodge them and seize the road.

Heck's men at Camp Garnett had no part in the engagement on the mountain to their rear, but by sunset, Heck knew things had gone badly for the Confederates. He called together some of his officers, including Hotchkiss, and told them that he did not know where Pegram was, but that the commander's last orders were for Heck to hold the line at Camp Garnett. Heck said he would follow his orders and directed his officers to return to their companies and prepare to defend the camp.

Just as the meeting was ending, Pegram rode up. He explained that the Federals had gained the road and that Camp Garnett was now sealed off. The Southerners were trapped, with Federals to their front and rear, rugged mountains covered by dense forests on either side, and the landscape shrouded in darkness. A cold rain began to fall.

Pegram had worked hard that day trying to salvage the battle on the mountain. He had been energetic in deploying troops to defend the road, but with the Federal success, which made Camp Garnett untenable, he ordered his troops nearby to retreat to Beverly, escaping however they could. To his credit, Pegram did not lead the retreat but rode deeper into the Federal trap to inform Heck of events. By this time, however, Pegram apparently had succumbed to fatigue and was a beaten man. Hotchkiss remembered Pegram standing in the rain at Camp Garnett, saying that "being exhausted by his efforts during the day and night, and having been injured by being thrown against a tree by the shying of his horse, he would remain in camp and surrender; but he directed Heck to immediately withdraw the small remaining force from the works and retreat in the direction of Laurel hill." [21]

It was then about 1 a.m. The men were tired from a day of tension. The rain was steady and the forests black, but Heck was game. He turned to Hotchkiss and asked if he could lead them out over the mountain to Confederate lines. Hotchkiss had ridden all over the area in his survey, and in the absence of a local guide, he was the best man to lead the escape. He had, in fact, reconnoitered the country around the proposed escape route just a few days earlier and felt confident he could find his way over the mountain without meeting any Federals. Heck immediately began preparations for departure.

With little or no deliberation, Hotchkiss had accepted perhaps a topographer's greatest challenge. The escape attempt would be the sternest test he would face during the war of his abilities and his nerve. He was charged with leading a column of tired men through a pathless forest and over a steep, rugged mountain in pitch darkness. Rain clouds filled the sky, so navigation by the stars was impossible. A pocket compass would be of little use in the wet blackness. Hotchkiss would have to proceed by memory and instinct, trusting to his sense of direction. His only navigational aids would be the flow of the mountain streams he would cross and the slope of the ground. Under ideal conditions, Hotchkiss could have taken an azimuth with his compass and positioned men along the route to point the column in the right direction, or he could have made blaze marks on trees to mark the trail for the rest of the column. But the retreat was decided upon and begun far too quickly to allow Hotchkiss to set up a guide system, and in any case, it was too dark and the woods too thick for him to take bearings with his compass.[22]

The column formed up quickly, Hotchkiss in the lead, followed immediately by Company C of the 25th Virginia under Capt. Robert Doak Lilley. Lilley was a native of Hotchkiss's Augusta County, a graduate of Washington College in Lexington, Virginia, and a former salesman of surveying instruments, in which capacity, perhaps, he came to know Hotchkiss. Lilley had recruited his company in Augusta County, and, though he was just twenty-five years old, with no military experience whatever, his recruits elected him their captain. They named the company the Augusta Lee Rifles.[23]

The forest was a dense tangle of evergreen and laurel, little more than a swamp in many places. Progress was slow. Even in daylight, a column passing through pathless woods might move at a speed of fifty yards per minute, but darkness and the density of the growth reduced the rate of travel to less than half that. The leaders had to blaze a trail through the interlocked pines, dogwoods, laurels, and thousands of chest-high maple saplings that bent and recoiled like whips as the men pushed past. "The rain pouring down in torrents and the night being very dark," Hotchkiss later recalled, "the line of march could hardly be kept but by a constant effort on the part of the men to keep almost in contact with each other, and our line was often broken by the fallen trees, dense thickets, and precipices that we encountered."[24]

The march continued steadily, the leaders forgoing the usual five- or ten-minute break each hour. The men concentrated so completely on working their way through the tangled woods that they were taken off guard by a low whistle coming from the woods to their right. Hotchkiss froze, and most of the line halted behind him. They had apparently strayed close to a Federal picket post. Not knowing what to do, Hotchkiss replied with a similar whistle and waited. Nothing happened. Quickly he set off again, passing word back down the column to keep moving.[25]

Soaked and weary, Hotchkiss led the slogging column onto the summit of Rich Mountain about dawn the next morning, July 12. There, in eerie gray light amid the dripping chestnut trees, Hotchkiss and Lilley were stunned to see just seventy men following them rather than the nearly five hundred that had trailed them out of Camp Garnett five hours earlier. The two men assumed that the rest of the column had lost contact and wandered off into the black woods. Only later would Hotchkiss learn that his column had split up as a result of confused orders from Pegram.

After Hotchkiss had led Heck's men out of Camp Garnett, Pegram changed his mind about surrendering and decided to try to escape to Garnett's camp at Laurel Hill. He sent a messenger to find Hotchkiss's column and bring it back. The messenger found the rear of the column and halted it; Heck obeyed orders and passed the word toward the head of the long column to about face. But the order only made it as far as the rear of Lilley's company. Led by Hotchkiss, the Augusta Lee Rifles continued the retreat unaware of events behind them. Pegram joined Heck in the forest and they struck off in a direction different from Hotchkiss's. The next day, lost and surrounded, Pegram decided to surrender his column, despite Heck's vigorous objections. In his official report of the incident, Pegram made no mention of his decision to remain at Camp Garnett and surrender. Instead, he made it seem as though he had always intended to escape over the mountain. He made no mention of Hotchkiss and said he himself led the column through the woods. Pegram also expressed surprise that Lilley's company, which he referred to as "Captain Silly's company," had strayed from Heck's column. It had "disappeared and has not been heard from since." In fact, Lilley's company alone escaped.[26]

About noon on the twelfth, Hotchkiss led his little company into Beverly, which had been abandoned by the Confederates during the night. Citizens were helping themselves to the food and supplies left behind by the army, and the weary soldiers also replaced their wet, torn, muddy clothes. Hotchkiss took new trousers, socks, and a coat before leading the column out of the village. Federals occupied the town shortly afterward.[27]

The small column was able to walk on a road now and made better time, marching through the day and finally halting at the western foot of Cheat Mountain in the evening. Wrote Hotchkiss, "We decided that an encounter from an ambuscade was preferable to a further retreat in our exhausted condition, having spent a whole day and half the night on our feet in the breastworks, and then retreated 30 miles through dense thickets, over fallen timber and ledges of rocks, through water courses and along muddy roads; but every man had his arms and ammunition and was ready for an encounter."[28]

The next morning, the refugees marched to the summit of Cheat, where they found a jumbled mass of Confederates: confused stragglers, survivors, and small remnants from other commands. No one seemed to be in command. Hotchkiss and Lilley met with the officers and discussed what to do. They decided to stay and defend the mountain should the Federals come after it. But after learning that John Letcher, Virginia's governor, happened to be a guest at a nearby home, the officers—apparently all of junior, company grade—sought to have their decision buttressed by the governor's sanction. Selecting someone to take their request to Letcher, they turned to the learned Professor Hotchkiss. Though tired and dirty after his long march, Hotchkiss accepted the mission and set off to obtain the governor's consent.

Hotchkiss found Letcher at the Greenbrier River at the foot of Allegheny Mountain with several hundred Confederate troops. The governor wavered but finally decided that the men on Cheat Mountain must withdraw to Allegheny Mountain, thus surrendering much territory to the Federals. Hotchkiss marched to the rear with Lilley's company, and a few days later, the Confederates withdrew to the town of Monterey to recruit, reorganize, and prepare to meet another Federal advance.

The Southerners had lost heavily at Rich Mountain, especially in men captured. Among the killed was General Garnett, who fell while supervising a withdrawal, and among the prisoners were 455 officers and men, including most of Heck's regiment, surrendered by Pegram.[29] Hotchkiss had escaped capture by the narrowest of margins, but suffered losses nonetheless. He had been forced to abandon his tent and all in it—the maps he had with him, including the Camp Garnett and Rich Mountain map on which he had been laboring so hard, all but a few of his personal effects, and most significant, his engineering equipment: the barometer, the measuring chain, and his compasses. It was not public property he had lost, but personal possessions, and he would eventually submit a claim to the Confederate government for eighty-three dollars. Some of what he lost had tremendous sentimental value. He wrote to Sara, telling her he "regretted the loss of my sweet little Testament, the gift of Mr. Gilbert at the time of our marriage, as much as anything I left behind, and next the loss of my fine Barometer and then of my old blue cloak. I could almost cry at the loss of such an old and faithful friend, one that has been my constant companion for 14 years, has shielded myself, my bosom friend and my children from the storm and comforted over many a weary mile."[30]

At Monterey, Hotchkiss was honored by the men he had led in the escape over Rich Mountain. His friends and neighbors in the Augusta Lee Rifles made him an honorary member of the company. He was also made adjutant of what was left of Heck's regiment, the 25th Virginia Infantry. The post of adjutant was usually filled by a lieutenant, but Hotchkiss told Sara he held the rank and received the pay of a captain.[31] He undertook the duties of adjutant, which consisted mainly of overseeing the preparation and flow of paperwork at regimental headquarters, perhaps as a prospectus, much as he had the engineering assignment under Heck. The position at headquarters of the 25th Virginia might lead to a better, more official, and permanent appointment, with the steady pay that Sara and the children needed.

While in Monterey, Hotchkiss made an acquaintance that led to an important acquisition. Col. William B. Taliaferro of the 23rd Virginia Infantry shared Hotchkiss's fondness for maps and openly admired the latter's work. The two men became good friends, and Hotchkiss eventually revealed that he coveted a particular map in Taliaferro's personal collection. The colonel agreed to trade the map to Hotchkiss in return for some others Hotchkiss possessed. The deal was struck, and Hotchkiss thus ob-

tained a cartographic resource of great value: the famous Nine-Sheet Map of Virginia.[32]

The original Nine-Sheet Map was produced under contract in 1829 by one Henry Boye for the Virginia legislature. It was an ambitious undertaking, for surveyors had to cover the entire state, traveling on foot, by wagon, and on horseback. Boye, an engineer, conducted his own survey, but also relied heavily on a series of county maps produced by John Wood in the 1820s. These maps showed county lines, transportation routes, and cities. Boye's colossal map—when the nine sections of the map were assembled they measured more than five feet by nine feet—made a very favorable impression on the politicians who had voted to fund it, but despite its attractiveness, the map showed the Commonwealth in only fair detail. Neither Boye's map nor any of those drawn by Wood was comprehensive. Still, the maps they produced were the most modern and comprehensive cartographic portraits of Virginia ever made, and for almost forty years they would influence virtually every other map of the Commonwealth.

A decade after Boye's monumental work, Claudius Crozet, a former officer in Napoleon's army, produced a transportation map of Virginia by using Boye's nine sheets as a base map. Crozet incorporated additional data of his own, but in conducting his survey, the Frenchman came to the alarming realization that Wood and Boye had both made substantial errors. Crozet was especially critical of Wood's county surveys, writing that "some are without scales, others give neither courses nor meridian lines, and all of them are generally filled up by guess, with streams, ridges and roads drawn at random, some of them even without real existence." Since Boye had based his maps partially on Wood's surveys, the errors were repeated in the great nine-sheet map, and Boye introduced many new errors with faulty arithmetic.[33]

In the 1850s, a former German army officer named

Ludwig von Bucholtz received state funding to overhaul Boye's mammoth Nine-Sheet Map, but the legislature tied his hands by insisting that starting from scratch and conducting a new survey would be far too expensive. The lawmakers told the German that he must simply make corrections to the original printing plates executed for Boye almost thirty years before. This edict ensured that Bucholtz's new version would be inaccurate.

And so matters stood at the outbreak of the war. That Hotchkiss so highly valued the Nine-Sheet Map, despite its flaws, indicates how desperately he and other military topographers needed information about Virginia. Most maps of Virginia produced before the war were either atlas-style maps, in which detail was sacrificed for clarity; road maps, which were concerned mainly with showing transportation routes; or cadastral maps, which showed property lines and state and county boundaries. Such maps were of great value to the travelers, businessmen, and tax collectors for whom they were drawn, but to soldiers they were virtually useless.

Most map users before the war were primarily interested in the locations of places and the distances between them—where Staunton was, for example, and how far it was from Richmond. Military men needed a different kind of map altogether, the kind in shortest supply: highly detailed topographic maps, which showed the natural and man-made features of the landscape. Army officers, North and South, from general to lieutenant, were charged with

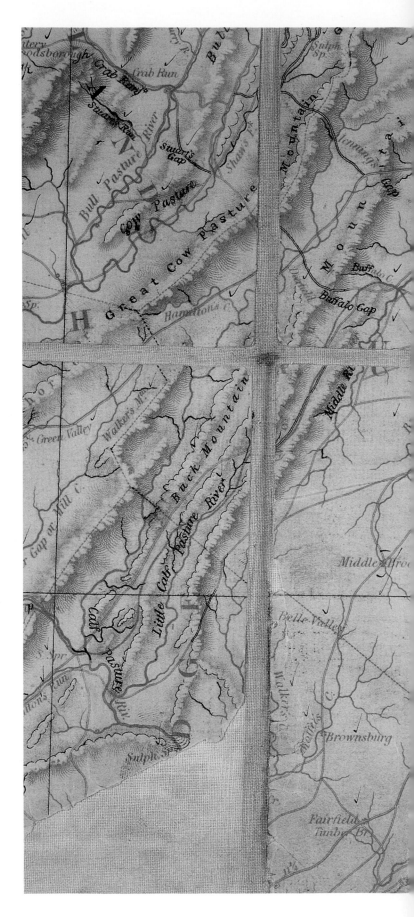

A SECTION OF HENRY BOYE'S NINE-SHEET MAP OF VIRGINIA SHOWS HOTCHKISS'S AUGUSTA COUNTY. THOUGH LADEN WITH ERRORS AND COMPLETELY INADEQUATE FOR MILITARY PURPOSES, BOYE'S MAP WAS THE BEST GENERAL SOURCE OF INFORMATION ABOUT VIRGINIA'S TOPOGRAPHY AT THE OUTBREAK OF THE WAR. THIS COPY BEARS HEAVY ANNOTATIONS AND CORRECTION MARKS.

leading men forward into unknown territory, and they needed to know not just the locations and distances between cities, but how to get to those places. They needed to know how long the journey would take and what obstacles they might encounter on the way. Generals needed to know of all the roads in a region, not just the major routes. They needed to know where the bridges were over rivers and streams, whether those rivers were fordable after rain, and if so, where. And they needed to know the location of mountains, swamps, forests, and scores of other topographical details—everything that might help or hinder them in getting to their destination. The absence of such maps led officers in both armies to feel that they were operating in the dark. An experienced surveyor and cartographer like Hotchkiss was a man bearing a candle who could show them where they were and where they might go. He immediately became important.

After less than a week at Monterey, the regiment withdrew farther eastward to McDowell. Hotchkiss, a member of the infantry now, and without the luxury of a wagon and team, suffered on the march and arrived at McDowell on the rainy banks of the swollen Bull Pasture River thoroughly worn out. Within twenty-four hours, he was seriously ill from exposure, fatigue, and poor food. "I found myself sick," he wrote to Sara a few days later, "truly sick, from head to foot, had a severe pain, all night, in my abdomen, was fainting sick. One of the boys gave me a dose of Radway's Ready Relief and I commenced vomiting and purging in earnest, but was still in much pain, so I took another dose, the hottest medicine I ever saw, it produced no nausea but vomited me in a moment and I kept on, then I bethought me of the tea you so kindly sent me and had one of the boys go to a house near by and get some made for me. It was good, but it did not stop my ailings, so Capt Lilley proposed, about dark, that I should go to Mrs. Alexander's, nearby, where I was very kindly cared

for, put in a clean bed, the first one I have been in since I left home, was very sick until midnight, lonely enough too in the midst of a house full of sick and well, but by keeping quiet my diarrhoea got checked some and I slept some. In the morning they gave me a nice cup of scalded bread and milk and it braced me up a good deal." [34]

Unfortunately, just as Hotchkiss was feeling better on that Sunday morning, the regiment received orders to return to Monterey. "It is too bad that they will always move here on Sunday, but there was no choice, and as I was the only staff officer here I was almost obliged to come, so I got Mrs. Alexander to give me a canteen full of boiled milk and laid down on the top of a baggage wagon and jolted over here, kept up by my canteen of milk." [35]

He arrived at Monterey too sick even to unroll his blanket for a bed. A young soldier "kindly fixed up things and made me a good cup of tea and one of the boys got me a nice piece of light bread and I ate quite a supper and slept very well." Hotchkiss regained his strength in the days to follow, but his constitution had suffered a severe blow, and amid the poor sanitation and illness of the camp, he was still at risk. Of Monterey, he wrote, "The pollution of the place is such that the waters are not in a condition to wash with, unless brought from some ways, it is the worst place in the state for men to be that are not well, there are few houses and they are full of all sorts and conditions and the sick have a hard time, some of them die daily." [36]

At Monterey, Hotchkiss met General Garnett's successor: Brig. Gen. William Wing Loring, a forty-two-year-old veteran of two wars and arduous campaigns in the West against Indians and Mormons. He had served with distinction in Mexico, gaining commendations and losing an arm. He remained in the service and became one of the youngest full colonels in the army. He came to western Virginia full of military knowledge and experience, but despite his empty sleeve, his small, soft, sleepy, eyes and huge, broad forehead gave him the look of a eccentric professor, not a captain of war.

The Federals had been slow to continue their advance from Rich Mountain, and when they finally moved, it was under a new commander. McClellan was called to Washington for promotion, and General Rosecrans took his place. Loring's Confederates prepared to meet the new Federal advances. Reinforcements and much-needed supplies snaked into the region from eastern Virginia to the staging area at McDowell.

Perhaps the clearest sign that the Confederates were determined to resist the Federals was the arrival from Richmond of President Jefferson Davis's military advisor, Gen. Robert E. Lee. He was fit and athletic for his fifty-four years and was highly respected in military circles—a career soldier, a son of a Revolutionary War hero, a graduate of and former superintendent at West Point, and the possessor of a distinguished record in the Mexican War. Lee's role in western Virginia was not entirely clear. He was not to command troops, but to provide some oversight of operations. Loring, also a soldier of the Old Army and a man of great pride, was offended by Lee's presence. He felt Richmond was looking over his shoulder. He reacted with stubbornness. Lee, for example, proposed a Southern advance against the Federals before the Federals moved upon the Southerners. Loring agreed to an advance, but made a point of conducting preparations in his own way, on his own schedule. He felt his wet, hungry, sick army lacked too many essentials to undertake an offensive, and he decided to wait until more supplies and reinforcements could arrive from the east. The result was disastrous for the Confederates.

Among the things Loring lacked were maps. To his credit, the general moved quickly to eliminate the problem, and having heard of the bearded, professorial topographer who had led an escape from Rich Mountain, sent for Jed Hotchkiss. Hotchkiss's military resume was short, but it impressed Loring, who asked him to map the area of operations. Hotchkiss was delighted. He liked Loring, at least initially, calling him a perfect gentleman, but more important, he had at last obtained the long-desired attachment to a general. He would now be able to use his unique abilities to make a real contribution to the war effort. He accepted the assignment and resigned the adjutancy of the 25th Virginia.

In his role as topographer, Hotchkiss was apparently present at some of the meetings between Lee and Loring and saw the latter's obstinacy. "General Lee," he wrote later, "was constantly urging General Loring to advance. General Loring was constantly hesitating, claiming that he was not ready for such an advance." Hotchkiss saw that Lee was conscious of Loring's sensitivity and delivered remarks "always in the nature of suggestions and inquiries as to the expediency of this or that movement." Loring was adamant, however, and pursued his preparations with meticulous care.[37]

One thing that Lee and Loring did agree upon was the need for a map of the Tygart Valley, the avenue by which the Confederates would advance whenever Loring felt ready to do so. Loring charged Hotchkiss with surveying and preparing a map of the valley, and to show approval and confidence, gave him a semi-official appointment as a lieutenant of engineers detailed to topographical duty. This appointment did not carry with it an official rank in the Confederate Engineer Corps, but Hotchkiss accepted it and went to work.

Unfortunately, the new assignment coincided with the onset of terrible weather early in August. Hotchkiss described the Cheat Mountain region as a damp, chilly, 5,000-foot-high watershed area "covered by a vast and dense forest of large evergreen trees." That summer, the region was especially wet, with "a steady downpour of rain

[and] intervals of heavy mists" that saturated the landscape. "Even the graded mountain roads," noted Hotchkiss, "cut up by the constant passing of heavy army trains, were converted into streams of axle-deep mud, making them practically impassable for vehicles of any kind."[38] The weather interfered greatly with Hotchkiss's work, especially since he was still feeling the effects of the illness and cramps he had suffered at McDowell weeks earlier. Despite the rain and his unsteady health, he began gathering all the existing maps he could of the region. Using what knowledge he had of the valley and what he could gain from a cursory survey and the reports of scouts and prisoners, he corrected the old maps. These updated maps would serve the immediate needs of the commanders. He then began a more complete survey with the aim of producing a comprehensive map. He was fortunate to have the assistance of a resident of the valley, a Mr. Conrad, who was not only a county magistrate, but also happened to be a surveyor. "His knowledge of the country was very remarkable," wrote Hotchkiss. "In fact he was a living notebook, giving me courses and distances which enabled me to construct the entire country in front of us that was quite sufficient for military purposes."[39]

But the advantages Hotchkiss gained through the assistance of Conrad were counterbalanced by the horrible working and living conditions at camp. Not only was the weather wet ("It is raining now," he wrote home, "it rains here every day and every night"),[40] making it difficult to find a dry place to work, but Hotchkiss had lost much of his equipment and had to make do with what was available. "My drawing board was the head of a barrel," he wrote to a friend, "my seat the half of another barrel." And there were the usual persistent hardships of camp life to endure—inadequate food and shelter and widespread disease. "The army was suffering terribly from sickness," he recorded later. "It was raining constantly, and the roads were impassable from mud, and more than half of the troops were sick: large numbers died daily, typhoid fever having broken out, and, as many of the troops were from the extreme South, large numbers of them were sick from the chill of the climate."[41] He was surprised and dismayed to see the behavior of many of the local residents, telling Sara that "more of the men have died for the want of nurses and proper diet than any other cause. The women here flee away from the army instead of coming to its aid and cheering up the men by their appearance. There are many of them here, but they seem to think it indelicate or beneath them, or something, I do not know what, to take care of the sick soldiers. There are a great many sick here. I can hear them groan, here where I am, from the upper story of the tavern which is converted into a hospital."[42]

Throughout those difficult weeks, Hotchkiss became impressed with the general quality of the men who served as Confederate officers, particularly Lee, who refused to let the weather deter him, and who was, according to Hotchkiss, "constantly in the saddle, riding to the front and reconnoitering the country."[43] In camp, Hotchkiss saw with approval that Lee ate the same rough and scant rations as the men in the ranks. Over the next four years, Hotchkiss and Lee would work together regularly, and each would come to have much respect for the other. But Hotchkiss had already formed a different opinion of his immediate chief, General Loring. After the war, Hotchkiss wrote that Loring "struck me as lacking in nearly all the qualities necessary for a commander of an army designed to carry on an offensive campaign in a difficult region. He was always hesitating what to do, was always suggesting difficulties in the way of active operations, and worse than all to my mind, he was always filling himself with brandy and thus incapacitating himself for his duties."[44]

Hotchkiss soon completed his map and presented it to Loring and Lee, but Loring continued to stall, and the rain continued to fall, and soon the condition of the roads made movement impossible. Hotchkiss thought that militarily the situation had hit bottom. "The commissariat was as bad as it could possibly be. At times the troops were entirely without food; the quartermaster's supplies were wholly inadequate, and the roads were in such a condition as to make it almost impossible to move wagons or artillery.... everything conspired to dishearten and to put it out of the power of any commander to accomplish results with such raw troops." [45]

Finally, with the cold, wet weather, poor sanitation, and indifferent food claiming more victims every day, Hotchkiss once again fell ill. It was typhoid fever, and for two days, all he could scrawl in his journal was "quite ill." When he rallied, he wrote optimistically, "I have been very sick for 4 or 5 days ... it was a typhoid attack, very bad headache, pains in my limbs and I have not slept any of consequence, but hope to tonight." [46]

On September 8, Loring at last moved his army forward. The rains, which had abated for a few days, long enough for the roads to dry, returned to drench the Confederate marchers and intensify the misery of the sick. Hotchkiss accompanied the army, but he was far from well.

On September 11 and 12, the Confederates made contact with the Federals at Cheat Mountain, and the planned attack for the 13th seemed to hold the promise of success. But on that day, the leader of the key Confederate column became confused and hesitant. The attack misfired and the offensive fizzled. Lee and Loring withdrew back down the valley.

As depressing and potentially disastrous as the defeat was, Hotchkiss had greater concerns. His health had worsened to the point where he was now seriously ill. On September 18, he wrote to Nelson at Churchville that he and the army had just returned from a foray against the enemy and that the expedition was a failure. "The exposure," he wrote, "used up a good many, myself among the rest. I came back completely exhausted and have been lying on my back for two days. Added to my previous state of weakness I will tell you I felt badly, and all alone ... twenty times did I cry like a child at the thoughts of home and the thousand attentions I should have. Oh! Brother, I never want to spend such a day again." [47]

Clearly, Hotchkiss was no longer fit for service: physically and perhaps emotionally spent, he had seen men sicken and die in the preceding weeks, so he knew that he must get home where he could recover under Sara's attention. He got permission to leave and was flattered when General Lee made arrangements to get him away from the camp. Hotchkiss took rides in the direction of home and wrote to Nelson to send a wagon for him. "If you can send there after me I shall be very, very glad, ... for I cannot think of jolting in the stage as my bones and flesh are now." [48] A few days later, he reached Churchville, where he went to bed. Militarily, his seventy-nine-day campaign on behalf of states' rights had been a dismal failure. But the acquaintances made and experience gained made it clear that he could be of great service to the Confederacy, if only his contributions could be put to better use. He would rest, recover his health, and try again.

BOTH
HOTCHKISS
AND MRS. JACKSON
CONSIDERED THIS
PHOTOGRAPH OF MAJ.
GEN. THOMAS J.
"STONEWALL"
JACKSON, TAKEN IN
FEBRUARY 1862, TO BE
THE MOST REVEALING
OF THE GENERAL'S
CHARACTER. GOV-
ERNED BY PIETY,
MODESTY, AND AMBI-
TION, JACKSON WAS A
MYSTERY TO MOST OF
THOSE WHO SERVED
UNDER HIM. SOME
IDOLIZED HIM,
OTHERS THOUGHT
HIM MAD, BUT
HOTCHKISS IMME-
DIATELY RECOGNIZED
JACKSON AS A MAN OF
RARE QUALITY.

CHAPTER THREE

"AND YE SHALL CHASE YOUR ENEMIES"

Throughout the unusually severe winter of 1861-62, Virginians in the Shenandoah Valley huddled by their hearths and wondered about the future. The armies in the Old Dominion passed the bleak months planning and organizing. The Federals, having suffered an embarrassing defeat at the Battle of Manassas, or Bull Run, in July 1861, reassessed their strategy and drilled hard in camps around Washington. The offensive role was clearly theirs in this war, and virtually everyone in Washington and Richmond, from president to private, understood that the offensive would come with the return of fair fighting weather. The war would surely begin in earnest in March or April of 1862.

The winter days were anxious ones in Washington, as the Lincoln administration and Congress joined legions of newspaper editors across the North in crying loudly for action. The commander of the huge Federal Army of the Potomac, Maj. Gen. George McClellan, the hero who had defeated Hotchkiss and his comrades at Rich Mountain the previous summer, resisted the clamor. He was an inspirational leader, but an exasperatingly slow and meticulous planner. He would move when the army was ready, he told the president, and his target would be Richmond, the capital of the Confederacy. He would capture it and end the war, he said.

Lincoln approved of McClellan's confidence, but had doubts about the general's plan of attack. McClellan wished to move his entire army by ship to a peninsula formed by the York and James rivers east of Richmond and advance on the city from that direction. Lincoln, remembering how the Confederates had done the unexpected at Manassas, wondered what might happen if the Southerners decided to attack Washington while McClellan's army was shipbound. And what would be Washington's fate if the general should be trapped, defeated, or destroyed on the Peninsula? The president declared that McClellan's plans must include provisions for the protection of Washington, which meant that the general must leave enough troops out of his offensive plans to control the avenues of access to the Federal capital, including the Shenandoah Valley.

Because the significant political barriers of the war ran generally east-west, dividing territory into north and south, the natural barriers of the Shenandoah Valley—the Allegheny Mountains on the west and the Blue Ridge on the east—formed a natural corridor that crossed the political boundaries between Virginia and the North. The northern end of the Valley at Harpers Ferry yawned invitingly at the very doorstep of the North, scant miles from Pennsylvania and considerably north of Washington. An aggressive Confederate commander in the Valley could use the mountains to shield his advance, cross the Potomac River into Maryland, and threaten Washington from the north. It was this possibility that worried Lincoln and caused him to require McClellan to control the Valley.

So as the cold and cloudy days passed away and the fair campaigning weather of 1862 drew near, the stage was set for a struggle in the Shenandoah Valley. It was a region of uncommon beauty, as the recollections of visitors who saw it for the first time attest. "The great Valley of Virginia was before us in all its beauty," wrote one Louisianian. "Fields of wheat spread far and wide, interspersed with woodlands, bright in their robes of tender green. Wherever appropriate sites existed, quaint old mills, with turning wheels, were busily grinding the previous year's harvest; and grove and eminence showed comfortable homesteads. The soft vernal influence shed a languid grace over the scene."[1] The Valley was a place so fertile, so temperate, and so fair that for generations, men had been driven to war to possess it. Native Americans had long fought over the territory, and continued fighting with European settlers almost into the nineteenth century. By the 1860s, little more than a hundred years after the first whites set foot in the Valley, a substantial white population had huge tracts of the rich soil under cultivation, providing food and fodder for Virginia. War had not touched this generation of Shenandoah farmers as it had previous residents of the region, but the people of the Valley were to learn that the same natural attributes that attract peaceful, industrious lovers of splendor also attract agents of destruction. The bottomlands of river valleys, so precious and productive for farmers, become commissaries to nations at war. Wide, glassy rivers full of fish become barriers to protect legions from their enemies, and wooded mountain slopes, so pleasing to the eye and spirit, become commanding fortresses and spy towers. So it has always been. Throughout

history, armies have occasionally strayed into swamps or deserts, but Mars, the god of war, generally chooses to lay waste to paradise. Eden, the scene of creation's first conflict, has remained man's battleground, and so it would be in the spring of 1862.

Ted Hotchkiss spent the winter in his warm house, surrounded by his loving family, slowly recovering his health. By March—the month the ancient Romans had named for their war god—Hotchkiss was ready to take the field. He sought, however, to avoid the confusion and embarrassment of the previous summer when he had reported to General Garnett's headquarters in search of an appointment. He wrote to a friend, William S. H. Baylor, an Augusta County resident serving on the staff of Maj. Gen. Thomas J. Jackson, the commander of the Confederate Valley District. Hotchkiss asked Baylor if Jackson needed a topographical engineer and, if so, whether there was a chance Hotchkiss might obtain the appointment. Baylor cordially responded that the chances were quite good, and he advised Hotchkiss to come to Jackson and tender his services in person.[2]

About this time, Governor John Letcher called out Virginia's militia in preparation for expected Federal advances into the state. Three regiments from Augusta County mobilized to march north and join Jackson's small army at Winchester. Hotchkiss decided to accompany the militiamen and see Jackson as Baylor had suggested. On March 12, 1862, a Monday morning, Hotchkiss kissed Sara and his two daughters good-bye and once again went off to war.

The militiamen received a disheartening introduction to campaigning. Rain and snow squalls soaked and chilled them as they marched. Everything was wet, and walking was an exhausting and unpleasant torment. Hotchkiss, however, remained cheerful, and if he experienced any discomfort on the trip, it was from anxiety over his future. The officers present had made him unofficial adjutant of the 160th Regiment Virginia Militia (his seventy-nine days of service the previous summer made him, in their eyes, a veteran), but with Jackson's command being reorganized to accommodate the consolidation and integration of the new troops, no position in a militia organization could be considered permanent. Hotchkiss kept his hopes low. "I have been very busy and have had to write a great deal," he wrote to Sara of his duties in helping to organize and muster men, "but expect to get through tomorrow, when I shall be a private, I suppose, as there are not enough men for a regiment."[3]

Still, he hoped for the coveted position at headquarters on Jackson's staff. On March 20, Hotchkiss and another officer rode to Jackson's headquarters to report the arrival of the Augusta militiamen. Jackson, who had performed well at the Battle of Manassas, where he had earned the nickname "Stonewall," was already among the more famous men in Virginia, so Hotchkiss must have been curious as he entered the general's presence. The two had met before, half a decade or more ago in Lexington, Virginia, where Jackson had been an instructor of natural philosophy and artillery tactics at the Virginia Military Institute. Hotchkiss had been a guest at the home of Jackson's father-in-law, the Reverend Dr. George Junkin, president of Washington College in Lexington, at which the distinguished Valley educator Mr. Hotchkiss was serving on a board of visiting examiners. The meeting in that peaceful college town must have seemed far in the past for both men as they met for the second time. Jackson received the news of the militia's arrival gratefully and chatted civilly for a time, but Hotchkiss made no mention of his desire to serve on the general's staff, perhaps wishing to speak with Baylor first.

Hotchkiss spent most of the following day with Baylor

William S. H. Baylor, Hotchkiss's friend and supporter, helped the cartographer gain a place on Jackson's staff.

mustering militiamen into Confederate service. Baylor, just two weeks shy of his thirty-first birthday, was a native of Virginia and a lawyer of considerable ability. At the age of twenty-six, four years after receiving his law degree from the University of Virginia, he was elected Commonwealth's attorney at Staunton. In 1861, he was made colonel of the 5th Virginia Volunteer Infantry and fought with the regiment at Manassas. Now, Will Baylor, "a good fellow— first rate, good natured and accommodating," thought Hotchkiss, was Jackson's inspector general, and Hotchkiss's prime booster.[4]

When Jackson finally came down to the militia camp to look over his new recruits, the observing Hotchkiss quickly decided that he liked the man. It was an opinion Hotchkiss would never alter, and in fact, his admiration of the general would grow and deepen with the passage of time.[5] Jackson was a thirty-eight-year-old Virginian from the highlands of what later became West Virginia. He had been an unexceptional student in his youth, but managed to gain admission to the United States Military Academy, where he made few close friends but many cordial acquaintances. A fellow cadet remembered him as "a tall, raw-boned young man, older than most members of his class and exceedingly shy and bashful." Classmates also remembered him as a tenacious worker. His efforts to solve mathematical equations at the blackboard were "sometimes painful to witness," recalled a fellow student. "No matter what proposition was assigned to him to recite on, he would hang on to it like a bull-dog, and in his mental efforts to overcome the difficulty great drops of perspiration would roll from his face, even in the coldest weather, so that it soon became a proverb with us that whenever 'Old Jack,' or 'the General' as he was once dubbed in honor of his name, got a difficult proposition at the blackboard he was certain to flood the section room."[6] The dogged determination paid off for Jackson, for he pulled himself up to stand seventeenth of fifty-nine at graduation in 1846. He served in the artillery in the Mexican War, garnering two brevets for gallantry. After the war, he resigned his commission and accepted a teaching position at the Virginia Military Institute. He would spend the next decade there.

He was, by all accounts, a poor teacher. His presentations lacked imagination, and he could not relate well to the undisciplined and high-spirited teenagers who made up the cadet corps. They, in turn, called him "Old Tom Fool" and played pranks on him whenever they thought they could get away with it. They laughed at his enormous feet, his ungraceful gait, and his grave manner. He seemed stiff and formal at the institute and maintained an almost absurd insistence on correct and truthful speech and proper behavior at all times. But the people of the town and the other members of the faculty who got to know him saw that the stiffness grew out of a natural intensity and a devotion to the task at hand. In all his dealings with people, Jackson was direct. He addressed problems, conversations, friendships, and assignments all the same way—head on. What he lacked in tact and social grace, he made up for in sincerity and earnestness. In time, his Lexington neighbors found him to be good-hearted, likable, and a loyal friend.

But being likable and companionable were two different matters, and Jackson never made much of a companion, partly because his standards of personal conduct were discouragingly high. He was respectability personified. He neither smoked nor drank, but admitted he had tried whiskey and liked the taste of it very much—which is the very reason he never touched it again. He selected his words carefully, and if he felt that in conversation he had said something that might have been misunderstood, he would immediately seek out the other party and explain what he had meant. He made and kept good friends, but his strict code of conduct made him a puzzle to many, which bothered him not at all. He was secure enough in himself to forgo the bother of trying to make others like him. He never cared for cronies.

Jackson married twice. His first wife, Elinor Junkin, died after delivering a stillborn infant little more than a year into the marriage. His second wife, Anna Morrison, had been Elinor's friend and had come to know Jackson well. The Major, as he was called in Lexington, grew completely and utterly devoted to Anna. Both were devout Presbyterians, and Jackson believed that their union had been "ordered" by God. Together they enjoyed a full life of service to the Lord and their community in Lexington; Jackson was a deacon at the Lexington Presbyterian church and taught a Sunday school class for black children.

The years at Virginia Military Institute, however, were not entirely blissful. There were sown the seeds of an unpleasant, and perhaps unearned, reputation that labeled Jackson an eccentric. His students, who saw him only in the classroom and around campus, recorded ample anecdotal evidence of his odd behavior, and the reputation followed him, as did many of his former pupils, into the Confederate army. The early months in the service of the Confederacy, in fact, seemed to bring more alleged peculiarities to the surface. Observers said he would not eat pepper because he believed it made his leg hurt; they claimed he would not mail a letter if it would be en route on the Sabbath. He sucked on lemons, they said. He could fall asleep in a moment, they said, in the midst of a church service, a conversation, or, if he was tired enough, at table with food in his mouth. How much truth there was in any of these claims is difficult to tell, but gossip cares little for truth, and once uttered, the stories about Jackson's peculiarities took on a life of their own.

But Hotchkiss and the other men who came to know Jackson best during the war always felt that too much was made of Jackson's few idiosyncratic habits and not enough attention given to the man's soul and character. One Winchester resident, in whose home Jackson made his headquarters for a time, declared that "if he possessed [eccentric traits] at all, he failed to exhibit them in the home. I never discovered them. The fact is that they did not exist to any observable extent. Whatever 'peculiarities' he had were just those simple individualities, which we all, in greater or less degree possess."[7]

There is also no disputing that Jackson was a hard man. Though cruelty was alien to him, he could be cold and inflexible. An officer told of seeing a mounted Jackson hit a skulking soldier on the head with his bridle reins to drive him back into the line of battle, the general shouting "Go back."[8] One of his men, commenting on the general's obsession with discipline, said Jackson would have a soldier shot at the drop of a hat, and drop it himself. Jackson would in all cases and under all circumstances perform what he considered to be his duty, and if that included having a man shot, then the man would die.

One incident during the war illustrates better than any other Jackson's sense of duty and rectitude—and his faith in himself. In January 1862, while Hotchkiss was home recovering his health, his past and future commanders clashed over a point of discipline, and Jackson showed his army and the Confederate War Department that he would neither accept nor condone a junior's insubordination or unwillingness to perform his duty.

In the dead of that frigid and dismal season, Jackson assigned General Loring, Hotchkiss's commander the previous summer, to occupy Romney in the mountains of northwestern Virginia. The town was a cheerless and uncomfortable place that winter, and Loring's men suffered. Loring protested, but Jackson would not change the orders. The strong-willed Loring then went over his commander's head to the secretary of war, and the war department ordered Jackson to withdraw Loring's command. Jackson complied because he considered it his duty to do so, but the next day he wrote to the war department: "Your order … has been received and promptly complied with. With such interference in my command I cannot expect to be of much service in the field, and, accordingly, respectfully request to be ordered to report for duty to the superintendent of the Virginia Military Institute at Lexington.… Should this application not be granted, I respectfully request that the president will accept my resignation from the army."[9] Faced with this ultimatum, and with the protestations of Jackson's friend and supporter Governor John Letcher, the bureaucrats in Richmond immediately relented and meddled no more with Jackson's command of his army. Loring was transferred a few weeks later.

Jackson's impatience, severe concept of discipline, and tendency to give terse, almost brusque replies to questions made him difficult to deal with at times, and some men simply could not understand him. But it seems the men who found him most baffling were the ones who had the least in common with him. Those who looked at the whole man could see that he was not as complicated as he was made out to be. Mystery surrounded him; it did not permeate him, for some men understood him quite plainly, Hotchkiss among them. From the outset, he saw the general as being, at heart, a simple, direct man, devoid of artfulness, whose sole desire in life was to do his duty and serve God. Perhaps Hotchkiss understood the essence of Jackson because it was, to a great extent, the essence of Jed Hotchkiss as well.

Federal advances southward in the Valley convinced Jackson that his small force could not long hold Winchester, the principal city in the lower Valley and the hub of a road network linking Jackson to Confederate troops east of the Blue Ridge Mountains.

Slowly and deliberately, the Confederates began to withdraw, and the Federals, under Maj. Gen. Nathaniel P. Banks, occupied Winchester on March 12. It seemed to the Federals at least, that the campaign for the Shenandoah Valley was ended. With control of Harpers Ferry and Winchester, the Federals had blocked the lower end of the Valley and could prevent Confederate movements against Maryland or Washington. The Valley was secure, and Banks began sending troops eastward over the Blue Ridge to support McClellan and his drive on Richmond.

But Jackson was not yet through; indeed, he had not yet begun. His mission was to prevent Federal control of the Valley if he could, and in any case he was to keep the Northern troops in the Valley from moving eastward to reinforce McClellan. Jackson had to act to halt Banks's transfer of men. On March 23, he struck.

The battle was joined at Kernstown, just south of Winchester. Jackson knew he was outnumbered, but had no idea what the ratio was. He had about 3,000 men, all

weary from having marched thirty-six miles in thirty-six hours.[10] Opposing him were 7,000 rested Federals.[11] The Confederates fought well, but the Federals repulsed them, and by nightfall, Jackson was in retreat. Tactically, Kernstown was a defeat for Jackson, but strategically it achieved everything he desired. His attack was a hard slap at the complacent Banks, who was compelled to sit up and reassess the decision to send troops to McClellan. Perhaps the Valley was not secure after all.

Hotchkiss had not been engaged. In the few hectic days since he had joined Jackson's army, many of the militiamen with whom he had come had entered veteran regiments, leaving just a small knot of 380 men, including Hotchkiss, to form their own unit, which they called simply the Augusta County Militia Battalion, even after they were mustered into Confederate service. While most of the army fought at Kernstown, Hotchkiss's little battalion lay unorganized and unarmed near Mt. Jackson, more than a day's march to the south. News of the engagement came to the recruits along with orders to draw weapons and march northward to reinforce Jackson's retreating brigades. On March 24, after marching all day on the loose, dusty stones of the Valley Turnpike past an intermittent flow of ambulances bearing wounded from the battle, Hotchkiss and his weary comrades crossed Tom's Brook and began climbing a long incline. It was there that they met Jackson sitting by the road alone. The general's orders to about-face and join the retreat of the army rattled the nerves of the already restive recruits, and panic broke out. Hotchkiss and other officers remained calm and quashed the panic, reassuring the men that all would be well. The Augusta militiamen regained their composure and did as ordered. General Jackson himself was an interested observer of Hotchkiss's self-possession.[12]

The retreat continued southward on the Valley Turnpike, an excellent, stone-surfaced road, until the beaten army halted for the night at the town of Mt. Jackson. Hotchkiss, who had been active in keeping the battalion

An 1885 view shows the Valley Turnpike just north of Middletown, Virginia. During the war, the road's macadamized surface made it passable in all kinds of weather. The stone walls aided drovers by preventing their livestock from straying off the road.

together and in good trim throughout the march, arrived at camp worn out by excitement and exertion. There, much to his delight, he found two letters from Sara waiting for him—the first news he had had from her since leaving home a week earlier. His joy was short-lived, however, for the letters brought terrible news. Scarlet fever had broken out in Augusta County, Sara wrote, and their daughter Nelly was gravely ill.

The next day he wrote back to comfort Sara. "My afflicted Wife—I read, with streaming eyes, by the camp fire … your two letters … sad, sad, may God forgive me for the sorrows of last night, and may He, in mercy, have spared my child—but I am now resigned. May you be supported in your extreme sorrow. I would that I could be with you, but it is forbidden me—and it is now too late to reach you before the crisis is passed.—I wait in painful solicitude the further news.… My love to all—and kisses to my children if any are spared to me." [13]

The next day another letter arrived, written two days after the first, telling of Nelly's continuing struggle and giving her father hope. "I gave up all hopes of hearing of her alive after your first letter," he told Sara, but now, his anxiety much relieved, Hotchkiss told her that he had put in for an emergency furlough and that his request was before Jackson. "I am in poor hopes of his approving it as he wants troops so badly, and Baylor trusts the Battalion to me more than to the other officers." That Nelly was alive and still fighting was enough to make her father optimistic. He could only wait and pray, "God grant that she may be spared to us." [14]

While this calamity troubled the Hotchkiss family, General Jackson had been thinking about the schoolmaster and his abilities, and three days after the fight at Kernstown, he came to a momentous decision. He summoned Hotchkiss to headquarters.

Hotchkiss repaired immediately to Jackson's office, which he found at a stone house near Narrow Passage Creek, not far from the village of Edinburg. Jackson welcomed him, and the two talked briefly about Hotchkiss's surveying and mapping the previous summer in the western mountains. Jackson then came abruptly to the point: "I want you to make me a map of the Valley, from Harpers Ferry to Lexington, showing all the points of offence and defence in those places. Mr. Pendleton will give you orders for whatever outfit you want. Good morning, Sir." [15]

At last, Hotchkiss had the long-desired staff appointment, and in addition, he had a worthy assignment that would keep him pleasantly occupied for weeks, if not months.

Pondering why Jackson had chosen that time to engage his services, Hotchkiss later felt that it was because the general had been impressed by his coolness in quelling the nervousness in the Augusta Battalion and asked Baylor for more detail about the schoolmaster from Churchville. Two days later Hotchkiss was hired. [16]

Hotchkiss wasted little time in gathering his possessions and bidding his friends in the Augusta Battalion farewell. He reported to Capt. Alexander Swift Pendleton, Jackson's acting adjutant general, and received orders for two horses, a wagon and driver, a tent, and some other miscellaneous supplies. [17] He shared the good news with Sara, but his excitement was tempered by worry over Nelly.

He went immediately to work on what he called the "big job." Mapping the region in any detail would take months. The Valley is about 140 miles long and from 12 to 24 miles wide, bounded on the northwest by North Mountain in the Allegheny Range and on the southeast by the Blue Ridge. For about fifty miles near its middle, the Valley is split by a huge mass of sandstone called Massanutten Mountain. The long mountain ridge towers 1,000 to 1,700 feet above the Valley floor and splits the Shenandoah River into two forks. The North Fork flows northward on the west side of Massanutten, and the South Fork, the larger stream, flows on the east. The presence of the river, numerous tributaries, and a few passable gaps in the mountains served by few good roads made maneuvering an army in the Valley complicated. It was Hotchkiss's job to study the region and paint a clear and understandable portrait of it for Jackson.

On March 28, Hotchkiss took to the field to do some surveying. That day, his first in the saddle in the service of Jackson, he made a startling discovery and a significant recommendation. He rode westward along Narrow Passage Creek, so named because the Valley floor at that point is pinched between a large loop in the North Fork of the Shenandoah River to the east, and the Allegheny Mountains to the northwest. Jackson had stopped his army here with the impression that it was a strong defensive position. Hotchkiss's long reconnaissance revealed otherwise.

"It was the general opinion in the country," Hotchkiss wrote later, "that at the Narrow Passage was a point where the enemy could easily be held in check and from the fact that Gen. Jackson had already halted there several times and that he kept his army in that vicinity, would lead to the conclusion that he entertained the same opinion. My reconnaissance westward showed that … [Narrow Passage] could be easily turned by several roads and that it would be difficult for an army to speedily fall back from that point." [18] Jackson received Hotchkiss's first report with interest and apparently accepted his judgment, for that afternoon, the general issued orders to abandon the Narrow Passage and move farther south. Jackson had not needed to wait long to learn the value of Jed Hotchkiss.

Despite unusually cold and raw weather, Hotchkiss was in the saddle again the next day, this time accompanied by a Mr. Hoshour of Woodstock, who was of great assistance in identifying the residences, roads, streams, and their courses. The topographer reported that night that his survey showed no defensible positions north of Woodstock, and this too was valuable information for Jackson.

Hotchkiss was enjoying his new work, but his thoughts were never far from home, especially in the first few days following his appointment, when Nelly was battling for her life. Finally word came from Sara that Nelly had passed the crisis. "I am truly thankful," he wrote, "that a Merciful God has spared us the sad affliction of depriving us of our first born—praised be his name that has granted it." [19] A few days later, Nelly sent him a gift. As he opened the letter, a single violet—one of the season's first—fell out before him. "I was very happy to think my little daughter was reviving and getting her new life again just as the sweet flowers are opening under the vernal sun. My little daughter must be very thankful to her God that her life is spared, and we will join her in thanking Him and hope she may live long to be a blessing to her parents and to her friends." [20]

The deliverance deeply affected him, giving him a bright flash of perspective on his life and circumstances. His daughter's brush with death showed him how precious life was and made him detest war more than ever. He loosed a torrent of pent-up frustration in a letter to Sara. "The birds are singing very sweetly here, and I suppose they are singing at Loch Willow, and Pa would like to sit out on the porch with the little girls and Ma and hear them sing rather than be where he has to see and hear so much of men killing and being killed, doing all the damage they can to one another, burning up bridges &c &c. O how I wish war would cease, and that we might all have peace in the enjoyment of our rights and liberties, but those rights we must have cost what it may." There was, of course, no satisfactory resolution to the unhappy caveat, so he forced down his revulsion of war and went to work in earnest. [21]

Hotchkiss spent his days riding over the country, usually alone, making sketches, measuring distances, following roads and cowpaths to their conclusions, and identifying places where the army might stand on the defense without fear of being flanked. A good topographical engineer was part scout, and Hotchkiss embodied all the best traits of the pathfinder: he was observant, intelligent, and of sound judgment, and he knew enough not to take unnecessary risks. All the information he gathered in his surveys was only valuable if he could deliver it to his commanding officer. If he were captured while surveying, his chief and his army would again be in the dark.

While he rode over the country, Hotchkiss not only made sketches of roads, rivers, and hills that he would later use in drawing his maps, but also noted a wealth of additional details—many of which could not be represented on any map. He noted the condition of the roads—were they wet or rutted? Would they support the army, or a brigade, or a regiment? How quickly could troops pass over unpaved Valley byways? As a geologist, he would have been able to tell something of the composition of the soil of the road surfaces and would know its properties when muddy. He noted how much the roads had been traveled lately and the type of vegetation that grew nearby. He recorded not just the location of woods, but their composition. A forest of hardwoods might make a better campsite than a pine forest; chestnut and oak burned cleaner than resinous evergreens, whose black smoke tainted food and faces. He also noted the type and condition of crops in nearby fields. Could they be harvested? Could they provide forage? He noted the strength and condition of bridges. How long would they support the weight of marching infantry? Would they support artillery and cavalry? How steep were the roads over mountains? Grades of more than about ten percent were too steep for wagons, and if the roads were wet and the wagons full, teams would have difficulty on much shallower slopes. What natural features—ridges, hills, woods, undulations in the ground—might conceal troops or screen their movements? What were the key points in a given area—elevations, depressions, fords, or bluffs—that must figure in tactical decisions? This information was valuable beyond price to Jackson, so Hotchkiss gathered and presented it, or was prepared to present it, when he delivered his maps to headquarters.

Hotchkiss came to understand that Jackson had a good spatial knowledge of the Valley from passing up and down in stagecoaches, which were a principle mode of travel, but the surveyor thought Jackson had not traveled much off the main roads and that his understanding of the Valley was limited. Hotchkiss, however, provided the knowledge and understanding of the region that Jackson lacked. After the war, Hotchkiss wrote, "I was thoroughly familiar with every portion of it from having walked and ridden over nearly every road in it, and gone along the crests of its mountain ridges during the dozen years or more preceding the Valley campaign. My knowledge of the Valley was such that I could from memory make [Jackson] a sketch of almost any portion of it, showing its detailed topography, and I may be pardoned for saying that my facilities for reproducing topographical details from memory was such that instead of asking me to make a map Jackson acquired the habit of 'please strike me off a map' as though it were a mechanical process."[22] Because of his familiarity with the Valley and its residents, many of whom were old friends or acquaintances who could answer specific questions about roads and rivers, Hotchkiss was uniquely equipped to reconnoiter and map the Valley. It is unlikely that any other man had the combination of skills, personality, technical knowledge, and work ethic that Hotchkiss brought to the task.

The rides were not always solitary, however. He befriended the companionable Sgt. S. Howell Brown, who was attached to headquarters on engineering duty. Brown, the county surveyor of Jefferson County, knew his job well, and the two men rode together when Brown was not otherwise engaged. Hotchkiss thought him "an excellent surveyor; a big stout fellow, accommodating and pleasant, but a mass of facts … fearfully exact, but I really like him nevertheless." The friendship would endure for the rest of their lives.[23]

Hotchkiss also often found company in Jackson's chief of cavalry, Col. Turner Ashby. Ashby was a Virginian ideal, a bold and courteous cavalier more prone to action than calm consideration. He had a reputation for courage and zeal, evidence of which Hotchkiss saw himself. "As Ashby and myself were riding along in front of the woods," Hotchkiss wrote in his diary of one episode, "a Federal sharpshooter … fired at him but hit, in the rear, and killed the horse that a little boy, they called Dixie, who followed Ashby, was riding. As the horse fell Dixie tumbled off, then jumped to his feet to run. Ashby called him back to get his saddle and coolly waited for him under a continuing fire from sharpshooters."[24]

Unfortunately, Ashby had also earned a reputation as a poor disciplinarian, evidence of which Hotchkiss would also witness. Jackson admired Ashby's bravery and vigor, but deplored his laxity in controlling his troopers, and the two men clashed on the issue several times. Throughout the weeks ahead, Ashby rendered Jackson brilliant and invaluable service, but would at times fail miserably.

A very pleasant side benefit to Hotchkiss's new position was that it brought him into contact with an extraordinary group of men. Jackson would one day tell Hotchkiss that he considered "the right sort of man" to be "one always striving to do his duty and never satisfied if anything can be done better."[25] It was with such men that Jackson had surrounded himself at headquarters. Jackson's staff was a galaxy of exceptionally bright—perhaps even brilliant—men of culture and accomplishment. At various times during the war, Jackson's official family included three present or future doctors of divinity or theology, at least eleven holders of master's degrees or more advanced degrees, a former congressman and diplomat, and at least four attorneys and nine educators, five of whom held or would hold professorships or chairs. All the more impressive is the extreme youth of the staff. Many were in their twenties, and at least three defy categorization by profession because they were too young—boys fresh out of college.[26]

Hotchkiss fit in very comfortably among these intellectual overachievers. The amateur naturalist-cum-academy principal could, and did, discourse intelligently with them on virtually any subject, from literature and geology to history and scripture. Scripture, especially, was a frequent topic, for the devout Jackson had made it a point to assemble around him Christian gentlemen who shared his devotion. It is not unlikely that Jackson inquired into Hotchkiss's past, and his faith, before selecting him for staff duty. Jackson required more of potential staff officers than mere ability. With rare exceptions, he required men with energy, moral strength, keen intelligence, and active bodies.

The friendships Hotchkiss formed with members of Jackson's staff were among the closest of his life. There was "Mr. Pendleton," as Jackson called him. Alexander Swift ("Sandie") Pendleton, a twenty-one-year-old prodigy who had been just a few weeks away from earning a master's degree at the University of Virginia when he resigned to enter the war. The son of a West Point graduate-turned-clergyman, Sandie had entered Washington College in Lexington at the age of thirteen, already fluent in Greek and Latin. He assisted professors in teaching Latin and mathematics, was graduated first in the class of 1857, received a gold medal for academic excellence, and was selected to deliver the commencement address, all before his seventeenth birthday. He believed that the purpose of his life was "not pleasure but service," a philosophy that surely endeared him to Jackson. He was a frail, unathletic figure,

L! Gen! T. J. Jackson & Staff

W. J. Hawks Maj. Chf. C. S.

R. L. Dabney Maj. A.A.G.

J. Hotchkiss Capt. Top. Eng.

W. Allan L! Col. Chf. Ord.

Hunter McGuire Maj. & Med. Dir.

A. S. Pendleton L! Col. A.A.G.

Photog'd by Vannerson & Jones
COPY RIGHT SECURED

Richmond V?

J. P. Smith Capt. A.D.C.

J. G. Morrison Capt. A.D.C.

H. K. Douglas Maj.

D. B. Bridgeford Maj. P.M.

Photographed by VANNERSON & JONES, from Original Negatives.

Taken at Richmond, Va.

not surprising for the son of an intellectual father and the sole brother of five sisters, but he had no shortage of courage. At the Battle of Manassas in July 1861, his horse was killed beneath him. He picked himself up, fell in with the men of the nearby 33rd Virginia Infantry and charged with them against a Federal battery. He was, literally and figuratively, the fair-haired boy at headquarters, and his hope was to enter the ministry after the war. Hotchkiss approved heartily of young Pendleton, calling him "a very fine young man—a gentleman in every way," and many shared his opinion.[27] Sandie Pendleton would become one of the more competent and beloved figures in the army.[28]

Jackson's medical director was twenty-six-year-old, mustachioed Dr. Hunter Holmes McGuire, the son of a Winchester physician. Young McGuire took his medical degree from Winchester Medical College in 1855 and taught anatomy at his alma mater, but eventually resigned to attend the University of Pennsylvania and Jefferson Medical College in Philadelphia. In 1859, the growing sectional tensions convinced McGuire and other Southerners at the college that they should return to the South. He and many of his fellow students went to Richmond and enrolled at the Medical College of Virginia. In March 1860, he received his second medical degree. When war broke out, he too showed he was willing to fight, and enlisted as a private in Company F of the 2nd Virginia Volunteer Infantry. Before long, he was commissioned as a surgeon and assigned to duty as medical director of the Army of the Shenandoah under General Jackson. The two men had been together ever since and had become intimate friends.[29]

McGuire, in fact, was fond of relating one anecdote about his sometime tent-mate Jackson that revealed much of the general. "Jackson," reported McGuire, "had gone over the battle field of Waterloo and spent several days in examining it. He said that it was the most interesting thing he found in Europe. One night in talking to me about it, he gave me a pretty clear description of the management of the English and French troops. I asked him whose disposition was the wisest, Napoleon's or Wellington's. He jumped up from the camp stool with a great deal of enthusiasm, and said: 'Napoleon's by all odds.' 'Why' said I 'didn't Napoleon then succeed at Waterloo?' He said: 'There is but one explanation of it, and that is that God Almighty intended Napoleon to stop right there. There is no other explanation.'"[30] McGuire and Hotchkiss became close companions, and their friendship would outlast all others among the headquarters staff. He was "blunt, good-humored and full of honest life," Hotchkiss told Sara, and he often entertained his fellows on the staff at evening sittings with medical lectures and diagnoses.[31]

Hotchkiss's immediate superior at headquarters was Lt. James Keith Boswell, Jackson's chief engineer. Not yet twenty-four years old, the dark-haired Boswell was from an old Virginia family prominent in Fauquier County. Despite his youth, he had already amassed significant engineering experience, laying out railroads in Missouri and Alabama, and had had little difficulty obtaining an appointment in the Confederate Engineer Corps. Before the war broke out, he had been an ardent secessionist, at least where his native Virginia was concerned, and hoped that the Old Dominion would not embarrass herself by remaining loyal to the Union while her sister states of the South broke away to form what he was certain would be "the greatest government which the world has ever seen."[32] Hotchkiss got to know him well in the early months at headquarters. Not only did they work closely, often spending long days together reconnoitering the country, but they were tent-mates. "Lieutenant Boswell," he told Sara, "is an excellent, good natured honest Presbyterian of Alabama, formerly of Fauquier County. He is well off—has a sweetheart in Fauquier, where the Yankees are and he talks much about her—he is my bed fellow—is one of your good fellows that everybody likes and of course I like him too." Like most young men of his age, Boswell was keenly interested in handsome young women, but he seems to have felt the attraction more strongly than did his friends. He was an incurable romantic, obsessed with comely females to the point of distraction. "Why am I such a slave to beauty?" he asked himself in his diary. Boswell's roving eyes and flighty heart would bring him trouble in the months ahead, and would help bring out a darker side of his nature that caused Hotchkiss great concern.[33]

Hotchkiss also enjoyed the company of Jackson's chief of artillery, Col. Stapleton Crutchfield. A Virginian, the twenty-six-year-old Crutchfield was graduated first in his class at the VMI, where he had been one of Jackson's pupils. He adored Shakespeare, and Sandie Pendleton considered him, "more conversant with it than anyone I ever saw and reciting by heart every passage that can be called for."[34] He apparently also had an un-Jacksonian relish of rest, for another member of the staff described him as a sleepy sort, "descendent of the man who invented sleep."[35] He was an expert artilleryman, however, and indeed would have to be to serve as chief of that arm under the stern old artilleryman Jackson.

Among the more likable men at headquarters was Maj. John A. Harman, the chief quartermaster. He was an exception to the profile of the typical Jackson staff officer in that he was not brilliant, highly educated, an intellectual, or even young. But he had his own kind of luster. He had been successful in business before the war and was one of those talented, tireless, indispensable people who always find a way to get a job done. His genius was in knowing how to get the most out of people. The thirty-eight-year-old Harman, exactly thirty days younger than Jackson, was a native of Augusta County, but had lived for many years in Texas, where he had been a Texas Ranger. After service in the Mexican War, he moved to Missouri and went into business, but at last came back to Virginia to farm and raise cattle. He was an active citizen, serving as a magistrate and as an officer in the local militia. He had been with Jackson from the outset of the war; they had apparently forged a relationship built on mutual respect, for there was a definite absence of affection.

Throughout the spring of 1862, the two men were constantly at odds. "He is the hardest master any man ever served," Harman wrote to his brother, adding that he thought "nothing but a mean-spirited man can remain long with him." As quartermaster, Harman bore a disproportionately heavy burden of responsibility when Jackson began ordering his troops to make long forced marches with little advance warning. Harman had to move the army's long, cumbersome supply trains just as quickly and have them present when the troops stopped to eat and rest. If Harman failed, the troops went hungry or perhaps could not fight because they were short of ammunition. Harman generally worked miracles, but thought Jackson routinely asked for more than any man could deliver and repeatedly submitted his resignation. Jackson, knowing the value of his quartermaster, refused to act on these gestures. Of one episode, Harman wrote to his brother, "The General found fault with me for the way in which the army had been foraged … and told me that I had not displayed the driving disposition that I had [previously]. I asked him to relieve me, but he said he had no one to put in my place.… I told him I would resign.… I will not serve him any longer. He says that I have attempted to pry into military matters. I thanked him for his candor and told him I would resign.

He afterwards took the blame upon himself for not having foraged for the 1,200 cavalry. I feel very much outraged and would not remain a day longer if I could help it. You had better look out or you will be ordered to fill my place. I shall press the resignation if he disapproves it; I can no longer be comfortable with him." It was an unhappy marriage, but Jackson thought a great deal of Harman's abilities and took unusual pains to make the relationship work.[36]

Jackson's impatience with Harman seems almost cold-hearted, however, in light of the personal tragedy the major endured that spring. The wave of scarlet fever that swept through parts of the Valley and that had brought Nelly Hotchkiss so close to death had visited Harman's home as well. The Harman household was enormous—thirteen children all told—but sadly, it was reduced that spring. "I feel sorry for poor John Harman," Hotchkiss told Sara, "he has lost two children and told me this morning that he expected two more to die today."[37] If anyone at that headquarters could be sympathetic to Harman, it was Hotchkiss, who had endured similar anguish just the week before. Harman, Hotchkiss wrote in his journal, "is completely unmanned, and I do not wonder!"[38]

Harman requested a furlough to go home. He got leave for forty-eight hours, rode fifty miles in five hours, found two of his children dead and buried, stayed for the death and burial of a third, and had to leave while the fourth was dying. Jackson would not extend the furlough. Despite their many disagreements, Harman did not blame Jackson. "The general is right," he told Hotchkiss, "the country needs every man at his post. We must think of the living and those who are to come after us. Some must suffer and why not I?"[39]

Of Jackson himself, the more Hotchkiss saw, the more he liked. "I am very much pleased with General Jackson and his staff," he told Sara. "He is at times very chatty, but usually has but little to say. Sunday he went through one of the brigades with a bundle of tracts and distributed them—he stays to himself most of the time—eats very sparingly—does not drink tea or coffee and hardly eats any meat." Jackson might have found excessive communication undesirable because conversation was difficult for him. "General Jackson does not say much, he is quite deaf—he spends most of his time in his room by himself, except when in the saddle—he is very pleasant though, and I like him."[40]

Not everyone shared Hotchkiss's admiration of the general—Harman, of course being the prime example. Jackson held his officers to a standard of routine excellence and did not believe in showering praise on a man who merely did his duty. This irked many subordinates. One staff officer recalled an instance when he had, "by almost superhuman efforts," moved a column of 160 army wagons "over icy mountain roads and through blinding storms of snow and sleet" to feed and supply Jackson's cold and hungry command. The chilled and exhausted officer found the general by a warm fire and reported the arrival of the provisions. Jackson's only response was, "That's good."[41]

Hotchkiss spent most of his days in the first weeks of April in the saddle, battered by horrible weather. Snow and ice storms made travel hazardous, and unseasonable cold made life miserable for the men of both armies. Whenever he could, Hotchkiss worked in camp, turning his notes and sketches into maps, and working on the big map of the entire Valley that Jackson had charged him with producing. The map would be large, that much Hotchkiss had already determined. To be of any military use, the map would have to include considerable detail—elevations, creeks, residences, etc.—which would require that the scale of the map be small. Hotchkiss envisioned the map as rectangular and perhaps as many as ten feet long. Jackson had not said when he wanted the map finished, but Hotchkiss worked on it steadily, only interrupting his work when Jackson gave him other assignments, which came with greater and greater frequency as the days passed by.

And with the passage of time came an increase in speculation at headquarters. What was to happen next? After Kernstown, the Federals had rather indolently pursued Jackson southward to the vicinity of Woodstock. Jackson, of course, wished to keep the Northerners occupied so they could not reinforce McClellan, who was now less than seventy miles from Richmond. Throughout the army, men wondered how Jackson could keep the Federals interested. Could he, with his small army of less than 4,000 men, give battle? If not, how long would the Federals remain to watch him? Would he, because of the great strength of the Federals before him, be forced to abandon the Valley? Opinions were legion, information from headquarters was scarce.

And the men of Jackson's staff thus became aware of their chief's most remarkable and most maddening trait: his obsession with secrecy. Jackson never let slip even the faintest hint of what his plans were, even to his most trusted officers. Never did he let so much as one person more than was necessary know what was afoot. "I think General Jackson is entirely too close about everything," wrote Harman, a judgment that would prove a marked understatement.[42] This predilection caused enormous frustration for many of the general officers with whom Jackson was to work, but the general's staff soon got accustomed to not knowing what was to happen and cheerfully made the best of what they could not change. They followed orders and asked no questions.

The staff enjoyed retelling a story at the expense of one of their own, Harman, who once bet the cost of an oyster supper that he could find out from "Old Jack" when they were going to move from their camp. Harman visited Jackson and asked, "in his blandest and most confidential tone of voice: 'By the way, general, when are we going to move?' The General, with his softest voice and his sweetest smile, replied: 'Major, can you keep a secret?'" Harman sincerely assured his general that he could, whereupon, "'Old Jack,' now with a grim smile on his earnest face, said: 'So can I,' and so the major had to pay soundly for the oyster supper."[43]

Virtually every member of Jackson's official family had some story to tell about the general's devotion to the security of important information. Jackson's chief commissary of subsistence, Maj. Wells J. Hawks, was a conscientious officer who sought to perform as efficiently as possible so as to waste neither time nor resources. On one march in 1861, after Jackson had halted the column for the night, Hawks moved his wagon train off the turnpike and into a field. Then, seeking to organize the train so as to be ready to move immediately in the morning, he went to Jackson to learn the direction of march for the morrow. "General," he said, "as we are going to make an early start tomorrow morning I would like to know which way to head the train." Jackson replied, "Arrange the wagon train with the heads of the horses towards the pike." Hawks persisted: "But shall I head it up the pike, or down the pike?" "I said *towards* the pike, Sir," fumed Jackson, refusing to divulge even the smallest bit of intelligence.[44] Jackson knew the importance of deceiving the enemy and took no chances in losing the advantage. He once told a staff officer, "Mystery, mystery, major, is the secret of success. Napoleon marched his men 50 miles in 24 hours and fought and won pitched battles, and ours can do the same."[45]

And as the army would learn, the general suffered little anguish about asking his troops to make such marches. War was a suffering business and nothing he could do within the scope of his duty could eliminate pain and discomfort from the foot soldier's life. As he saw it, he and the men of his army had left their homes to do a difficult job, and the sooner they finished their work, the sooner they would get home. Some of them would die—perhaps even he—but he could not help that, for such was the nature of the task at hand. His duty was to defeat the enemy, and he could only do that by hard fighting and marching. Speed was a weapon, and Jackson knew it could save lives. A Valley woman who saw Jackson's tired men marching continuously over the dusty Valley turnpike berated the general for driving the poor boys too hard. Jackson's reply was terse and succinct: "Legs are cheaper than heads, madam."[46]

On April 17, Jackson moved at last from his positions around Rude's Hill and headed south, the Federals close behind him. Still, none of his staff knew where the army was bound. As the column reached Harrisonburg on the morning of the eighteenth, Jackson turned east, toward the Blue Ridge Mountains and roads leading over the mountains. To many in the army, this could only mean that Jackson was abandoning the Valley, which was an unpopular decision indeed, for most of the men in the ranks were natives and disliked leaving their homes undefended. In a letter to his brother, John Harman was almost despondent: "I have time to say to you that my worst fears are realized," he wrote from Harrisonburg as soon as the army turned east. "We cross the mountain at

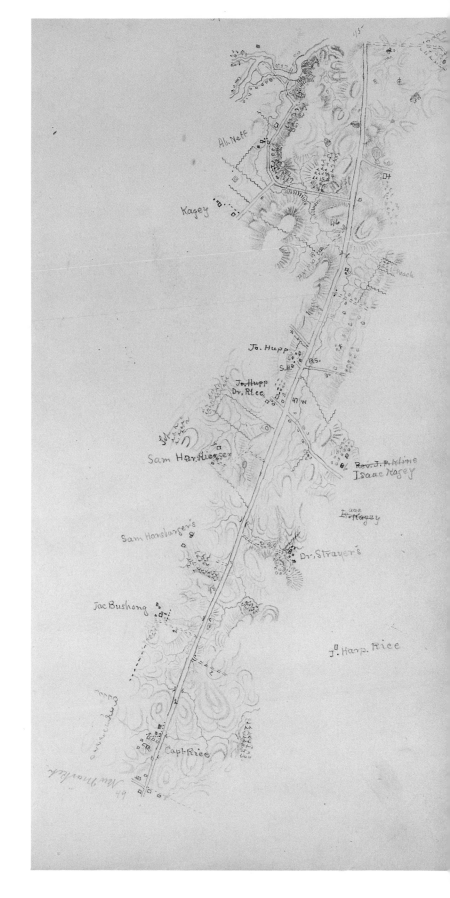

HOTCHKISS'S SKETCH OF A ROAD NORTH OF STRASBURG, VIRGINIA, REVEALS HIS ATTENTION TO DETAIL. HE TOOK COMPASS READINGS TO DETERMINE THE DEGREE OF EACH TURN IN THE ROAD. HE MEASURED THE ALTITUDE OF ALMOST EVERY ELEVATION AND DEPRESSION. HE PAINSTAKINGLY RECORDED RESIDENTS' NAMES—A DIFFICULT TASK, AS THE NUMEROUS CORRECTIONS SHOW.

Swift Run Gap.... It is great confusion here and it looks more like a rout than an army. I reckon things look gloomy to me at best." [47] A few days later, Hotchkiss wrote to Sara to allay her fears of Federal depredations. "If the foe should come to your door, outwardly submit, but coldly, and abhor to the last those that seek [to bring to] our firesides slaughter and devastation.... I hope the foe may not visit you—but if they do, try and keep them from destroying by claiming protection as a lady from the officers, and they may give some heed to it." [48]

But Jackson was not leaving the Valley and had no intention of doing so soon. He moved to the foot of the Blue Ridge, through the town of Conrad's Store (later renamed Elkton), and encamped his army below Swift Run Gap. This was a strong defensive position where he could take protection from the mountains and the South Fork of the Shenandoah River. There he would wait, gather his strength, and watch what the Federals decided to do. But first he had to take one precaution to secure his position. The bridges downstream on the South Fork had to be destroyed to keep Federals from moving on his flank. He sent a party of cavalrymen to burn the spans and a member of his staff to ensure the work was done properly. The assignment went to Hotchkiss.

In the months ahead, Jackson would often assign Hotchkiss to guide expeditions to their objectives, reasoning, perhaps, that Hotchkiss knew the region and the roads better than anyone else available. If the objective could be reached, Hotchkiss would get there, even if it meant finding an alternative route. Furthermore, Hotchkiss had already shown himself to be cool-headed and responsible, a trustworthy man in a crisis. On this, his first extra-topographical mission, all of the erstwhile schoolmaster's abilities would be tested.

In a hard rain, the worst possible weather for arson, Hotchkiss led 150 of Ashby's cavalrymen northward toward their targets. A portion of the troopers were under the command of Capt. Macon Jordan, a former student of Hotchkiss and son of a prominent family in the town of Luray. The column rode about ten miles to the first bridge, referred to locally as the "Red" bridge, and there Hotchkiss left a detachment with orders to take up the planking and prepare to fire the stringers. He then went on the remaining six miles to the "Columbia" bridge, stopping just short and sending a scout. The cavalrymen under Jordan grew restive. Hotchkiss already knew that Ashby enforced little discipline in his command, but he was shocked to learn that a large number of the troopers with him that day, including Captain Jordan, were drunk on "apple-jack whiskey."

The scout returned to say no Federals were in sight, and Hotchkiss immediately sent a captain and three men to burn the bridge. But one target remained, and Hotchkiss ordered another small party to ride on downstream and torch the "White House" bridge. As the arsonists went to their work, he moved off a short distance with the rest of the cavalry to feed their horses in preparation for the ride back to the "Red." Within minutes, he wrote to Sara later, all was chaos. The men at work on the Columbia "had put hay in the mouth of it and set it on fire, when a column of the enemy appeared and fired a volley and their dragoons charged, a messenger at once reported that they were coming, and I ordered the men to their horses and told Jordan to front his men—and I went forward to reconnoiter, when Jordan followed me instead of attending to his men, and the enemy came charging up and firing when our men broke at once, except some 3 or 4, and a perfect stampede of them took place, the enemy pursuing for 3 miles, every attempt to rally [Jordan's men] was unavailing, some actually throwing away their guns, many their coats, blankets &c, &c—I never saw a more disgraceful affair." [49]

Hotchkiss gave up trying to rally the fugitives and went

on to ensure that the men at the first bridge completed their work of destruction, which they did. He then returned to headquarters and made his report. Hotchkiss was embarrassed by the incident, not for himself, but for Jordan and his troopers—"All owing no doubt to the state of intoxication of some of the men, and to the want of discipline." The incident allowed him a greater understanding of Jackson's complaints against Ashby. "I am sorry, truly sorry, that Jordan was in such a condition," he told Sara, "and I do not know what may come of it to him, but I am sure the general will see that he is properly looked after. When Ashby's men are with him they behave gallantly, but when they are away they lack the inspiration of his presence, and being undisciplined they often fail to do any good—only a few days ago a company of 50 of them were taken prisoners through lack of care in guarding themselves."[50]

On April 24, there arrived at headquarters a man who would have an important influence on Jackson, Hotchkiss, and history. The Reverend Dr. Robert Louis Dabney, one of the more prominent theologians in Virginia, came to headquarters at the invitation of Jackson to become chief of staff.

Dabney was a forty-two-year-old Virginian with military genes. Two ancestors had been officers in the American Revolution, and his father had been a private in the War of 1812. Educated at Hampden-Sydney College, the University of Virginia, and the Union Theological Seminary, where he was a professor of theology, Dabney seems to have been a man of pronounced conservative opinions on virtually everything and was outspoken in expressing his beliefs. As pastor of the Tinkling Spring Presbyterian Church in Augusta County, Virginia, for example, he declared his views on church music: "Believing as I do that vocal religious music is a part of worship of divine appointment, and that the articulation of words conveying divine truth is its essential, I cannot but regret the introduction of instruments into church music. With the worldly ostentatious intention, with which it is usually done, I have no doubt that it is a very great sin.... I wish ... a fair specimen of Presbyterian worship in its original simplicity and strength, without the popish accessories of choirs and organs."[51]

Dabney was also strongly proslavery, and detested what he believed were the ignorant and misguided efforts of Northern abolitionists. "This question of moral right is at the bottom of the whole matter.... If we want to affect the general current of national opinion on this subject, 'Is slaveholding intrinsically immoral or unjust?' We must go before the nation with the bible as the test, and the 'Thus saith the Lord,' as the answer. The policy is wiser, because we know that on the bible argument, we are, logically, impregnable.... The bible being found to stand on our side, they will have to come out, and array themselves against the Bible."[52] Hotchkiss liked Dabney, declaring him "a fine man." The two might have been acquainted from Augusta County before the war.

Jackson's army stayed holed up in Swift Run Gap for ten days as the Federals slowly sallied forward. Jackson's dilemma was substantial. Maj. Gen. John C. Frémont, commanding a total of 15,000 Federals, drove two columns totaling about 6,000 through the mountains west of the Valley. Banks remained with his 19,000 men at Harrisonburg between Jackson and Frémont. If the Federals joined at Harrisonburg, Jackson would be outnumbered by almost five to one. Jackson could call upon Brig. Gen. Edward ("Allegheny") Johnson, who was between the two Federal forces. But Johnson had only 3,000 men with him, roughly half of Frémont's two nearest columns. Jackson also hoped to be reinforced by Maj. Gen. Richard S. Ewell's division of 8,000 men, but even with that addition to his force, and counting Johnson's, the Federals would have almost a two-to-one advantage if they came together. Jackson's only hope of defeating the Federals, or even of keeping them occupied longer, was to keep them apart. How to do that with his vastly outnumbered army was the knotty problem before him.

Jackson was stymied in the last third of April by rain, which made the roads all but impassable and swelled the rivers and streams. Late in the month, a plan crystallized in the general's mind, and Hotchkiss was to play an important role. Jackson, of course, kept his plans to himself, but tipped his hand to his topographical engineer. Hotchkiss requested a short leave to visit his home across the Valley and secure his family and some important papers against depredations from Federal cavalry, which had been seen just a few miles from Loch Willow. Jackson routinely discouraged his officers from taking leave, but in this case, he approved the request—he wished Hotchkiss to visit General Johnson, who had his headquarters near Churchville. Hotchkiss could learn from Johnson the exact position of the enemy, the condition of the general's troops, and the state of the roads in the vicinity. Was Old Jack planning a move to Augusta County?

The bad weather continued, making most of the ride to and from western Augusta miserable, but Hotchkiss obtained the desired intelligence from Johnson and returned to Jackson just three days after setting out, having covered more than ninety miles. The general had another assignment waiting for his topographer. The next morning, April 30, Hotchkiss was to climb to the Peak, at the southern end of Massanutten Mountain, which loomed above the Valley pastures in Jackson's front and stood between him and Banks's army at Harrisonburg. From the summit, only six miles from Banks, Hotchkiss was to observe the Federals' dispositions and actions. Then, from a concealed place on the height, he was to convey what he saw to Jackson by signaling with a bed sheet. Hotchkiss selected as his escort Company E of the 10th Virginia Infantry because, he explained to Jackson, the men were from the vicinity and were "familiar with the country and its paths and byways." [53] The infantrymen knew the area even better than Hotchkiss had hoped; indeed, at the formation of their company, they had named themselves "The Peaked Mountain Grays" after the eminence they knew so well, so it was especially appropriate that they be a part of the mission. In addition, Hotchkiss knew and liked the company commander, William B. Yancey, yet another of his former students. [54]

They set off at 1 a.m., marching five miles or more to the base of the mountain and heading up into a water gap. So well did Yancey's boys know the sloping woods that even in the black night they led Hotchkiss to a path "used by parties visiting the Peak to enjoy the fine prospect from it." Hotchkiss described the climb as "rough, but comparatively easy," thanks to the trail, and reported reaching the summit about 5 a.m.

As the sun reached over the Blue Ridge and chased the shadows out of the southern reaches of the Page Valley, which lies between the Blue Ridge and Massanutten, Hotchkiss saw that Ashby's cavalry was already on the march. He signaled that Banks was quiet, and Ashby continued the march around the base of the mountain and

A DETAIL FROM THE "MAP OF THE VALLEY" JACKSON REQUESTED OF HOTCHKISS IN MARCH 1862 CENTERS ON PORT REPUBLIC. THE MAP WAS NOT FINISHED UNTIL AFTER JACKSON'S DEATH, BUT IT AIDED HIS SUCCESSORS. OVER NINE FEET LONG AND MOUNTED ON DURABLE LINEN, THE MAP SERVED AS A PRIMARY SOURCE FOR TOPOGRAPHICAL INFORMATION ABOUT THE VALLEY. THE INK GRID WAS ADDED LATER TO ASSIST CARTOGRAPHERS IN COPYING OR ENLARGING SECTIONS.

then westward toward Harrisonburg. Hotchkiss watched the Confederate column snake over the white road toward the Federals, who, he could see, still lay unsuspecting around Harrisonburg. Eventually, the Northerners awoke to what was happening and Hotchkiss noted couriers racing about and wagons setting off for the rear. Banks formed a line of battle. Hotchkiss waved the sheet according to the prearranged code he and Jackson had decided upon and informed his general of the Federals' arousal. Ashby continued the march, planning to draw Banks into a fight. From his vantage point, Hotchkiss could see the shrewdness of Jackson's movement. The general had split his army, sending the larger portion off to the vicinity of Port Republic, a few miles south of Ashby's column's left flank. From that point, it could march in support of the other, smaller column moving directly on the Federal position. If the Federals took the bait offered by the small column and attacked, Ashby's column could withdraw, thus bringing the flank of the pursuing Northerners within reach of the strong Confederate force near Port Republic. Hotchkiss watched with interest, but late in the afternoon, he finally had to signal Jackson that Banks was not budging from his defensive positions. He would not bite.

Jackson's infantry had broken camp that afternoon and had marched toward Port Republic. Hotchkiss descended the mountain and joined him on the march, relating in great detail all he had seen from his perch. Hotchkiss then learned that Old Jack's foray had had another purpose. A division of reinforcements under Ewell had come over the Blue Ridge during the day to occupy Jackson's camps at Swift Run Gap. Ashby's march on Harrisonburg had been a diversion to distract the Federals and occupy their full attention so they could not see Ewell's arrival. Hotchkiss, by Jackson's order, briefed Ewell on what he had seen from the Peak, and then rode through a hard rain to join Jackson at the new camp three miles north of Port Republic.

The march on April 30 was the first move in Jackson's offensive. The movement continued, but progress was slow, and the army covered only ten miles in two days.[55] But more troubling to the men in the ranks than the slow progress was the direction in which they were moving: eastward, over the Blue Ridge and out of the Valley. To their surprise, Jackson was abandoning the Valley. Depression made the going even slower as the men turned their backs on their homes and marched to they knew not where.

Jackson's weary, muddy men trudged down out of Brown's Gap and onto harder, drier roads that led them to Mechum's River Station, a depot on the Virginia Central Railroad, where they bivouacked for the night. In the morning, May 4, to the surprise and delight of his army, Jackson issued orders for the wagon trains and artillery to turn west and head back into the Valley by way of another gap in the Blue Ridge. The general then had his infantry board trains and ride over the mountains. By the following evening, Jackson's army was reunited at Staunton, positioned to join forces with General Johnson and divide Banks and Frémont. The sad, slow march out of the Valley had only been a ruse intended to mislead Banks. It had worked perfectly, but, having seized the initiative, the Valley Army now had to press the advantage and defeat one of the divided Federal columns. On May 7, Jackson, now commanding an army of 9,000, moved westward into the mountains toward Frémont. His men were ready for a fight. "Started this morning for Buffalo Gap and the Shenandoah Mountains," wrote one in his diary, "to give the enemy a taste of Jackson."[56]

The march was swift, and on May 8, as the army neared the Federals' expected position, Jackson detailed Hotchkiss to lead the advance. He moved forward with skirmishers up the winding mountain roads, over which he had driven as a teamster less than a year before. At each turn in the road, Hotchkiss stopped to ensure the way was clear of Federals. He then turned and waved his handkerchief as a signal to Jackson, who led the van of the main column forward.[57]

The slow, cautious process continued to the summit of Bull Pasture Mountain. On the crest, Jackson asked Hotchkiss for information about the valley before them, at the bottom of which lay the town of McDowell. The town was occupied by a portion of Frémont's army under Brig. Gen. Robert C. Schenck. Having spent time at McDowell the previous summer, and having made good use of that time by scouting and surveying the region, Hotchkiss could respond to Jackson's request quickly and fully. He took the general to a "projecting ledge of rocks on the right hand side of the road from which the enemy's position was visible and pointed out to him the details of the locality." To help illustrate his descriptions, Hotchkiss sketched out a map for Jackson on the spot.[58]

The terrain was too rugged to permit artillery to move quickly into a position to fire on the Federals, and the afternoon was well advanced, so Jackson decided that the guns should be moved up during the night to support an attack in the morning. This delay would also permit Jackson's men some rest. They had marched the last thirty-four miles to McDowell in twenty-three hours.[59] He directed Hotchkiss to find a road by which artillery could be brought up into the field near the rock ledge on which they stood. That accomplished, said Jackson, Hotchkiss and the other staff members should go down the hill to headquarters and get some rest.

Hotchkiss soon found a route for the artillery and informed the necessary officers. He then wearily returned to his tent and lay down to rest before eating dinner. Almost immediately, he heard firing up the mountain. "I at once jumped up and … galloped back to the top of the mountain, a distance of about three miles, where I found Gen. Jackson … alone in the road, the firing on the left having well nigh ceased. He expressed his gratification at my coming and at once said in his usual incisive rapid way, 'Go up on the mountain and give my compliments to Gen. Taliaferro and tell him he must hold on there until I come with the Stonewall Brigade, which I have sent for.' "[60] Hotchkiss was off immediately, riding as far as the terrain would allow, then climbing on foot. He found the battlefield in chaos. The Federals, declining to wait for Jackson to attack them in the morning, had stealthily climbed the mountain and attacked Jackson's infantry. Wounded men were everywhere, and officers ran about trying to prepare the lines to repel another attack. Hotchkiss found his friend Brig. Gen. William Taliaferro and delivered Jackson's message, then scrambled back down the mountain and found Jackson still waiting in the road in the gap. "We remained there some time until he became satisfied that there would be no further fighting that night," Hotchkiss recalled. Darkness had ended the fighting, and Jackson and Hotchkiss together rode back to headquarters, where the topographer ate and immediately retired, "giving instructions to have my horse ready and myself awakened a little before three the next morning." Before dawn, he oversaw the movement of the artillery to the summit, but sunrise on May 9 showed that there would be no fighting that day. Schenck had retired from the mountain and abandoned McDowell. Jackson's first fight against Frémont's Federals had been a victory.

Hotchkiss rode over the battlefield, which he described as "sickening," and made a few sketches for future reference, but for most of Jackson's army this was a day of rest.[61] On May 10, Jackson set his army off in pursuit of the outnumbered Schenck, chasing him deeper into the mountains. But Jackson was not one to pursue mindlessly. As he rode, he mulled over possibilities, and decided that even if his pursuit was swift, the prey could still escape. He needed to hem Schenck in, and he called upon Hotchkiss to do it.

"Sometime during the afternoon of the 10th," remembered Hotchkiss, "I should say between three and four p.m., while we were waiting developments in front, the General beckoned to me then turned and rode back along the road by which we had advanced, I following him, until we reached a wood road that turned into the woods to our left. We rode up that a little ways when he turned and addressed me, emphasizing his words, shaking his long index finger towards me, and said, in his quick, rapid way: 'General Banks is in Harrisonburg, Gen. Frémont is at Franklin, there is a good road between them. Gen. Frémont ought to march to Gen. Banks, but I don't think he will do it, I want the road between them and Dry River Gap blockaded by daylight tomorrow morning so he cannot do this. Please take a squad of couriers and ride back to Churchville, by way of McDowell, and take Capt. Sterrett's company of cavalry, which you will find near Churchville and go and blockade Dry River Gap. Send me back a messenger every hour telling me where you are and what you have done.'" Hotchkiss asked if Sgt. S. Howell Brown might accompany him. Jackson assented, and Hotchkiss set off at once, trailing a long string of couriers behind him.[62]

The incident is remarkable for several reasons. It shows just how serious Jackson was about maintaining secrecy. He took Hotchkiss away from the staff, away from the marching column, and into the woods, where no one, not even friendly ears, could hear the assignment. If secrecy was so crucial, presumably Jackson did not tell any other members of the staff where Hotchkiss was even after he had left. No one at headquarters knew what Hotchkiss was up to, nor anything about the North or Dry River gaps, except Jackson.

The importance of the mission, in Jackson's mind, is indicated by the requirement that Hotchkiss report every hour. Jackson had to know the status of Hotchkiss's mission to know how he was to deal with Schenck and Frémont. If Hotchkiss failed and Fremont slipped out through one of the gaps into the Valley to join Banks, Jackson would be trapped in the mountains and vastly outnumbered by the combined Federals. The assignment also showed Jackson's supreme confidence in his topographical engineer.

After a ride of about fifty miles, Hotchkiss's party reached Churchville near midnight. He found Franklin F. Sterrett's cavalry—about sixty men—and told Sterrett to bring his troopers to Loch Willow. Hotchkiss then took Brown home with him, joyously awoke Sara, fed his horse, and got something to eat. Sterrett arrived soon after and the party again set out into the darkness, northeastward, bound for Dry River Gap.

Before dawn, the riders approached the town of Rawley Springs at the eastern end of the gap. Before entering the gap, Hotchkiss sent pickets out to the east, toward Harrisonburg, only twelve miles away, where Banks still sat with his army. Then the rest of the party rode up into the gap about three miles to a rocky gorge. Just at daylight, Hotchkiss stopped, left one detachment with the horses, and sent the rest of the men up the steep slopes to fell trees and roll rocks into the road. Within a few hours, the road was obstructed and the gap closed. The same destruction soon closed the North River Gap, and finally, his work done, Hotchkiss relaxed. He returned to Churchville to see his family, eat, and rest his horse, which he had ridden well over a hundred miles in little more than twenty-four hours.[63]

Meanwhile, Jackson's pursuit of Schenck was frustrated when the retreating Federals set fire to the woods by the road. The heat, billowing smoke, and flying ash slowed the Confederates to a standstill, and Jackson declared, according to one of his staff, that the smoke was "the most adroit expedient to which a retreating army could resort to embarrass pursuit and that it entailed upon him all the disadvantages of a night attack."[64] Though Jackson would have liked to have struck Schenck again, he was satisfied that these Federals would be no more trouble as they fled deep into the mountains with no open route by which they could join their friends at Harrisonburg. For the time being, Jackson had put Frémont out of the game. The Southerners about-faced and marched out of the mountains and once again to the Valley.

Hotchkiss rejoined Jackson and Ewell, who had stayed behind in the Valley to detain Banks.[65] The Federal general had cooperated, remaining quiet while Jackson dispensed with Frémont. In fact, the long stretch of inactivity in the Valley following the Battle of Kernstown induced Federal administrators in Washington to view the Valley as secure. On May 8, as Jackson was preparing to attack Schenck at McDowell, Washington ordered Banks to detach 11,000 of his 19,000 men and send them east of the Blue Ridge. His force reduced by more than half, Banks no longer was secure at Harrisonburg, and began to withdraw down the Valley toward Winchester. After a brief consultation, Jackson and Ewell decided to pursue and, if possible, attack Banks.

The pursuit immediately struck an obstacle on May 18 in high water at the North River. At the town of Bridgewater, ironically enough, Jackson puzzled over how to get his men across the swollen flood. He turned to Hotchkiss for suggestions. Once again, the topographer offered valuable intelligence that perhaps he alone possessed of all the men with Jackson. He had lived for many years just a few miles distant at Mossy Creek, he explained to Jackson, and knew the country and its residents intimately. He recalled that many of the farmers nearby owned sturdy four- and six-horse wagons. If enough vehicles could be gathered, they could be trundled into the stream to serve as trestles. The army could cross over planks laid on top of the wagons. Jackson approved the idea, the wagons were found, and the army crossed the same day.

Banks's withdrawal from the upper Valley allowed Jackson and Ewell freedom to choose their lines of march. Ewell moved northward on the east side of Massanutten through the Page Valley. Jackson moved northward through the main valley west of Massanutten on the Valley pike.

At New Market, the Confederate commander turned east and crossed Massanutten at New Market Gap to join Ewell. Reunited, the large column continued northward, now screened from the Federals by Massanutten. The marches were rapid, so swift, in fact, that Jackson's infantrymen would come to be called "foot cavalry." They maintained a brisk pace for fifty minutes each hour. After a ten-minute rest, they would be off again through one of the more beautiful portions of the Valley. Fresh spring grass covered the broad floodplain, the rounded knobs of the Blue Ridge stood in ranks three or four deep to the east, the sawtooth skyline of Massanutten stood silhouetted behind them, and the South Fork, flat and wide, coiled in silty brown whorls below them to the left. It was glorious country, and must have given the men in the ranks an even greater love of their valley, inspiring them, perhaps, to want even more to drive out the invaders.

Jackson had sent Hotchkiss and Boswell ahead of the army to scout the country and learn Banks's location. Hotchkiss sketched the area north of Woodstock, while Boswell climbed Signal Knob at the extreme northern end of the Massanutten ridge to spy on Banks, who had stopped his retreat at Strasburg and Front Royal.[66] On May 23, Jackson's combined force, now numbering about 17,000, attacked a portion of Banks's force at Front Royal, at the northern end of the Page Valley. The Confederates drove

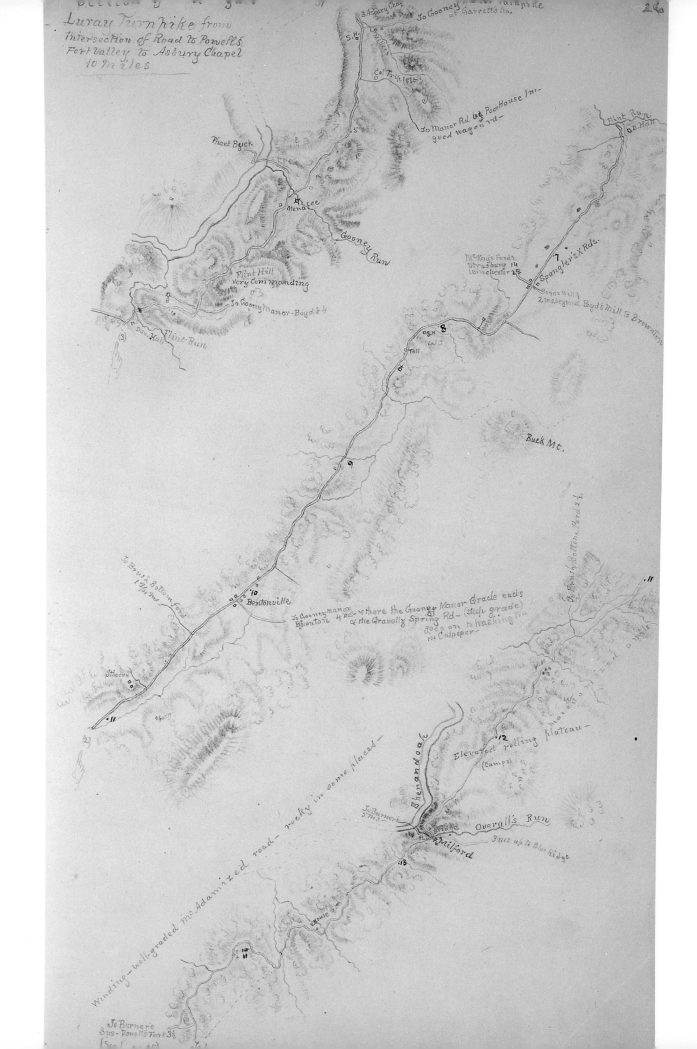

Luray Turnpike from
Intersection of Road to Powells
Fort Valley to Asbury Chapel
10 miles

To Gooney Manor Turnpike
at Garrett's Ho.

Asbury Chac.

S.H.

Col Trip lett

To Manor Rd to Poor House In—
gued wagon rd—

Flint Run

O.D. Hall

Phaet Buck

Mc Lee
Mena

Gooney Run

McKay's Ford
Strasburg 14
Winchester 18

Spangler's X Rds.

Boyds Mill 4
2 ms. beyond Boyds Mill to Brownton

Flint Hill
Very Commanding

To Gooney Manor - Boyds 4

5.H 8

(3)
Dan Hall Flint Run

Toll

Buck Mt.

9

To Brush Bottom Ford 2½

To Brush Bottom ford
1¾ ms

10
Bentonville

To Gooney Manor
Browton 4 ms—where the Gooney Manor Grade ends
of the Gravelly Spring Rd— (steep grade)
goes on to Washington
in Culpeper—

11

Stinton

II

11

(2) a farm

Winding—well-graded macAdamized road—rocky in some places—

Shenandoah

12
Elevated rolling plateau—

(Camps)

To Burners
5 ms

Bridge

Milford

Overall's Run
3 ms up to Blue Ridge

13

a house

14
H

To Burners
Sps—Powells Fort 3½

the Federals back in confusion, and the next morning, Banks, his force now reduced to about 7,000 men, abandoned Strasburg, five miles west of Front Royal, moving quickly northward toward Winchester. But Banks had waited too long. Jackson was upon him.

Jackson split his force, sending one column directly to Winchester in an effort to beat Banks there. The general led the second, larger portion of his army toward Banks's retreating column, which he assumed was to the west on the Valley Turnpike. Jackson sent Hotchkiss ahead of the column with some cavalrymen to find Banks. After less than a half a mile, the topographer was fired upon and returned quickly to tell the general he had found the Union commander. Jackson advanced on the side road, drove off the skirmishers who had fired on Hotchkiss, and came to a rise of ground east of Middletown. There, where the Valley Pike passed through the town, lay a portion of Banks's column—a wagon train and cavalry. Jackson deployed some artillery and opened fire.

"As soon as the shell fell among the Yankee cavalry they began to stampede," wrote Hotchkiss, "and as there was a Regt. of some 700 they filled the road for some distance, the companies of the 8th La. moved promptly forward and just gained the crest of a low ridge, along one side of which the road ran, as the cavalry passed, and poured into them a deadly volley, and such a tumbling of men and horses, as the General afterwards remarked, 'it looked too bad to see so many of them disposed of at once.'"[67]

SKETCHES FROM HOTCHKISS'S NOTEBOOK SHOW A SECTION OF THE MAIN ROAD THROUGH THE PAGE VALLEY. HOTCHKISS CAREFULLY NOTED DISTANCES, THE CONDITION OF ROAD SURFACES, AND THE SIZE OF HILLS. JACKSON'S VALLEY ARMY MARCHED OVER THIS STRETCH OF ROAD ON MAY 23, 1863, IN PURSUIT OF BANKS.

The Federals were routed and fled in all directions. Jackson moved in quickly to take prisoners and secure the supplies in the abandoned wagons. Hotchkiss was astounded and delighted by the appearance of the prisoners, writing that he saw "hundreds of men and richly caparisoned horses, the pride of the Yankee army, its superbly mounted Vermont, N.Y. and Pa. cavalry, that had exultingly and insolently ridden over our Valley." Before the Confederate guns, these brash Yankees had "melted like snow before the sun.... I am not vindictive, but I really did not feel sorry to see the horse and his insolent rider laid low. It seemed a just retribution for the evils they had inflicted on an innocent people."[68]

Jackson sent his cavalry northward on the Valley Pike in pursuit of the rest of Banks's column, and followed with the infantry. The general soon overtook Ashby, who had stopped the pursuit when many of his troopers had fallen out to loot the captured Federal wagons. Jackson was furious. This was just the sort of problem he had feared would happen in Ashby's undisciplined command. His cavalry scattered, Jackson could do nothing but push on with his foot soldiers. One infantryman remembered "dead Yankees and horses lying all along the road" and "Wagons strewn from Strasburg to Kernstown."[69] It was an exhausting and enervating march, for the Federals withdrew slowly and sullenly. They set fire to their abandoned wagons, and as dark came on, the two armies skirmished by the light of the long string of flaming vehicles that marked the destruction along the Valley Pike.

Jackson's and Ewell's columns did not merge until the morning of the twenty-fifth. Jackson's men had marched through the night and had but one hour's sleep in the morning. The 5th Virginia Regiment, now under the command of Hotchkiss's old friend Will Baylor, got no rest before Jackson had his men up and readying for an attack. Ewell attacked at dawn, and the exhausted Confederates of Jackson's column pitched in soon afterward. The Federal resistance was stiff, but did not last long. Banks's lines broke, and his command fled northward in chaos, through Winchester and on to the Potomac River and the safety of the Maryland shore.

Hotchkiss was exhilarated by the victory and the pursuit of "the haughty and insolent foe" through the streets of Winchester. It was a glorious moment, and it reminded him of the triumphs of arms in scripture. For Sara he described in soaring, almost Biblical rhetoric the climax of the battle and the liberation of the town. "At that moment the intrepid leader, in front, amid the roar of musketry and artillery, devoutly raised his hands to heaven, as if for Divine aid, when the enemy's line wavered, fell back, and fled. 'Now' says the General, swinging his plain gray cap, 'let's shout,' and at his shout went up that of the host with him and all dashed forward in pursuit. The day was won and through the streets of Winchester we pursued the foe, that had gloried in its pride and power but two short days before, amid the huzzas, shouts, tears, thanks, looks of unutterable delight, waving of Confederate flags and handkerchiefs of its whole liberated population.… It was a proud entry, and through we went, the sons of Winchester in the lead dealing death to the foe at every corner; and when we reached the other side of the town, the General, now thoroughly aroused, turned and said, 'Order the whole army to press on to the Potomac,' and on it came, and on sped the foe and after them we hurled shot, shell and iron hail, for miles, until the General ordered our men to halt, and the cavalry to be brought up to pursue. He then turned to go back to meet the cavalry passing along through our 3 united armies who had eagerly sought the ordered rest after 40 hours of exertion, but they felt not the labors they had endured, for all, even the dullest, now saw the consummation of the long marches, the short rations, the sleepless nights, interdicted furloughs—victory had come

from them, and as the hero of it turned back there was one shout of triumph, one spring up, one waving of hats from one end of the long line to the other, all murmurs were hushed, and 'old Jack' was the greatest of warriors to them and the idol of the hour's affections." [70]

The victory could scarcely have been more complete. Jackson's loss in killed, wounded, and missing in the fights at Front Royal and Winchester did not exceed 400, while Federal losses in prisoners alone came to more than 3,000. [71] So much materiel was captured that the Confederates would have trouble getting it all away. The booty included 103 head of cattle, more than seven tons of bacon, three tons of hard bread, and almost a ton and a half of sugar and salt. [72] "Major Harman, my chief quartermaster," Jackson wrote later in his report of the battle, "had but one week within which to remove it, and, although his efforts were characterized by his usual energy, promptitude, and judgment, all the conveyances that within that short period could be hired or impressed were inadequate to the work." [73]

Among the items captured were some baskets of champagne, and Major Hawks, commissary of subsistence, thought that the magnitude of the victory might induce General Jackson to make an exception to his strict abstinence from alcohol and perhaps lead the staff in a celebratory drink. Hawks sent a basket to headquarters. It was returned with a terse, mildly disapproving note from Jackson: "Major Hawks will send this wine, and all the wine captured, to the hospital." Thus scorned, the well-meaning Hawks complied. [74]

As Banks crossed the Potomac, Jackson allowed most of his weary army two days of rest around Winchester, where they basked in the gratitude of the relieved citizens. On the third day, the general moved off in pursuit of Banks, a movement that might have been interpreted as an attempt to follow the beaten and confused Federals into Maryland. This, of course, is how he hoped the Federals would see his advance, but he had no intention of crossing the Potomac. He sent one brigade—his old brigade, which now shared his nickname of Stonewall—in advance of the main column. Brig. Gen. Charles Winder, commanding the Stonewall Brigade, marched to the river to ensure that Banks crossed.

But the campaign was not yet over, and events were about to take a dramatic turn. On May 27, Jackson received news that two strong Federal columns were moving on his rear. Maj. Gen. Irvin McDowell was marching westward toward Front Royal with 30,000 men, almost twice as many as Jackson commanded. General Frémont, who had been moving slowly northward through the mountains while Jackson had throttled Banks, had been ordered into action by President Lincoln himself and was now approaching Strasburg from the west with 15,000 or more men. Frémont had had a long march out of the mountains; the most direct routes back into the Valley were still blocked, thanks to the efficiency of Hotchkiss and Sterrett two and a half weeks earlier. In addition to McDowell and Frémont, a strong Federal force was forming across the river at Harpers Ferry.

Jackson saw the door closing behind him and acted quickly to slide out before it slammed shut. He set his army in motion back to Winchester and thence on to Strasburg. His rear guard, the Stonewall Brigade, remained at Halltown, near Harpers Ferry, through May 30, when he recalled it. To guide the brigade in its retreat, Jackson once again called upon Hotchkiss.

"I want you to go to Charles Town and bring up the first brigade," Jackson told Hotchkiss. "I will stay in Winchester until you get here if I can, but if I cannot, and the enemy gets here first, you must bring it around through the mountains."[75] Hotchkiss said he understood and departed immediately. "I rode rapidly and reached Charles Town… quite early in the morning," Hotchkiss wrote,

"and at once found Gen. Winder … and gave him Gen. Jackson's orders." Winder sprang into action and the march began at once. And it was a brutal march. The rain fell in sheets and the roads turned to mud. After long hours filled with anxiety about whether the column was marching into a trap, Hotchkiss reached Winchester at about dusk. The brigade continued on through town in the gathering darkness, with orders to reach Jackson at Strasburg that night. But the soldiers had nearly reached the limit of their endurance. One officer who was present recalled that "by this time our men were straggling fearfully. Four regiments of the brigade had marched that day 34 or 35 miles, through mud and rain, and the 2nd Regiment had marched continuously, under worse conditions (for no rations had been issued to them for at least two days) from Loudoun Heights, which fact made the march about 5 miles more than the other regiments marched."[76] It was about 10 p.m. when Winder decided his men could go no further that night.[77] Hotchkiss, too, was worn out and slept in the hay of a stable beside his horse.[78]

In the morning, Winder and Hotchkiss led the advance south again toward Strasburg. But even after rejoining Jackson, the Stonewall Brigade could have no rest, for Jackson was pulling out of Strasburg, prodding his army southward to elude the ever-so-slowly closing jaws of McDowell and Frémont. The Confederates moved hastily, Ashby's cavalry acting as a rear guard, and when the Federals finally reached the Valley Pike, Jackson's escape route, the Confederates were gone. Jackson had escaped by marching twice as far as the Federals had in less time.

By June 4, the Southern column had almost reached Harrisonburg. But Jackson was not in headlong retreat. He was, as always, looking for a way to retrieve the initiative, and as the plan formed in his mind, he turned to his topographer for detailed information. On June 4, Jackson consulted Hotchkiss twice on the terrain around Port Republic, and at 10 p.m. dispatched him once again to the Peak to watch the pursuing Federal columns advancing on both sides of Massanutten.

Hotchkiss spent the day on the mountain with a man from the signal corps, finally coming down in the evening to report to Jackson. The Federal column east of Massanutten under Brig. Gen. James Shields was in camp near Conrad's Store and looked to be staying that way. This intelligence permitted Jackson to make a bold decision. The Federals had apparently decided to remain separated, thus offering the aggressive Jackson the opportunity to attack both forces. He immediately began preparations.

The 11,000 Federals under Frémont on the west of Massanutten and the 10,000 men under Shields in the Page Valley east of Massanutten remained idle, permitting Jackson a few days to rest his army at Port Republic. John Harman was still angry and had neither been relieved nor allowed to resign. He had been worked almost to the point of exhaustion during the campaign and took a few moments to babble a stream of acid complaints to his brother. "If I get through this safely, General Jackson must either relieve me or reduce the train. I will not be worked so any longer through this trip. All things are disagreeable, but where there is confusion I cannot help it. Oh for a few days rest."[79] Hotchkiss, too, was fatigued, and wanted desperately to go home. Despite the exhilaration of the marches and victories of the past weeks, and despite the satisfaction of knowing how much he had contributed to the preservation of the Valley so far, after little more than two months of service, he was heartily sick of war. To his brother Nelson he wrote, "I am every day more and more impressed with the belief that of all human evils war is the greatest, the most degrading and horrible, one from which all engaged in it long to be delivered. Misery and suffering all around them, suffering and anxiety at home. Nothing but the preservation of our dearest rights could ever induce me to have

anything to do with it, but we must fight out our destiny, come weal, come woe, and leave those that war does not sweep away to prove whether blood has been shed for good or evil."[80]

But the fighting continued, as did the dying. In a rearguard skirmish near Harrisonburg on June 6, Turner Ashby fell, apparently killed accidentally by his own men. Despite his professional disagreements with Ashby, the commanding general had respected the cavalryman as a man and fully appreciated his worth to the army. Jackson, and indeed all who knew Ashby, were saddened by his death, which Hotchkiss called "a loss irreparable."[81]

Early on the beautiful morning of June 8, Federal cavalry launched a surprise attack and seized a portion of Port Republic. At the sound of the firing, Jackson started walking toward it, too impatient to wait for his horse to be saddled. When his mount came up, he rode into the town with Pendleton, Boswell, Crutchfield, and two other staff officers toward the crucial bridge over the South Fork of the Shenandoah. So close were the Federals that they overtook Jackson's little party and captured Crutchfield and another officer.

Hotchkiss was unfit for duty that day, lying in his tent, "sick with a violent headache … exhausted from duty." When the attack came, Hotchkiss helped break down headquarters and pack it up in wagons to be moved to safety. He then mounted his horse and rode quickly away from the fight, too sick to be of any use. He rode to Weyer's Cave, which he had first visited fifteen years earlier on his walking tour of the Valley. There, high above the valley, he sat and watched the fighting at Cross Keys, a few miles west of Port Republic, where General Ewell had attacked Frémont."[82] Later still, sick and weary, Hotchkiss went to a house near the cave, lay down, and slept.

The fighting resumed in the morning, but this time Jackson was the aggressor. He attacked Shields in the morning, hoping to deal with Frémont in the afternoon. The Stonewall Brigade opened the attack but was repulsed. "Just about that time," wrote an improved Hotchkiss, "I came up and the General asked where I had been. I informed him; then he said: 'Take General Taylor around and take those batteries,' pointing to the enemy's batteries … which were making sad havoc among our men." [83]

The Louisiana brigade of Brig. Gen. Richard Taylor, son of President Zachary Taylor and brother-in-law of Jefferson Davis, followed Hotchkiss on roads and through a dense woods to the flank of the Federal artillery. The brigade charged and finally took the guns. Another Confederate brigade added its fire, and the Federals broke. Frémont, who had advanced toward the battle, found that the bridge over the South Fork had been burned. He could only watch as Jackson thrashed Shields. Later both Federal forces retired, and Jackson's Valley Campaign was over.

Jackson rested his men for five days in the rich fields of the Valley near Mount Meridian, and on June 13, he congratulated them. "Beset on both flanks by two boastful armies," he told them in a written order, "you have escaped their toils, inflicting successively crushing blows upon each of your pursuers. Let a few more such efforts be made, and you may confidently hope that our beautiful Valley will be cleansed from the pollution of the invader's presence." [84]

Jackson's campaign in the Valley had in many ways been a miracle. Vastly outnumbered, hampered by rain, mud, and snow, and sustained on several occasions more by luck than ability, Jackson had created a military masterpiece. His actions perfectly illustrated the principles of speed of movement and concentration of force so important to military success. He had made the best possible use of his resources, asking much of his men and officers and getting more from some of them—John Harman, for example—than even they felt they could give. Hotchkiss had

reason to be proud of his contribution. Jackson had used the terrain of the Valley superbly, and Hotchkiss had been the general's main source of topographical information. The role of topography had been so important, in fact, that it might accurately be said that the Valley Campaign would have been impossible without the detailed information Hotchkiss supplied. He had cast a brilliant light on the Valley, enabling his general to see and understand its features and characteristics. Without Hotchkiss, Jackson would have moved in comparative darkness and lacked the swift confidence that characterized his marches and was crucial to the success of the campaign. Jed Hotchkiss had been indispensable.

And being the student of the Bible that he was, and knowing, as Jackson did, that all earthly successes derive from heaven and the will of God, Hotchkiss must have pondered over the meaning of the great campaign. Perhaps he recalled a passage from scripture that he had read with his Sunday school class on an October morning just before the start of the war. If he remembered it, he would have marveled over its accuracy, for in the twenty-sixth chapter of Leviticus, verses 3-8, Hotchkiss and his students had seen foretold an outline of Jackson's Valley Campaign:

And ye shall chase your enemies,
and they shall fall before you by the sword.
And five of you shall chase an hundred,
and an hundred of you shall put ten thousand to flight:
and your enemies shall fall before you by the sword.

And perhaps, in recalling the events of the campaign just finished, in which the devout general had driven enemies from the beautiful Valley, Hotchkiss saw the great irony in the verses. Or, more likely, perhaps he saw no irony in them at all.

GEN. ROBERT E. LEE STANDS BEFORE HIS RENTED HOUSE IN RICHMOND IN APRIL 1865. LEE CONSIDERED HOTCHKISS'S TOPOGRAPHICAL ABILITIES EXTREMELY VALUABLE, AND HE OFTEN BORROWED THE SURVEYOR FOR SPECIAL ASSIGNMENTS. TWICE DURING THE WAR, WHEN ARMY RED TAPE THREATENED HOTCHKISS'S POSITION AT HEADQUARTERS, LEE ISSUED A SPECIAL DISPENSATION TO KEEP THE TOPOGRAPHER ON THE JOB.

CHAPTER FOUR
CAMPAIGNING WITH LEE

Jackson had no leisure to savor his success in the Valley. McClellan and his army were closing in on Richmond, and Lee needed help. If Jackson expected a summons from Lee, he kept that expectation to himself. His staff, however, was not as easily fooled as the Federals and surmised what was afoot. "Jackson," recalled Hotchkiss, "made constant use of all maps … but made a particular study of those of the region where he made marches or where he expected to have encampments.… one of the things that annoyed him was the necessity of calling for maps and map information which would in any manner suggest or reveal his intentions as it was a cardinal principle with him to tell no one what he intended to do. This led him to resort to strategy."[1]

Jackson called Hotchkiss to his tent one day and asked for maps of the country from Port Republic to Lexington. Hotchkiss retrieved some maps of the upper Valley from his tent and brought them to the general, spending about a half hour talking about roads and streams and defensible positions "just as though he had in mind a march in that direction," Hotchkiss recalled. Jackson suddenly said, "Good, very good," and, knowing he had been dismissed, Hotchkiss returned to his tent to continue working on a map. About half an hour later, an orderly announced that Jackson wanted Hotchkiss again. This time, Jackson "remarked that they had been having some fighting down

about Richmond … and that he would like to see the map of the field of operations, so I brought the maps of the country around Richmond." The two spent almost an hour this time going over the maps, long enough to convince Hotchkiss that the first interview with the Lexington area maps had been a ruse.[2] The next day, the Valley Army moved eastward, having been called by Lee to Richmond.

Hotchkiss, however, would not be accompanying his headquarters comrades. Jackson still wished for maps of the Valley and thought his topographer's time would be better spent working up the desired charts. The general ordered Hotchkiss to stay behind in the Valley and draw. Hotchkiss moved his tent and his maps to Augusta County, where he could work in relative comfort. As much as he would have liked to, however, he did not set up his office at Loch Willow, where distractions would have made working difficult. Instead, he pitched camp at Staunton, where he could get regular news from the war and the rest of the Valley and transmit it to Jackson if necessary, which was part of his assignment.

The weeks that followed refreshed and rejuvenated Hotchkiss. He found relaxation in working on maps almost constantly. On Sundays, he stayed with Sara and the girls and attended services. The weather was fine, and friends and neighbors hospitable. Here was a respite from the madness of campaigning, for Staunton was an island of civilized repose where a man might eat wholesome meals without fear of being shot at, sleep regular hours without fear of being called from his bed at any moment, and shun inclement weather if he had a mind to. Hotchkiss did have rather more interruptions to his work than he cared for as well-meaning but curious friends stopped by to ask about General Jackson or to look at maps of the area near Richmond where the armies were fighting, but by and large these weeks in Staunton were like a dream.

But there was no mistaking that the war continued. Signs of the conflict were everywhere. Women worked in the fields, for many of the men were in the army, and remarkably, on clear days, cannonading could be heard from battlefields east of Richmond—more than 125 miles away. His friends at headquarters wrote to "Hotch," as they called him; Boswell shared news of events around Richmond—and of the pretty girls spoken to and good meals eaten, all of which was "most important" to young officers.[3] In the first week of July, Hotchkiss knew that the fighting had ended at Richmond, that the Federals had been driven back, and that a new campaign could not be far off. It was only a matter of time before he would rejoin the army. Then, on July 14, no trains came from Richmond. The cars were being held at the capital, and Hotchkiss knew that "some movement is on hand." Sure enough, the next night, while working in his tent, he received a message from Jackson ordering him to Gordonsville at once. The army was returning.[4]

The abrupt end to the happy month in Staunton failed to dampen Hotchkiss's spirits. He was anxious to see his friends and hear of the adventures around Richmond. Hastily he wrote to Sara, broke camp, and went back to the war.

Jackson arrived in Gordonsville looking, Hotchkiss thought, the worse for his trip to the Peninsula. While his topographer was basking in the idylls of Staunton, Jackson was undergoing the greatest ordeal of his military career.

He had entered the fighting around Richmond physically exhausted after the campaign in the Valley, but General Lee, who now commanded the main Confederate army in Virginia—the Army of Northern Virginia—gave Jackson the most demanding and important assignments in the effort to drive McClellan's army away from the Confederate capital. On the first day of the attack, Jackson failed to get his army in position and could not support other elements of Lee's forces, which faltered greatly as a result. On the second day, Jackson was late again, and at least twice more that week he failed to fulfill expectations.

Certainly a contributing factor to the mysterious lapse was Jackson's unfamiliarity with the Tidewater region east of Richmond. He had never been there, and his staff and most of his army were from the Valley and other parts of Virginia. What was worse, maps were scarce, and Jackson might not have had any. Before leaving the Valley, Jackson had looked at whatever maps of the Tidewater Hotchkiss had, but apparently did not take any with him, expecting that Lee would have an ample supply. Lee had one map, but it is not clear whether enough copies were made for his lieutenants. Other maps that might have been available would have been of questionable value. The region had not been extensively surveyed, despite its proximity to the state capital, and existing maps varied widely in their placement of roads and watercourses. Even with the map he had, Lee had difficulty getting his troops to where he wanted them in the dense, dark, marshy forests and swamps along the Chickahominy River. The best hope for navigation in the Tidewater lay with a guide who knew the country. In the absence of such a guide, the next best thing would be an experienced and responsible topographer with a keen sense of direction. But Jackson had left Hotchkiss in the Valley. For his part, Hotchkiss always lamented that he had not been present around Richmond. Many years later, he would tell a comrade, "I think I may also add without egotism that if I had been with Jackson he would have been much better provided for with maps and other information which he so sorely needed during the Richmond campaign."[5]

Despite Jackson's curious failures, Lee had succeeded in wresting the initiative from McClellan and pushing the Federals back from Richmond's doorstep. The Federal War Department recalled McClellan and his Army of the Potomac to Washington, and Lee planned his next move. While McClellan had lain outside of Richmond, a smaller Federal army under a new commander moved into central Virginia. Lee would now devote attention to this force, and among his first moves, he sent Jackson to Gordonsville.

But developing a strategy to meet the Federals would take time, and meanwhile the army entered its own idyll. Flushed with victory first in the Valley and then outside of Richmond, the Confederates in Virginia had good reason to seek repose. The region around Gordonsville was a smiling country plump with orchards of ripening fruit, its rolling meadows painted green and amber by fields of standing corn and wheat. Blackberries covered the hills, and the whole army, Jackson included, took time to dally in the sunshine and sample the sweet taste of summer in Virginia. Water was clean and plentiful, and shade trees grew tall and broad. Jackson's men could see the Blue Ridge to the west, which, the general remarked, reminded them all of their homes in the Valley. Here, Hotchkiss thought, "Our worn-out and exhausted men can be refreshed after the toils and dangers of the Richmond fight."[6]

Toward the end of the month, the period of solace and rest came to a close—at least for Hotchkiss. Jackson needed maps and put his cartographer to work. Hotchkiss wrote Sara for his bottle of blue ink, which was "very precious," and he asked that it be packed up carefully. He worked hard on the maps Jackson requested, staying by his tent, "preparing maps for future use if not immediate." His creations were put to use more immediately than even he expected.[7]

The new Federal commander in Piedmont Virginia was Maj. Gen. John Pope, a forty-year-old professional soldier who had enjoyed some military success in Missouri, Tennessee, and Mississippi in recent months and was brought east by Lincoln to work his magic in Virginia. Pope was not well liked among his brother officers and soon would be loathed by thousands of men in both armies. Upon assuming command, he issued a boldly worded address to his troops that contrasted them unfavorably with Federals in the western theater, where, he said, "We have always seen the backs of our enemies." Having thus offended many of his men, Pope then angered his opponents, Lee in particular, by issuing orders that gave his men liberty to confiscate the property of Virginians and to arrest any citizen suspected of abetting the enemy. Lee called Pope a "miscreant" and looked for a way to crush him.

The Confederates bided their time in the Gordonsville area, watching for Pope to make a mistake. Finally, in early August, Jackson moved against an isolated portion of Pope's army. The commander of the Federal wing was Jackson's old opponent from the Valley, Nathaniel Banks. Jackson must have been delighted at the chance to meet Banks again on the battlefield. On August 9, in the pastures near Cedar Run and in the shadow of Cedar Mountain, Jackson's force stumbled onto Banks and the battle was joined. Though he had the initiative, Jackson was caught off guard by the Federal positioning and strength, and his brigades entered the battle off balance. It was a bitter and terrifying contest, Hotchkiss calling it "as desperate a fight as I ever saw."[8] In fact, along with the rest of Jackson's staff, he was in the middle of the fight throughout the afternoon, "exposed for some time to a horrid fire of artillery and musketry on nearly three sides of us, the balls falling as thick as I ever saw them, reaping their harvest of death on all sides." But strangely, the awful hail of bullets held no terror for Hotchkiss. He attained that day the sort of detached, completely irrational calm that men who have been in combat have described for centuries. He held fast to his faith and became perfectly fearless. "I never felt the protecting goodness of God more forcibly," he told Nelson, "and never looked upon a scene with more calmness, though in the very vortex of destruction."[9]

This sketch from Hotchkiss's survey of the Cedar Mountain battlefield includes prominent features of the terrain and notes on the positions of the troops engaged.

The Confederates held the field and claimed victory, but they had suffered fearful casualties. As Hotchkiss conducted his usual post-battle survey of the field, he witnessed "ghastly horrors," and heard "agonizing shrieks and groans from the many wounded Yankees that were lying exposed to the full blaze of the sun." He saw Confederate burial parties move the helpless Northerners into the shade and give them some water, but the Southerners gave most of their succor to their own wounded.[10] "God save me from such spectacles," he wrote to Nelson, "the dead, the dying, the mangled, the screaming, the blackened living and the dead humanities. I looked upon them all without a feeling of sorrow for my foes, (though I could in faith say Father

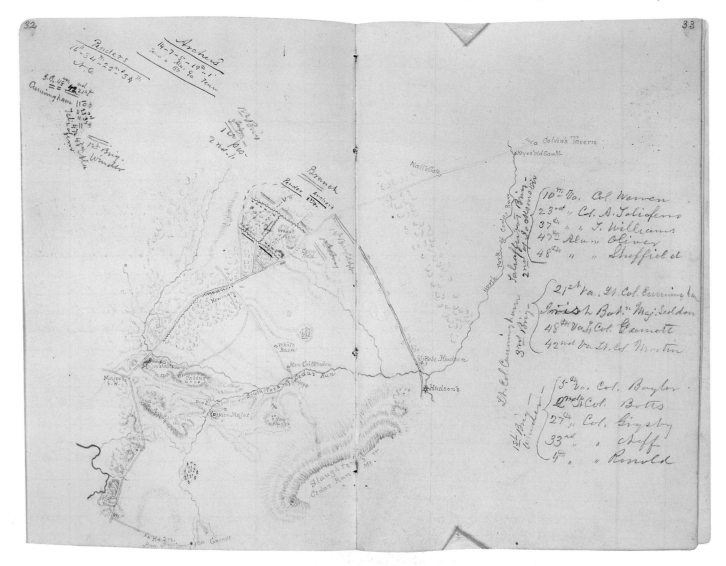

forgive them,) for they had come of their own will upon our soil to waste and burn, and kill, but my heart grieved for every son of the South that lay there weltering in his gore; that poured out his life blood to rescue our land from a worse than Egyptian bondage. May God help them with salvation, and their friends with consolation and may they live forever in the memory of a people that will one day be free and happy."[11]

But even as Hotchkiss worked on the battlefield map, Jackson needed other charts more urgently. He beckoned to Hotchkiss while they were riding with the staff one day and said, as Hotchkiss remembered, "As soon as we got back to camp he wished me to prepare maps covering the whole country from Gordonsville to Washington, saying that he wanted several copies of this I think five. As it was about the middle of the day and on Sunday, and we would soon be to our camp ground, I asked him if this work should go on on that day, knowing his great antipathy for doing anything on Sunday that was not of necessity. His reply was that it was important to have it done at once, consequently as soon as we got into camp I went to work."[12] The next day, Jackson reinforced the importance and urgency of the assignment, telling Hotchkiss not to be afraid of making too many.[13]

Hotchkiss, of course, deduced what few others in the army were privileged to know: Jackson was planning a move north. But it soon became apparent that the move would be even bigger than Hotchkiss could realize. Lee moved his headquarters nearby and called a meeting of his principal lieutenants. Jackson took Hotchkiss's maps to the conference, giving one to Lee and another to General J. E. B. ("Jeb") Stuart, the chief of cavalry, and the generals together discussed how to get at Pope.[14] Lee and his officers arrived at a bold plan that would at least move the war farther north so that the all-important harvesting in central Virginia could proceed undisturbed, and at most lead to another Federal defeat. Lee's plan called for Jackson, with roughly half the army, to march around Pope's right flank and strike his supply depot at Manassas Junction. With his supply line broken, and with a large enemy force in his rear—between him and Washington—Pope would have no choice but to fall back. Lee and Longstreet would then follow with the rest of the army and join Jackson near Manassas. The plan depended on secrecy and swift marches, and Jackson had shown a talent for both in the Valley.

On August 25, Jackson set his column in motion. For two days, the Confederates toiled over hot dusty roads, losing many infantrymen to heat and thirst. Jackson pushed on, using maps prepared by Hotchkiss and following a route scouted and selected by Boswell. Finally, fifty-four miles from their starting point, Jackson's weary "foot cavalry" arrived at Manassas Junction and looted and burned the Federal depot with little opposition. His task completed, Jackson moved on to the old battlefield at Manassas, where he had earned his nickname just over a year earlier, and hid his men near an unfinished railroad cut. There they waited for Lee and Longstreet.

Hotchkiss, however, was not with his chief. He had remained behind by Jackson's order to work on maps. After drawing all day, he packed up each night and followed in the wake of the army, quenching his thirst on the hot, dusty roads by munching on some onions Sara had sent him.[15] As he gained on the army, he heard firing in the distance.

Jackson had been unable to wait for the rest of the army. Around dusk on August 28, he attacked a target of opportunity, a Federal column passing unawares along the turnpike before the railroad cut. The fighting began that evening and would continue for the next two days. Longstreet and Lee arrived in time to support Jackson's hard-pressed line, finally falling on Pope's exposed left flank and driving the surprised Federals off the battlefield, across

Bull Run, and back toward Washington thirty miles away. The Confederate victory was complete, but the destruction of life was almost beyond comprehension. More than 18,000 men fell dead or wounded in little more than fifty hours. On September 1, Jackson attacked the retreating Federals at Chantilly in a violent thunderstorm, but the Northerners made good their escape, and Lee finally reined in Jackson so his men could rest.

By the close of the fighting on the final day at Manassas, Hotchkiss had rejoined the army and reported to Jackson. The general ordered him to map the battlefield, and to do so quickly, for they would soon be moving on. Hotchkiss was unprepared for what he saw. The Federals, he told Sara, lay "in thousands over the battlefield, rotting and enriching the soil they vainly boasted as their own." [16] It was the greatest slaughter he had ever seen, or ever cared to see: "Never have I seen such horrors. I thought I had seen war and bloodshed in its worst shape at Port Republic and elsewhere, but that was nothing … their dead were strewn over a space of 5 miles long and three wide, piled up in many places, sometimes in long lines as they stood in the ranks, and upon one another where they attempted, seven times, to break Jackson's line, and were as many times repulsed." [17]

One of the dead was Hotchkiss's good friend Col. Will Baylor of the 5th Virginia, who had been so important in getting Hotchkiss the position on Jackson's staff. Baylor's widow took the loss very hard, and Hotchkiss sent comforting words via Sara. "It is well to grieve for the dead, but half the pang is removed when one dies as Baylor did, at the head of his troops, bearing the colors and cheering them on when he was met by a volley from a whole regiment of the enemy." [18] Hotchkiss was not impressed because Baylor died gloriously, but because he died doing his duty. Baylor had disregarded danger, and if he had felt fear he had ignored that as well, and strode forward into harm's

way because it was his responsibility to do so. That the man was killed was unfortunate, Hotchkiss believed, but he had died a man's death—fulfilling his duty—thereby increasing the value of his life.

Barely had Hotchkiss begun to survey the field when Jackson moved on, rescuing the mapmaker from the scenes of carnage and directing him to guide a portion of the army northward. The army buzzed with speculation. Would Lee attack Washington? Would the Federals evacuate their capital and flee from victorious Confederates? Was the army bound for an invasion of the North? The answer came quickly. Lee swung his powerful and supremely confident army westward and headed for the fords on the Potomac River. The Army of Northern Virginia was taking the war to the Northern people.

As the army moved closer to the Potomac, Hotchkiss was in an exultant mood. "I am in excellent health," he told Sara, "and enjoy this excitement." [19] Everything in this region was superb, he thought. The countryside was "magnificent," the food was plentiful, including "some of the finest apples I ever saw," and when they camped at night it was by "a splendid spring." Finally, on September 5, they came to the Potomac, and the army's excitement reached its zenith. Hotchkiss recorded a vivid picture of the historic crossing: "We started about sunrise and went, by a private road, to White's Ford and there crossed the Potomac into Maryland, Gen. Jackson on a cream-colored, or 'clayback' horse, and riding on the left of the front. The 10th Va. Regt. of infantry, preceded by a band and bearing a Virginia flag, was in the advance; as the band reached the Maryland shore it struck up the air, 'Maryland, my Maryland,' amid shouts of the soldiers. It was a noble spectacle, the broad river, fringed by the lofty trees in full foliage; the exuberant wealth of the autumnal wild flowers down to the very margin of the stream and a bright green island stretched away to the right." [20]

It was a thrilling moment, and the great adventure put the men in the ranks in high spirits. On the northern bank, fortune immediately smiled on the invaders as they came upon a canal boat full of melons enroute to the Washington markets. The soldiers swarmed forward to purchase the cargo, and Jackson and his staff enjoyed their first meal together outside of Virginia.

The welcome in Maryland could not have been warmer. "People came from every direction, as the news spread," Hotchkiss wrote to Sara, "and offered us anything they had for the use of the army; did not object to the burning of rails and the using of roasting ears, which was the only food our men had, save the quantities the people gave them."[21] Jackson, in fact, was concerned about his troops' short rations, and ordered his officers to purchase a field of standing corn, the ears to be distributed to the men and the husks and stalks to the horses. He then ordered the troops to have one day's rations of roasting ears cooked and in the haversacks by dawn the next day. Hotchkiss heard one soldier muse, "Wonder if the General has roasting ears in his haversack too?" Not long afterward, when the staff stopped for dinner, Hotchkiss smiled when he saw Jackson pull a large roasting ear out of his haversack and sit down to gnaw off the kernels.[22]

Those first days in Maryland were, for Hotchkiss at least, one of the emotional high points of the war. Never again would he be so thrilled, excited, and confident of victory as in the second week of September 1862. He was part of a strong and splendid army beneath brilliant and admirable generals, a combination that seemed to make them unbeatable. He saw that at last, after the long months of campaigning and the slaughter of thousands of young men, the end might be very near indeed. And after the Federals made peace, he mused, he could return to Sara and the girls. "Be of good cheer," he wrote to her from Frederick, Maryland, "the skies are brightening for an end to this

bloody war. We have to fight once more and no doubt soon."[23]

Lee hoped that the climactic battle would occur somewhere in Pennsylvania. He hoped to strike north into the Keystone State and capture its capital, Harrisburg, breaking up the recruitment and supply depots there and severing the Pennsylvania Railroad, the main link between the Midwest and the East. Lee's line of supply and communication would run through the Shenandoah Valley, so before he moved farther north, he had to secure the Valley by eliminating the Federal garrisons at Martinsburg and Harpers Ferry. He sent Jackson to accomplish this crucial mission.

Jackson moved his command westward over the Catoctin and South mountains toward Martinsburg. From there, he would turn south to Harpers Ferry, and thence rejoin Lee and Longstreet on the march to Pennsylvania. It was on this grand sweep through Maryland and Virginia that Hotchkiss acquired his most precious war relic, which would be treasured in his family for decades. While riding with Jackson one day, he remarked that he would like to return to a town through which they had just passed to purchase a new hat from among those he had noticed in a shop window, because his was worn out. "Good!" said Jackson, "Do so and please get me one also." Hotchkiss asked what size he wore and handed him his own hat to try on. "He said that is exactly the size," recalled Hotchkiss. "So I went back and got two hats and when I overtook him I gave him one of them and he put it on." Hotchkiss asked if he should take care of the old cap, and Jackson replied, "If you please," and Hotchkiss put it in his saddle bags full of drawing materials and maps. Reminded of the hat months later, Jackson made a gift of it to his topographical engineer.[24]

In the town of Boonsboro, a roving party of Federal cavalry made a bold charge at the head of the Confederate column, almost capturing a pair of officers, but the troopers soon withdrew, and Jackson ordered a halt for the night. That evening, an old friend unexpectedly returned to headquarters with an amazing tale of adventure and deceit. Twenty-two-year-old George Junkin, formerly aide-de-camp to Jackson, had escaped from a Northern prison and made his way south to rejoin his comrades. Junkin was, like Hotchkiss, a native Northerner. He left his Pennsylvania family to attend Washington College in the Shenandoah Valley, at which his uncle, the Reverend Dr. George Junkin—Jackson's father-in-law—was president. Young Junkin was a cousin of Jackson's first wife. Like Hotchkiss, he remained with the South when war came, and became aide-de-camp to Jackson in February 1862, but was captured at the Battle of Kernstown.

Junkin's father, a clergyman, visited his son in the Northern prison and soundly criticized him "for having become a 'rebel' and joining the enemies of his country." The Reverend Junkin said that his wife had been "crazed" by the treason of her son, and that now only her son could save her from insanity by taking the oath of allegiance to the Union and going to see her. Young Junkin was horrified by what his actions had done to his poor mother and immediately did as his father asked—he took the oath of allegiance to the United States and returned home to see his mother. At his home, he found, to his "utter amazement," that she was not insane or even sick. Outraged, he proclaimed his revulsion at his father's deceit, and at once headed south, on foot, intent on rejoining the "Rebels" so loathed by his scheming father. It was on his long walk back to Virginia that he happened upon his old friends at Jackson's headquarters. Hotchkiss, who had not known the boy before he walked into camp, was impressed by his story and his courage, knowing that he would be treated harshly by the Federals if captured again after having sworn allegiance to the Union.[25]

The march continued, with the Federals falling back before Jackson's advance through Maryland and back into Virginia. "We ... swept around by Frederick, Middletown and Williamsport," Hotchkiss wrote to Sara, "swept them out of Martinsburg and gathered them all into Harpers Ferry."[26] The Confederates turned south and soon came upon Harpers Ferry, the quaint and picturesque little town at the confluence of the Potomac and Shenandoah rivers. This was the northern extremity of the Valley, and it was here that Hotchkiss had first set foot in Virginia on

his walking tour fifteen years earlier. Now the town was occupied by 12,000 Federal troops, preparing to defend themselves.

But Harpers Ferry was indefensible, completely surrounded by high hills and wedged in the fork of the two rivers. There was no practical way to keep enemy artillery off the dominating hills, and there was no easy escape route from the town itself. Once Jackson's men were in position on the three heights that commanded the town, the Federals in Harpers Ferry were trapped.

Jackson's force was separated by the two rivers, so the general sent Hotchkiss to establish a line of signals between headquarters and the wing of the army on Loudoun

A TROOP TRAIN STANDS IDLE ON THE TRACKS OF THE WINCHESTER AND POTOMAC RAILROAD AT HARPERS FERRY WHILE ANOTHER TRAIN HEADS SOUTH. THE TOWN REMAINED A TRANSPORTATION HUB THROUGHOUT THE WAR, DESPITE THE DESTRUCTION OF BRIDGES AND MILES OF RAILROAD TRACK.

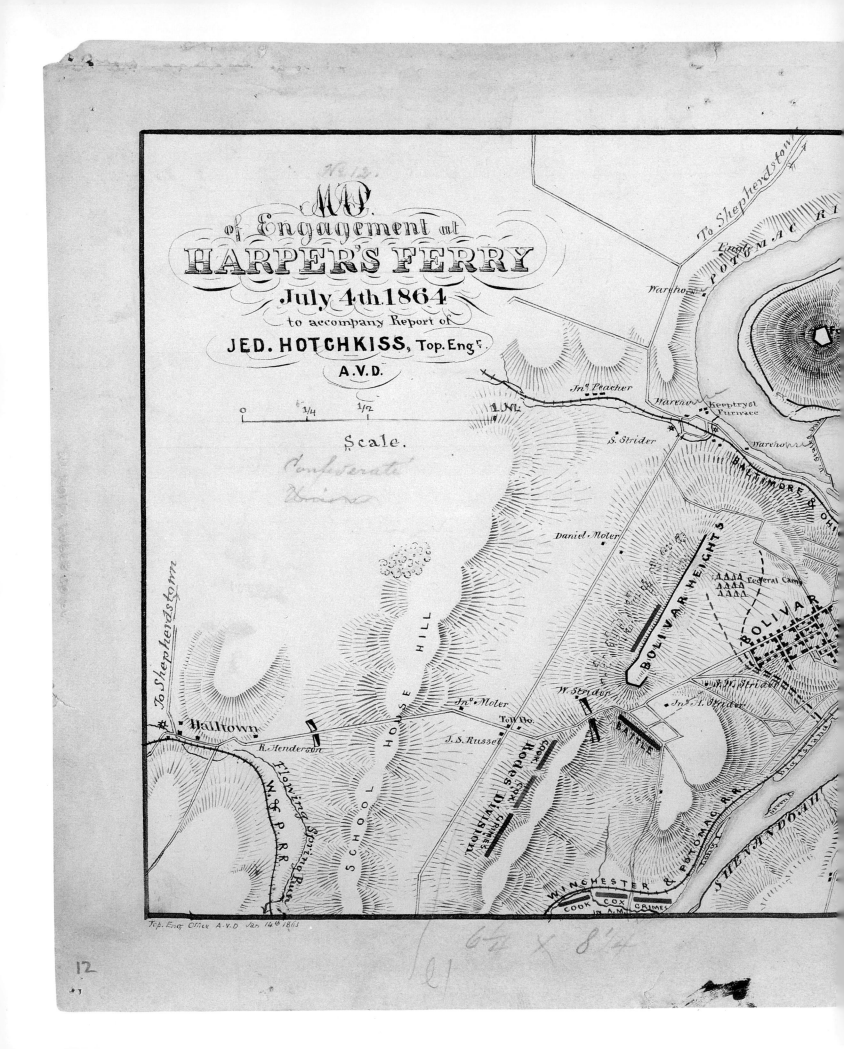

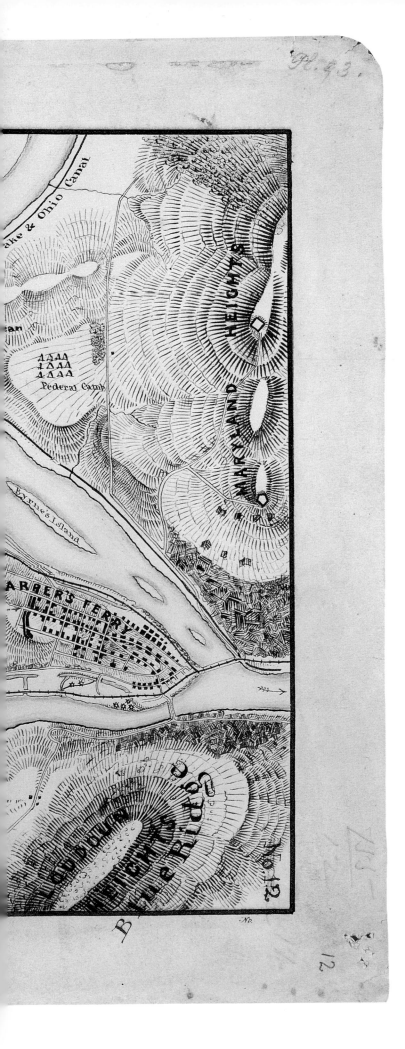

Heights under Brig. Gen. John G. Walker. From the heights he could see the enemy waiting under arms throughout the day on September 14. The Federals refused to surrender, but after Jackson shelled the town and advanced his infantry, the Northerners saw the hopelessness of their position and capitulated.

The size of the capture was enormous: wagons, provisions, blankets, muskets, ammunition, overcoats, medicines, bandages, camp kettles, artillery pieces, and 12,000 Federal soldiers. It was the greatest single capture of Federal troops during the war. Curious to see and talk to the Northerners, Hotchkiss went into the town at the first opportunity. He was astounded at what he saw. "I never saw a more splendidly dressed set of men, the officers were all splendidly equipped and everything there was new, artillery and all." [27] He was also surprised by what he heard. He found a lot of prisoners from his home state of New York and talked to them about the war. "I found all the New Yorkers glad they were taken, and anxious to go home. The officers, many of them, intend to resign at once. A major from Palmyra gave me his revolver and told me four weeks was enough for him and had altered his opinions completely." [28]

Jackson had little time to review the prisoners, however, for he was behind schedule in rejoining Lee. More worrisome, the Federal Army of the Potomac had left the safety of Washington's defenses and was pursuing Lee's fragmented army. McClellan was in command and was pushing through Maryland more rapidly than Lee had expected him. Forced to modify his plans and forgo, for

---

HOTCHKISS CAREFULLY RETAINED ALL HIS NOTES AND SURVEY DATA FOR FUTURE REFERENCE. THIS 1864 MAP OF HARPERS FERRY, ONE OF HOTCHKISS'S FINEST PIECES OF WORK, WAS BASED IN PART ON INFORMATION GATHERED IN 1862.

Though he probably did not see these dead soldiers at Gettysburg, Hotchkiss often had to ride among the dead and wounded while he made post-battle surveys. The sights and sounds depressed him and convinced him that General Jackson was right to call war "the greatest of evils."

the moment, a move into Pennsylvania, Lee summoned Jackson to the town of Sharpsburg, where the Army of Northern Virginia would make a stand.

Jackson moved most of his command out of Harpers Ferry but left some of his staff and A. P. Hill's Division behind to attend to the administrative details of the surrender and the removal or destruction of captured supplies. On September 16, he joined Lee at Sharpsburg, near

Antietam Creek. Lee had taken the best defensive position he could find, but it left much to be desired. The wide Potomac was at his back and there was only one practical escape route. If his army were beaten on the field, it would have no place to go and would face complete destruction on the banks of the river.

Hotchkiss was among those Jackson left behind. He assisted the engineers in destroying two bridges over the Potomac and helped Jackson's ordnance chief, William Allan, collect arms and ammunition. By the seventeenth, he was making plans to rejoin Jackson, for a battle seemed imminent, but he could not get across the Potomac. His horse, exhausted from long rides with short rests, broke down. He had seen its collapse coming, and had noted a week before that the poor animal was "quite used up." But for the failure to come just at that time was an unlucky coincidence. Hotchkiss would not go into battle that day.[29]

What Hotchkiss missed on September 17 was the greatest slaughter in American history. The fighting at Sharpsburg was desperate. Never before had America seen anything like this mass destruction of life. The fields and swales above Antietam Creek became a slaughterhouse as the armies lost a total of nearly 23,000 men in a single day of combat. Jackson's men had staved off attacks all morning, suffering some of the heaviest casualties of the day, before the fighting shifted to another part of the battlefield. Lee's army had fought to the point of collapse, and only the timely arrival of A. P. Hill's troops after a forced march from Harpers Ferry saved the Confederate army from a resounding defeat.

On the day after the battle, Hotchkiss crossed the river and found that Jackson wanted him to make a reconnaissance upriver, beyond Shepherdstown, Virginia, to determine if the known fords on the Potomac were practical, given the stage of the river, for artillery and wagon trains. Hotchkiss found a guide and spent the day in the saddle, locating approach roads and scouting the fords and Federal outposts, finding that the fords were suitable for infantry and cavalry only.[30] He wearily returned to Shepherdstown late in the night and found, to his surprise, that the army was retreating. "The road was full of horses, wagons, ambulances, etc., and very narrow, with a bluff above and below and the river beneath. I found the ford full of wagons and the bank on the other side densely packed with them. I saw some pushed into the canal by the press."[31] He tried to ride back toward Sharpsburg and find Jackson, but he found movement slow against the tide of retreating wagons. He met Gen. Jeb Stuart, who asked that Hotchkiss accompany him as a guide. Hotchkiss surrendered any hope of finding Jackson that night and did as Stuart wished, but the going was still treacherous on the dark,

crowded roads, and Stuart's horse stumbled and fell beneath a wagon. Finally, Hotchkiss lay down to sleep in the street at Shepherdstown with a group of soldiers by a campfire.

On the night of September 18, Lee started his army across the river to Virginia. Fears that McClellan would fall upon the army's rear heightened the normal complications and confusion of such a large movement. "It was a night of suspense," wrote Hotchkiss to Sara, "for our immense train and large body of troops had to pass the river by one ford with McClellan's vast army close behind and watching our movements, but it was all accomplished safely. Providence blessing us with a fog to aid us.... The movement was equal to a great victory and left us free for new plans."[32]

The escape of Lee's army was indeed a victory of sorts, for the battle-weary Confederates, having marched so far on short rations, and having lost more than one-quarter of their strength at Sharpsburg, might not have been able to resist McClellan had he attacked with vigor. The men, horses, and equipment in Lee's army were worn out. Even Hotchkiss, who rode almost everywhere he went, was "almost barefooted" and a great many of the infantrymen were literally so.[33]

But the Southerners returned home in good spirits, not feeling the least bit defeated. Many, including Hotchkiss, felt that they had accomplished much. "It was a great thing," he wrote to brother Nelson with his customary optimism, "a glorious achievement, to free our state from the enemy and drive him beyond the Potomac."[34] But the army had suffered much, and not only had the Federal army survived the invasion, but the Northern people had barely felt the effect of the incursion at all, and now the war would continue. As the Army of Northern Virginia returned to Virginia, it could expect the Federal army to follow. Once again, Virginia would be a battleground.

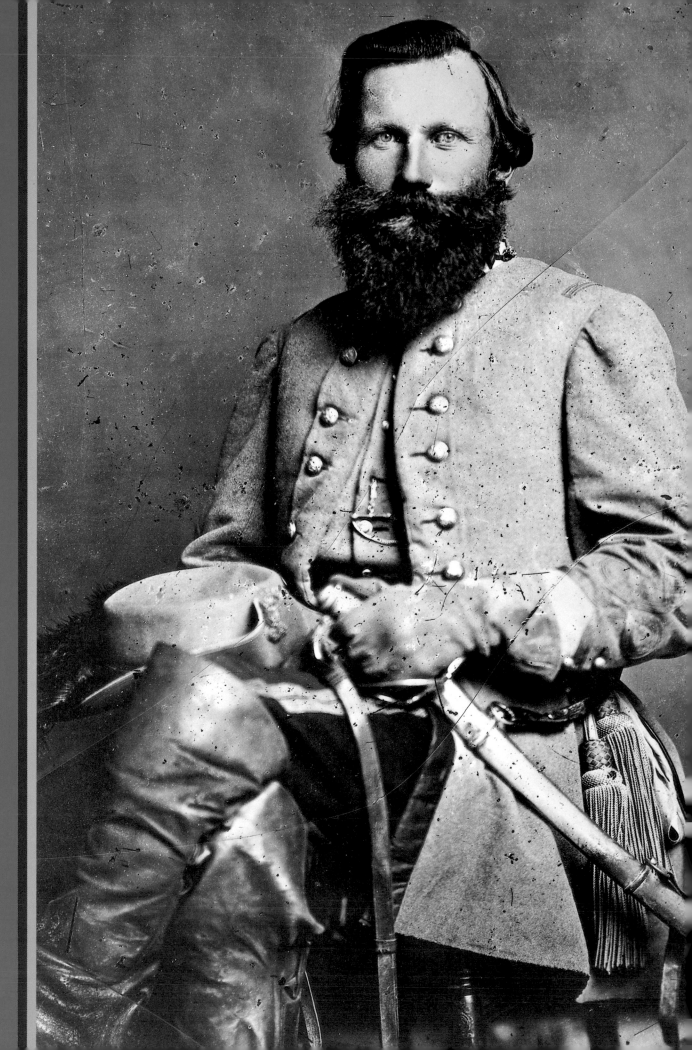

Maj. Gen. James Ewell Brown "Jeb" Stuart, Lee's chief of cavalry, and Jed Hotchkiss were both in the business of gathering information, but they approached their jobs from different perspectives. The charming Stuart did everything with a certain dash. Hotchkiss cared only for accuracy. The cavalier and the schoolmaster became good friends, and Hotchkiss was always greeted warmly at cavalry headquarters.

CHAPTER FIVE

"THIS WINTER OF OUR SORROW"

As tired and worn out as the Confederates were, the Federals were even more so, at least in the mind of their commander, General McClellan. He took his time recrossing the Potomac into Virginia and then waited some more as his army rested and drew new equipment. His deliberation greatly benefited his army, but the respite allowed Lee's army to recoup much of its vitality as well.

Jackson established headquarters in the lower Valley near Winchester while his troops rested and refitted. He kept Hotchkiss busy making maps of the region and the just-completed Maryland Campaign, and General Lee requested maps as well. Lee, of course, remembered Hotchkiss from the Cheat Mountain campaign in western Virginia a year earlier, but the maps the topographer had supplied on short notice after the battle of Cedar Mountain (or Cedar Run as Hotchkiss called it) impressed the general even more, greatly assisting him to plan and execute the movement around Pope to Manassas. Lee was now confident of Hotchkiss's abilities and of his value to the army, and in the months and years ahead, would often requisition the mapmaker's assistance, occasionally even "borrowing" him from Second Corps headquarters for a specific assignment.[1]

But as valuable as Hotchkiss was to the army, he had

faults, and Jackson, always commander first and friend and comrade second, privately discussed with his topographer what he saw as shortcomings. Hotchkiss recorded in his diary that he "had a plain talk with the General; he said he thought my great fault was talking too much."[2] Jackson, of course, was abnormally close-mouthed and obsessively secretive about military matters, so it is not surprising that he worried about loquacity on his staff—especially in a member of that staff who, because of his job, knew or could forecast what the army's movements might be by his assignments from the general. Jackson probably did not care that Hotchkiss was garrulous about personal or nonmilitary matters, but he was obviously anxious that his chatty and companionable topographer might accidentally let slip some important information. Jackson made clear that his comments were not meant as a criticism, for he expressed great satisfaction with Hotchkiss's work, writing a recommendation for his appointment to the Engineer Corps that read in part, "The facility with which he collects topographical information has been unequaled by any other person whom I have had with me during the present war. Should he be appointed I hope that he will be directed to report to me for duty."[3]

The testimonial went a long way toward assuaging any hurt feelings, if indeed Hotchkiss had any. By this time,

Hotchkiss thought so much of Jackson that he immediately took the general's words to heart. "I can but admire the General's candor in telling me what he did," he wrote, "and I intend, with God's help, to get rid of the fault complained of."[4] Hotchkiss was not an insecure man, but he obviously understood that he had much to learn, especially about war, and that Jackson meant his comments professionally. Try though he might, however, Hotchkiss apparently could not curb his gabbing, for after the war, his friend and fellow staff member William Allan told him, "Talking will be the death of you yet."[5]

As the days stretched into weeks after the Battle of Sharpsburg, or Antietam, the Federals' name, it became apparent that McClellan intended no determined offensive before winter (though he assured President Lincoln that he would strike Lee "when the army was ready to do so"). Jackson saw the Federal inactivity as an opportunity to catch up on a backlog of work, so he instructed Hotchkiss to complete several dormant mapping projects, particularly the large, detailed map of the Valley that Jackson had requested in his first interview with Hotchkiss in March. Hotchkiss had more surveying to do south and east of Winchester and in the Page Valley, so he went to work immediately.

He set off on a long, solitary reconnaissance on horseback, scouting and sketching the Valley from Winchester to Staunton. He paid close attention to the battlefields where Jackson had fought the previous spring, spending two days sketching the Kernstown battlefield. He was absent from headquarters for weeks at a time, working at his own pace, which was brisk, and taking refuge at friendly homes with warm fires whenever the weather turned bad, which was often that autumn.[6]

As Hotchkiss worked, riding to and fro over roads, measuring distances, sketching river courses and elevations, he aroused considerable curiosity among the local citizens.

"The people have many surmises as to the object of my passing along taking notes," he wrote to Sara, "and I heard many strange reports. One that I had selected a hill near Dayton for our winter quarters. That report had spread widely. I could hardly make them believe that I only wanted to make a map of the country. They suffered so much from the Yankee invasion of the Valley that they live in constant dread of a repetition of it and interpret everything that looks like a backward movement as ominous of danger."[7]

But in parts of the Valley where Hotchkiss was unknown, he stirred not curiosity but suspicion. He recorded one amusing incident in his journal: "A boy saw me sketching, by the road side, and reported me to the Provost Marshal, at Luray, as having on blue pants, etc., so he got Capt. Macon Jordan and some others to come and take me prisoner. When the Captain rode up he broke into a big laugh, recognizing me, having been one of my Mossy Creek pupils, and insisting that I should go to his house."[8]

Hotchkiss saw much of the Valley that autumn, and to his dismay, he found the countryside almost barren. All the crops and forage had long since been harvested and consumed by the ravenous armies that had occupied the region for so long. In addition, the weather had been dry for weeks, and the fields had turned to dust. "The Great Valley is almost desolate from the drought," he wrote in his journal, noting that the huge clouds of dust that billowed up and blew down the Valley Turnpike were almost unbearable and made travel next to impossible. Worse, the harvest looked small. "The crop of corn is fearfully short where I have been, and not much wheat sown." Virginia appeared to be in for a hard winter.[9]

On the last of October, he returned to a hearty reception at headquarters near Berryville. As a matter of fact, Jackson had just begun to wonder about his topographer, for he had a new mission for him. Hotchkiss had been serving on Jackson's staff without rank and virtually without military status, though he received the pay of a first lieutenant. Jackson assigned him to duty at headquarters, but still no commission came. He served with Boswell as an engineer but held no appointment in the Engineer Corps. His position, then, appears to have been that of a civilian employee or perhaps a private detailed for special duty.[10] Jackson, a stickler for military correctness, certainly looked at Hotchkiss as a civilian, for he never referred to him as anything but "Mister Hotchkiss." When Jackson commanded the Valley Army, an independent command, he felt justified in paying Hotchkiss from the Confederate treasury. By the autumn of 1862, however, commanding the Second Corps of the Army of Northern Virginia, Jackson was no longer an independent commander, entitled to make all his own judgments in such matters, at least according to his strict sense of rectitude. He therefore told Hotchkiss that if he were to continue at headquarters as a member of the Second Corps staff, he would have to obtain permission from General Lee. Hotchkiss wished for an officer's commission, but this was not within the power of Jackson to give. The general did write to the secretary of war, praising the topographer's work. Jackson made clear to Hotchkiss that if a commission came, he could certainly remain at headquarters, but in the meantime Mr. Hotchkiss had better go see General Lee.

So early in November, Hotchkiss squared his accounts, collecting three months' pay ($300), and set off for Lee's headquarters in Culpeper County.[11] He rode slowly, enjoying the scenery and feeling little concern about what Lee would say. "I knew General Lee too well to have any fears about my place," he wrote to Sara a few days later. "I took my time and mapped the roads as I went."[12]

He reported to Lee on November 6 and enjoyed a long talk with the commander. As expected, Hotchkiss received permission to remain with Jackson. His position was safe, but he still wished for a commission. What he did not know is that the testimonial Jackson sent to the Confederate War Department would bear fruit—of a sort. Though he would not receive notification for some weeks yet, Hotchkiss was to receive a temporary appointment from the secretary of war as a captain of engineers, which entitled him to military rank and pay. He would henceforth be Captain Hotchkiss.[13] The appointment was still in the future, however, as he thanked Lee and began the long ride back to headquarters. Once again, he kept a leisurely pace, taking a roundabout route and mapping as he went.[14]

The next day, a tremendous blizzard blew in over the mountains, driving Hotchkiss to shelter in "the rickety quarters of a humorous old widower, for he kept a good fire and one of his married daughters had come home for a few days and made the eating very good, so I thanked a kind Providence that had so well provided for me." He was dumbfounded, however, by some straggling soldiers who trudged through the storm, not on a march, but in search of liquor. "But it is almost incredible to believe when I tell you," he wrote to Sara, "that soldiers, many of them barefooted, passed by that day from 8 miles off, going a mile or so beyond after liquor at 12 dollars a gallon—to what straits will not men go for the vile stuff—they said that apple brandy sold that day in camp at 48 dollars a gallon."[15]

That snowy November 7 was a momentous day for the warring armies in Virginia, for through the blizzard rode a messenger from Washington with orders for Gen. George McClellan relieving him of command of the Army of the Potomac. President Lincoln had had enough of Little Mac's inactivity and decided to replace him with a subordinate, Maj. Gen. Ambrose E. Burnside. The new commanding general was capable enough at times, but was crippled by a lack of self-confidence. The men of Lee's army received the news gratefully, for though they felt they could have beaten McClellan, they were even more sure that Burnside would be no match for Lee and Jackson.

Hotchkiss summed up headquarters opinion in a letter to Sara: "Lincoln has damaged his cause much by this act, but it is a good thing for us."[16]

When Hotchkiss returned to headquarters, Jackson greeted him warmly and expressed pleasure that Lee had permitted him to stay.[17] The two men chatted for some time, and Jackson approved Hotchkiss's proposal to continue surveying the Valley while reasonably good weather prevailed, adding that he might go into winter quarters at home at Loch Willow and spend the cold weather fixing up maps. The plan depended on what the Federals did, of course, and on that subject there was no end to the speculation. Jackson, however, paid no attention to the camp gossip. "The General dislikes rumors, exceedingly," wrote Hotchkiss in his diary; "unless he can get substantial facts, I don't believe he likes to hear anything."[18]

So Hotchkiss set off on his third long survey of the season, moving south toward the prospect of a winter at home. The weather was not as good as he had hoped it would be, though, and he fell ill. When he arrived at Staunton, he found orders from Jackson waiting for him, but he felt "too unwell to obey."[19] He went home to Loch Willow and bed.

The orders from Jackson had been prompted, at long last, by Federal activity. Burnside had begun the first phase of an ambitious march toward Richmond. He shifted his army southward around Lee and planned to cross the Rappahannock River on pontoon bridges in the vicinity of Fredericksburg, Virginia. Once on the southern shore, he would have a head start on the Army of Northern Virginia in a race to the Confederate capital. As Burnside moved, Lee reacted, rushing men to Fredericksburg. When the movement began, Jackson summoned Hotchkiss.

Though too sick to respond immediately, Hotchkiss did comply with his orders two days later when he felt better. "War is a hard thing, every man a slave to power

and can have no will of his own."[20] He rejoined Jackson on December 4 and was glad to be back amid the bustle and activity of headquarters, sharing news and exchanging opinions with his comrades. A principal topic of discussion was President Lincoln's address to Congress, in which he discussed his plan for emancipation of the Confederate states' slaves, for the preliminary Emancipation Proclamation, issued just after the battle at Sharpsburg, would go into effect on January 1, 1863. Hotchkiss shared the views of most of his fellow staff officers and thought little of Lincoln, terming his argument on emancipation "claptrap,"[21] and thought the current Congress would "long be remembered as the creature of a tyrant."[22]

Burnside's army arrived on the hills opposite Fredericksburg in good time, but the pontoons did not. By the time the bridge materials arrived, so had Lee's Confederates, and the prospects of an unmolested crossing and a head start on Richmond were gone. Lee arrayed his army of just under 80,000 men south and west of Fredericksburg. Longstreet's corps occupied heights behind the town itself, and Jackson's corps stretched for more than twenty miles downstream on Longstreet's right.

Burnside actively attempted to get his troops across the river, but was not especially efficient. Finally, on December 11, Federal engineers began laying bridges, but they were driven back by sniper fire from the basements and windows of the town. The Federals responded with an artillery bombardment from 150 guns, setting the city afire but failing to root out the snipers. Finally, Federal infantry paddled across the river under fire and slowly pushed the Confederates out.

While this street fighting occupied attention on Longstreet's front, Jackson was hurrying his far-flung troops closer to the city. Jackson seemed to be spoiling for a fight. His staff thought him anxious in the days before the battle, and he regularly sent scouts and messengers to Lee and to

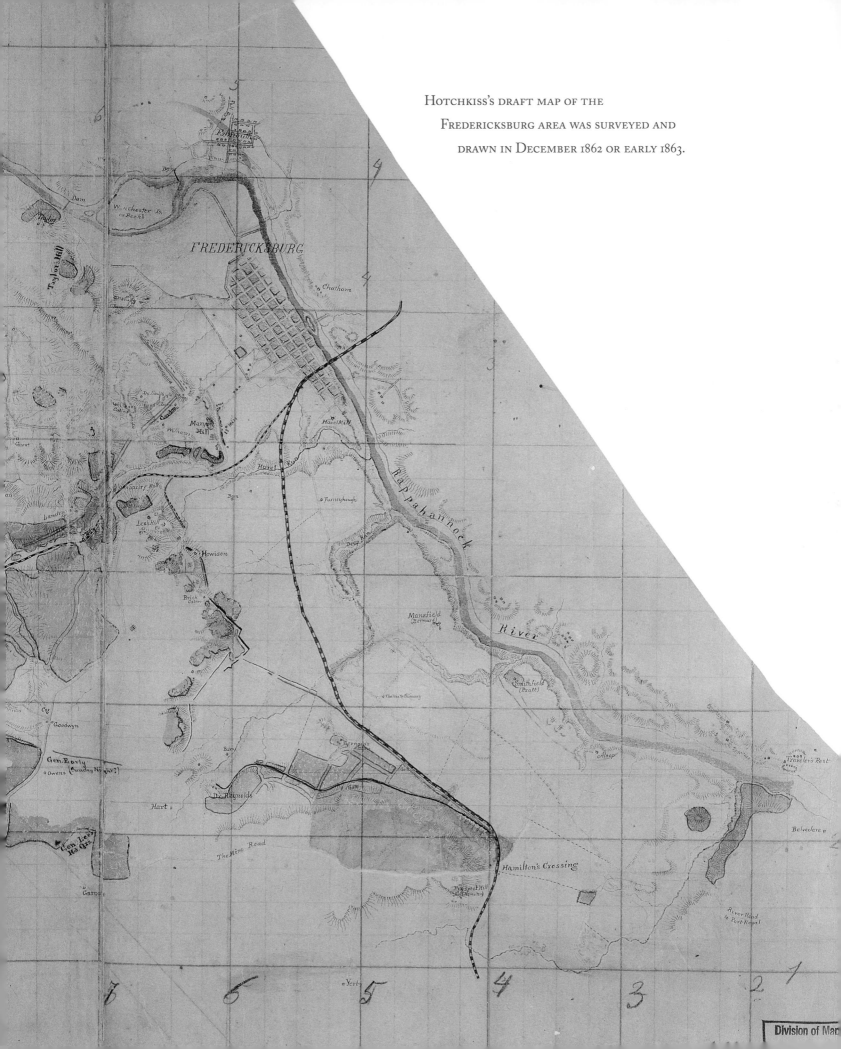

HOTCHKISS'S DRAFT MAP OF THE FREDERICKSBURG AREA WAS SURVEYED AND DRAWN IN DECEMBER 1862 OR EARLY 1863.

other commanders in search of news about the Federals. On December 12, he went on a long survey of the lines with Hotchkiss, returning to headquarters in high spirits, whistling gaily, apparently happy with what he saw.[23]

That Jackson's blood was up in expectation of a battle might have taken a tangible form in his donning of a completely new outfit. He wore a handsome coat, the gift of General Stuart, a new hat from his wife, and sword and spurs from a friend in the cavalry. The transformation was marked. His men, who nurtured a strong affection for him, were energized by the new Old Jack. His aide, James Power Smith, remembered the scene on the morning of December 13, as the men prepared for battle: "As Jackson rode back along the lines, the enthusiasm of the troops was simply boundless. It was impossible to restrain the cheers, which rolled like waves up and down the ranks and broke out again and again.… Altogether he looked so 'spick and span' that the boys could scarcely believe their eyes, so unlike was he to the battered, sunburnt 'Old Jack' of the Valley. But the sorrel horse he rode, and the same following of staff and couriers reassured the troops and they were more than ever delighted with him. The unwonted splendor of their great general was greeted as a great omen on the morn of battle. Everywhere there was confidence, impatient expectation, and the best of spirits."[24]

Jackson's appearance had provided a needed psychological boost for his troops, who had rolled out of their blankets that morning to a cold, damp, cheerless dawn. Languid clouds of mist lay in the river basin and in the hollows of the fields west and south of the town. All through the gray morning, Hotchkiss and the staff listened to the shouted orders of Federal officers and the squeaking and rumbling of Northern artillery as it moved into position, invisible in the fog.

The tension was high, perhaps too high for Hotchkiss, who, for the first and only time in the war, lost his nerve. He experienced a presentiment of death, and he wrote a fearful and frightening letter to Sara: "What my fate may be I know not, I can only trust in a merciful God, whose favor has never forsaken me, and hope for his protection. May he grant us victory, and may it be the means of bringing peace to our distracted land. If it should be my lot to lay down my life for my country's cause I can only hope that God and my country will befriend you and my children, my only legacy, I am sorry to say so, will be a father's blessing, and, I trust, an example they need not be ashamed

FEDERAL ARTILLERY REDUCED THE HANDSOME COLONIAL RIVER TOWN OF FREDERICKSBURG TO RUINS. HOTCHKISS JOINED WITH OTHERS OF JACKSON'S STAFF TO DONATE $850 TO THE IMPOVERISHED RESIDENTS.

96 *Mapping for Stonewall*

of. I will not send this until after the day has passed."[25] Never had he written in such tones to his anxious wife, and had he mailed it before the battle was done, she would have been justified in worrying.

As the sun climbed, "red and firey,"[26] the mists dissipated, and there on the plain lay what one of Jackson's staff thought was "as grand a martial array, perhaps, as has ever been seen in America."[27] Rifle barrels glinted in the sunlight and colored banners rippled in the breeze above 60,000 blue-coated Federals. Two Northern divisions stood in advance in line of battle.

About 10:30 a.m., Federals in Jackson's front stepped off on their assault. Confederate artillery raked their flank, but the Northerners—many of them Pennsylvanians under Maj. Gen. George G. Meade—pressed forward. They struck Jackson's line in a patch of woods that extended from the rest of the forest into the fields. Miraculously, they had hit upon a great weakness in the Confederate position—a gap of several hundred yards, unoccupied by any Southern troops. Meade pressed the attack, funneling his men through the breach and calling desperately for reinforcements to capitalize on the advantage. But no supports came, and Jackson reacted quickly, organizing a counterattack that sent the Federals tumbling back out of the woods. A cold, biting wind stung faces and ears, and Jackson and his staff stayed close to headquarters most of the day, near a big open fire in an open field.[28]

The fighting on Jackson's front had been severe, but it paled beside the combat before Longstreet's troops closer to the city. Throughout the day, line after line of Federal infantry advanced and was thrown back with horrible loss, the day ending with the Northerners back where they started, taking shelter in Fredericksburg and along the bank

of the river. The Battle of Fredericksburg had been a resounding Confederate victory.

But Jackson was not yet satisfied. He wished to attack, immediately, that night, and prepared to strike the Federals as they lay licking their wounds with their backs to the wide, icy river. The general approached Dr. McGuire and indirectly sought information. McGuire recalled that "he asked me that day how many yards of bandaging I had, and when I told him that I did not know exactly how many I had, that I had enough for another fight, he seemed a little worried at my lack of information on that point and showed some little feeling about it, and I answered him very tersely 'I have plenty for another battle' meaning to imply that this was all he had any necessity for knowing. I asked then 'What do you want to know how much bandaging I have for?' He said, 'I want a yard of bandaging to put on the arm of every soldier in this night's attack, so that the men may know each other from the enemy.' I told him I did not have enough cotton cloth for any such purpose, that he would have to take a piece of the shirt tail of each soldier to supply the cloth, but unfortunately … half of them had no shirts."[29]

Despite Jackson's eagerness, the night attack was not made, and when morning came, the Federals still huddled on the river bank. Lee saw the advantages of remaining on the defensive and waited. The Federals, however, were beaten, and they quietly and secretly retired across the river under cover of darkness. Their only accomplishments were to level much of the city of Fredericksburg and waste thousands of lives in futile attacks. Hotchkiss felt little emotion for the dead Federals lying about, "mere boys in appearance, slowly wasting away this far from their homes, killed in a vain attempt to subjugate us," but he was disgusted by the wanton destruction of Fredericksburg and was filled with sorrow for its people. "I had no idea before how a bombarded, sacked city would look," he wrote to Sara, "and

I do not wish to see it again, unless it would be right to sack Washington, that sink of iniquity, after bombarding it with all 'old Abe's' horrid crew in it."[30]

In the gathering dusk of December 15, Jackson, now convinced that the Federals planned no more offensive movements in the near future, led his staff in search of a place to eat and rest. One officer suggested a nearby plantation, Moss Neck. Jackson assented, until the party arrived at the gate to the mansion and he saw the size and elegance of the house. It was far too elaborate, much too comfortable, and he ordered that they move on and sleep in a soldier's bed on the floor of a nearby woods.

Couriers built a fire in the base of a hollow tulip tree, and the general and his staff stood for a while watching the bright sparks sail up into the cold, black sky. Hotchkiss remembered that the staff tried to convince Jackson to find shelter, "as the air was sharp and raw and we had nothing to eat; but he refused and we soon laid down, in a circle around the roaring fire in the tree, with our feet towards the fire."[31] Young Lieutenant Smith recalled later that he for one was angry that Jackson had rejected the hot food and dry beds of Moss Neck, and when Jackson asked him if he had any food in his haversack, the young man, who had not eaten since dawn, replied truthfully, but "with extreme pleasure," that he had none. So the men and their mounts in that dreary campsite went to sleep hungry, Smith sharing a blanket with Jackson. The general could not sleep, however; even his formidable will soon bowed to hunger and the cold. He sat up, apparently prepared to sit awake by the fire for a while. But moments later the chimney tree cracked and crashed down into the camp, nearly hitting Jackson and showering sparks and ashes everywhere. A short time later, after trying again to sleep, Jackson surrendered, sat up again, and ordered his staff to move to Moss Neck for the night. All were relieved, but bitter young Lieutenant Smith almost gloated with an "I-told-you-so" air until he wrapped himself in a rug by a blazing fire at Moss Neck and went to sleep beside his general.[32]

Moss Neck was the home of Mr. Richard Corbin, who had inherited the estate from his father. The younger Corbin was not at home to greet Jackson and his staff, for he was in the army, serving as a private in the 9th Virginia Cavalry. But Jackson did not long avail himself of the cozy accommodations of the manor house. He refused all offers of quarters in the mansion, but assented to pitching the headquarters tents in the yard, where he could share some of the discomforts of his troops. Eventually, a bad cold forced him out of the tent and into the Corbins' small plantation office, but his staff remained under canvas.

As soon as he was established in his tent, Hotchkiss wrote to Sara, telling her where he was, how he was, and expressing regret for having worried her: "I wrote you a gloomy letter the day before the big fight of Saturday, in which I indulged in gloomy anticipations of what might happen on the morrow, but my gloomy mood passed with the day, although that day brought sadness to many hearth stones—gloom to many a household; yet God's good Providence spared me, and I am thankful, truly thankful, for my own sake and ten thousand times more on my family's account—and may God for his Son's sake still shield me. Pray that it may be so, my dear, and teach our little ones to ask protection from Our Heavenly Father for me from the 'arrow that flieth at Noonday'."[33]

And at the same time he sympathized with her and the hard life the war had imposed upon her. "I see, by your letter, that you are worn down by care, and so have the 'horrors.' You will say that I do not appreciate your troubles, but I know I do, and fully feel for them all, but words are of little use and I can only hope for days of peace and respite from the stern demands of cruel war to enable me to fix myself and family as I would desire."[34]

Jackson's little office was the subject of much good-natured kidding among the staff and the other generals. Besides books and agricultural catalogues, the tiny house had a fire, a table, and a cot. The walls were covered with prints of horses and hunting scenes, many of them in bad taste, all of them thoroughly un-Jacksonian, and some of the general officers who visited Jackson, notably Lee and Stuart, teased him about the rustic art and what they claimed were luxurious accommodations. "Come to my headquarters," Lee had tweaked, "to see how real soldiers live."

Stuart was one of the great characters of the army. Capable and brave, he was chief of the army's cavalry, adored by his men and valued by Lee. Jackson came to know Stuart, and, though the cavalier was everything Jackson was not—effusive, ebullient, witty, socially graceful, and exceptionally fond of entertainment—Stonewall eventually developed a warm affection for him. The two men had worked together well when called upon to do so, but they remained stark contrasts. Lieutenant Smith recalled Stuart's first visit to the office at Moss Neck: "With clanking saber and spurs and waving black plume he came, and was warmly greeted at the door. Papers and work were all hastily laid aside. No sooner had Stuart entered than his attention turned to the pictures on the wall. He read aloud what was said about each noted race horse and each splendid bull. At the hearth he paused to scan with affected astonishment the horrid picture of a certain terrier that could kill so many rats a minute. He pretended to believe that they were General Jackson's selections; with great solemnity he looked at the picture and then at the general. He paused and stepped back, and in solemn tones said he wished to express his astonishment and grief at the display of General Jackson's low tastes. It would be a sad disappointment to the old ladies of the country, who thought that Jackson was a good man. General Jackson was delighted above measure. He blushed like a girl, and hesitated, and said nothing but to turn aside and direct that a good dinner be prepared for General Stuart. All the genial humor and frolic of that splendid cavalier were enjoyed exceedingly, with utter incapacity for response."[35]

Hotchkiss also came to know and like Stuart, who, like all good cavalrymen, valued men who knew the country. The two men enjoyed each other's company, Stuart playing the role of wit and Hotchkiss the appreciative audience. "He is the genuine soul," wrote Hotchkiss, "always full of life and humour. He has gotten two sets of hoops which he sent to his wife, who was at a house near by, and told the boy to tell her only one set was for her, he wanted the other for his sweetheart—and when the boy came back and reported that she said she would see about the other set, he had a very hearty laugh. Major Von Borcke, a Prussian on his staff is a fine looking intelligent German and Stuart jokes him every now and then to see him blush—he does it so charmingly."[36]

In the quiet days after Fredericksburg, Hotchkiss began thinking of home and grew bold enough to ask Jackson for a furlough. Jackson never took leave himself, believing it was his duty to remain at headquarters, and he attempted to infuse his staff with the same single-minded devotion, but dedicated though they were, they were divided in their sense of duty between the army and their families. Jackson accepted this somewhat grudgingly, and would occasionally grant furloughs. Finding Jackson in a pliant mood, Hotchkiss received permission to travel to Staunton on "business from the Engineer Corps," though the absence was tantamount to a Christmas leave.[37]

Hotchkiss spent the holiday with his family, but the joy was tempered by the news that Nelson no longer wished to remain at Loch Willow, and that he planned to purchase a new farm. This was an unsettling development for Hotchkiss and Sara, for without Nelson to run the farm, Jed could not afford the payments on the Loch Willow property. He was deep in debt, as were many families,

North and South, and he soon realized that he would have to sell the farm and find someplace else for Sara and the girls to live. The arrangements were too complex to make immediately, and he was due back at headquarters, so the great upheaval in the Hotchkiss family would have to wait.

He started back toward the end of his eight-day leave, having to fight huge crowds on the trains, as it was the last day of the year and the last day of the contracts for thousands of hired servants and slaves, who were heading for new quarters and new masters. He arrived at Moss Neck to a warm welcome, especially once all his comrades saw the bounteous supply of food and delicacies that Sara had prepared and sent with him.

With the beginning of the new year, the troops settled into their winter quarters for a long stay. "What a transformation of our quiet country home!" wrote Roberta ("Bertie") Corbin, mistress of Moss Neck. "Thousands of soldiers around! The hills echoing with the sounds of army life. The fife and drum, brisk tattoo and reveille! The sound of many axes, the falling of great trees; for in less than six weeks, great forests were literally mowed down! Almost Phoenix-like sprang into life settlements of little log huts, dotted here and there with white tents. The smoke curled from hundreds of camp fires! It was a moving panorama. Those sounds of camp life, they haunt me now! The hum of voices, the bands playing, the old 'Stonewall Brigade' right in front of the house."[38]

Hotchkiss also mentioned the regrettable destruction of the fine old trees: "The trees have disappeared, and houses that never looked at each other, in the almost century they have been standing, stare at each other, impudently, in the face—having barely the trees that surround them left to tell of the lordly race from whose destruction they are spared—so it is here—but across the river they too are gone and whatever new generation shall live in that land they cannot say they sit under the trees their fathers planted."[39] In describing the atmosphere at Moss Neck for Sara, Hotchkiss wrote, "Under the shade of the oaks, cedars and hollys … we build our fires, eat our meals, read the papers, talk and work, in the most humdrum way imaginable, everything going as if wound up to run down and then wound up again—a dreamy sort of existence, a sort of trance, after our perpetual motion, … ever since last spring."[40]

The winter at Moss Neck would be a pleasant time, always looked back upon with some fondness. Jackson's officers found they could work in relative comfort and security among the friendly and attentive citizens of the neighborhood. They remained busy catching up on unfinished work and preparing the army for campaigning again in the spring, but they were able to enjoy the civilizing influences of good books from the Corbin library or social visits to other camps or neighboring homes. Especially welcome was the company of the ladies at Moss Neck, and for one member of the staff, Sandie Pendleton, the evenings in the Corbin parlor grew ever more serious as the weeks passed. Captain Pendleton had lost his heart to Kate Corbin, Richard Corbin's twenty-three-year-old sister, who lived at Moss Neck with her sister-in-law and her niece. Other members of the staff had paid attentions to Miss Corbin, but in the end, the young and brilliant Pendleton won her over. They soon announced their engagement, and Jackson reportedly said, "If he makes as good a husband as he has a soldier, Miss Corbin will do well."[41]

General Jackson himself became especially interested in one of the young ladies of Moss Neck—five-year-old Janie Corbin. "He would send for her every morning to come to the office to see him," recalled Jane's mother, Bertie. "She would play there for hours, sitting upon the floor with a pair of scissors cutting paper and entertaining him with her childish prattle. One favorite amusement was folding paper and cutting a long string of dolls, which she called her 'Stonewall Brigade.' "[42]

Jackson's wife had sent him a new hat, which was surrounded by an ornamental band of gold. Jackson disliked the glittering decoration, but left it alone out of consideration for Mrs. Jackson's feelings. One day, however, he saw an opportunity to please his young friend and dispose of the unwanted gilt at the same time. He cut the band from his cap and bound it around her hair "like a coronet," her mother thought. The general told her, "Janie, it suits a little girl like you better than it does any old soldier." Mrs. Corbin recalled that the delighted girl fairly flew to the house. "She came running in, her eyes sparkling, to show it to me and to tell me what he said. After that she always wore it for an ornament, in the same way."[43]

But for all the pleasures and comforts of Moss Neck, the stay there was not altogether happy. Many of the men, especially Hotchkiss and the others from the Valley, disliked the Fredericksburg area intensely, finding the weather much harsher than in their own region between the mountains. "All concur in the opinion that this is a hard country and hope we may not have to stay here long," Hotchkiss had written early in their stay, describing the region as "the low lands, flat lands, swamp lands, pine lands, sand lands, endless woodlands of eastern Virginia where, as I supposed, the Gen. wants me to make a map for him, for no one can get along here without some guide. Ask any one the direction to a place and he will tell you two or three ways, any one of which is twice as far as it ought to be."[44]

Hotchkiss got used to the climate, but found it harder to adapt to the gloom brought about by the emotional travails of Jim Boswell, his messmate and best friend. Like all of Jackson's staff officers, Boswell was competent and devoted to his duty. But he was also a complete romantic, as were many young men of his age. He was deeply, almost madly, in love with a young woman in his native Fauquier

James K. Boswell, Hotchkiss's love-lorn tent-mate and close friend, posed for this portrait before he entered the service in 1861.

County, whom he had known since boyhood. But she had yet to declare her affections. He wrote in his diary what she had meant to him through his first year of war: "I loved with all the strength of my nature a young and beautiful woman; one who combined with the perfection of female beauty and grace, a bright and well cultivated mind, a voice of surpassing sweetness, and a heart as warm as her nature was delicate and refined. I hoped that the heart might be mine; and this hope, together with an intense desire to become worthy of so pure a thing has sustained me through all of the trials and dangers of the past campaign. Her bright image has risen before me when the battle raged hotter and the missiles of death flew thickest, and bade me do my duty if I would be worthy of such a love as hers. And that injunction has never been unheeded."[45]

Boswell wore his affections on his sleeve, having told

Hotchkiss of his love for Sophia deButts Carter in March, immediately after the topographer had joined Jackson's staff. By the turn of the new year, his preoccupation with her had become consuming. "In fact," Hotchkiss recalled, "he was so mad with love that he was constantly talking about her day and night and wearying me with his lamentations."[46] Boswell was every bit the swooning knight of romantic legend. Not only was he away from her, she behind enemy lines, but he could no longer bear the uncertainty of not knowing how she felt about him. He knew she had other suitors.

Hotchkiss, though certainly no cupid, hated to see his friend so distressed and offered to help. For Boswell, of course, nothing could help but seeing her, and he asked Hotchkiss to help him implement a scheme by which he might go to her. Hotchkiss agreed and recorded what happened next: "I mounted my horse one day and rode over to the headquarters of my gallant and lady-loving friend, Gen. J. E. B. Stuart, and told him the tale of my friend Boswell's woes and besought him to aid me in relieving him. He at once ardently entered into the spirit of the situation." Hotchkiss explained that though it would be risky for a Confederate officer to travel so deep behind enemy lines, the nature of Boswell's illness was "desperate." He knew the country where she lived, for it was near his boyhood home, and he was willing to "take any risk to have an opportunity to see her."

The crafty Stuart, himself an incurable romantic, became more enamored of Boswell's adventure with every passing moment, and soon suggested how he could help. He would write Hotchkiss a letter asking for a map of upper Fauquier County. Hotchkiss should then "take that letter to Gen. Jackson … and tell him that I was very sorry that I could not comply with Gen. Stuart's request as I had but meager information about that part of the country that when Jackson expressed his regret that we could not furnish this information that I should suggest that he send Capt. Boswell over to secure such information as was needed to enable me to make this map."[47] Hotchkiss thought the plan might work and returned to tell Boswell. "The 'love-sick' fellow fairly danced with delight," he told Sara. "It would have done your heart good to have seen how happy he was in anticipation of his visit to 'the loved one.' "[48] Stuart's letter came and the "flank movement on 'Old Jack' " worked perfectly, for the general issued Boswell orders to survey the Piedmont Valley. Boswell was filled with joy, but nervous with apprehension, writing in his diary, "Tomorrow morning I start towards the goal of all my hopes and fears. A kind heaven look propitiously on my suit for my happiness for life depends on a favorable answer."[49]

Jackson unintentionally provided a humorous ending to this scene in the drama. A few days after Boswell had gone, Jackson needed a line of earthworks laid out. Since Stuart had borrowed Boswell, he simply requested a similar favor, asking his cavalryman friend to send his engineer for a few days. It was Stuart, then, and not Jackson, who wound up shorthanded. Stuart took it all in good humor, as usual, laughing at Hotchkiss and saying, "You caught me once, but you won't again."[50]

At Sophia's home, Glen Welby, Boswell was greeted cordially, but with a marked lack of warmth. She was "extremely kind but cold as ice; inexplicable girl."[51] Still, he was not yet prepared to show the white flag, and, indeed, he was so in love with her that he could not have surrendered on his own. He remained as a guest at Glen Welby for almost two weeks, scouting and sketching the roads during the days and enjoying Sophia's company and that of the other young people who stopped by on social calls. Some of the visitors, however, were quite clearly on missions similar to Boswell's. The engineer found the competition a bit harrowing, especially after the dreadful events of January 21, which Boswell called "the most eventful day

of my life and one which I shall ever remember with intense horror."[52]

Boswell had been joined at Glen Welby by his cousin, James Keith, also a Confederate officer. A young clergyman, identified in Boswell's diary only as "J. S.," was also present, and he obviously had intentions of pursuing Sophia's affections. While a storm blew hard outside, Sophia and her sister, Fannie, entertained the young men and a few neighbors in the warm parlor with songs and refreshments. Sophia sang and played the piano. Boswell recounted in his diary the events of the afternoon and evening. The preacher "requested her to sing 'No One to Love' but she slipped the song aside. I had previously asked for 'God Save the South.' He opened the music book and selected it and turning to her said 'Sing that, Mr. Boswell likes it,' and she sang one verse beautifully and turning to me asked if she should sing more. I requested another verse and she sang it.… I was happy.… I was intensely happy."[53]

The tense atmosphere continued until 7 p.m., when the company gathered for evening prayer, with J. S. reading the Eighty-eighth Psalm. "After prayers," Boswell continued in his diary, "I took my place near Miss S. and commenced a conversation with her in a low tone. I was very happy, though in a state of doubt. I had determined to make known my feelings that evening and I hoped for success." J. S. left the room, and one of the other visitors leaned close to Boswell and said, "The Green-eyed monster has possession of him."

Boswell resumed his talk with Sophia, but they were soon interrupted by loud noises upstairs. "I heard a rapid step across the floor above, a loud report, then a heavy fall. Cousin F[annie] rose from her seat instantly and said in a most excited manner, 'Mr. Keith, Mr. Boswell, please run upstairs, that man has done something rash.' We rushed up the stairs. J. K. entered the room first, and started back and said, 'Great God, Jim, he has shot himself.' We went

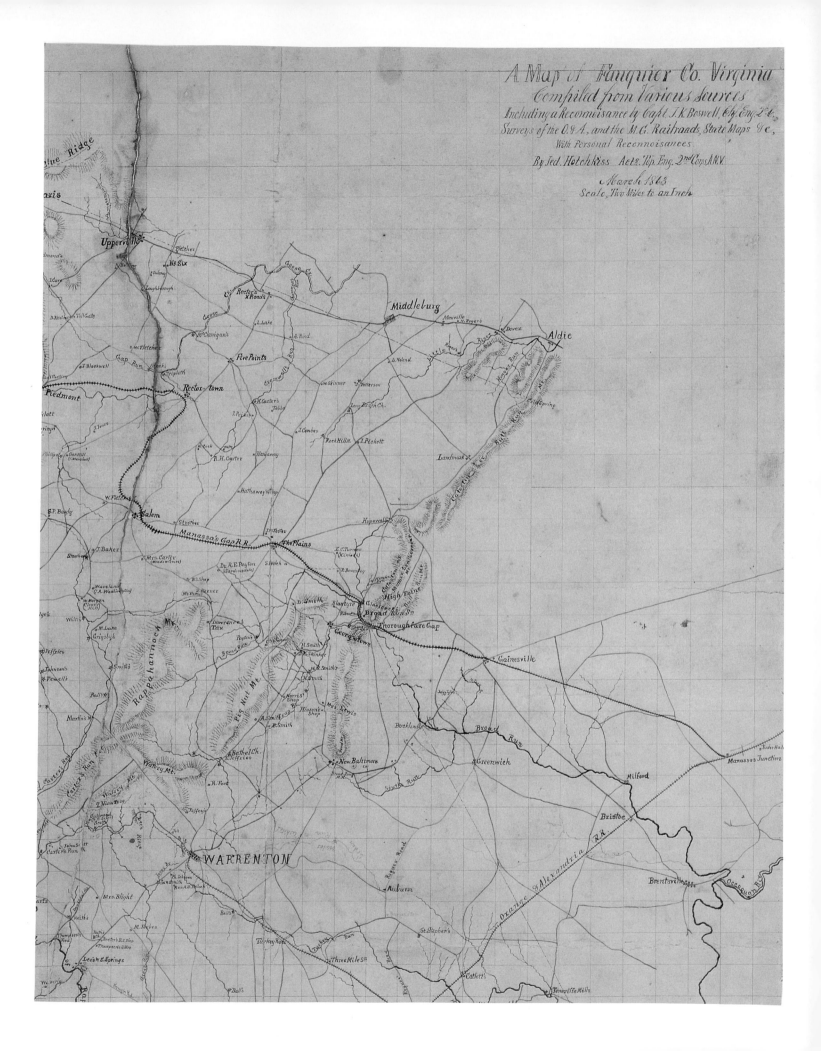

A Map of Fauquier Co. Virginia
Compiled from Various Sources
Including a Reconnoisance by Capt. J. K. Boswell, Chf. Eng. 2d C.
Surveys of the O. & A., and the M. G. Railroads, State Maps &c,
With Personal Reconnoisances
By Jed. Hotchkiss Actg. Top. Eng. 2nd Corps A.N.V.
March 1863
Scale, Two Miles to an Inch

into the room and Great Heaven, what a sight. He lay stretched on the floor, his feet toward the mirror, before which he had evidently been standing when that unnatural deed was committed, in his right hand he still held the pistol."

Boswell went immediately to tell the others. Sophia came to meet him at the foot of the stairs. "Oh! what intense feeling did her countenance express. I saw that she knew the worst and the incentive. I felt at that moment 'The Green-eyed Monster has possession of him' run through my brain like molten lead. I felt I was the cause of this terrific scene. Oh, at that moment I would have given worlds to have been anywhere rather than at this house.... Oh, the horror of that night, I would not spend another such for all this world could offer."

The assemblage at Glen Welby all struggled through the awkward feelings and oppressive memories of the next few days, the women being especially kind to Boswell, knowing perhaps what he felt. It was torture for him not to be able to tell her he loved her, but to do so seemed impossible considering the circumstances, yet to remain silent any longer seemed equally impossible. Finally, word came that Jackson wanted him to return, and Boswell realized that the time had come. He tried to speak to her in private, but she avoided him. The next day, the same thing happened. On the third day, he rose early and sent her a note to meet him in the dining room. She could postpone it no longer.

"She came down looking so beautiful, yet so sad."

MUCH OF THE SURVEY DATA FOR HOTCHKISS'S COMPOSITE MAP OF FAUQUIER COUNTY, AN AREA HEAVILY TRAVERSED BY BOTH ARMIES, WAS COLLECTED BY J. K. BOSWELL DURING HIS VISIT TO SOPHIA deBUTTS CARTER AT THE HOME OF HER FATHER, MR. R. H. CARTER, BETWEEN SALEM AND RECTORTOWN.

wrote Boswell. They talked for a while, and then Boswell declared, "I must know my fate." After months of pressure, the dam burst, and he poured out professions of love to her, finally asking her, "Can you ever learn to love me?" Boswell could see she was pained by the situation, but she remained calm and said, "It can never be." As the truth came crashing down upon him, Boswell blurted out, "Then farewell forever," and after bidding the others good-bye, immediately set off for the long, dangerous ride back to headquarters.[54]

He arrived at Moss Neck far worse off than he had left it. Hotchkiss recalled that he "looked and acted almost like a lunatic and I found it very difficult to bring him to himself again." The young man went on about one of Sophia's suitors whom he believed held her affections, Lt. Col. Welby Carter of the 1st Virginia Cavalry. Boswell, Hotchkiss remembered, "felt very bitter towards Col. Carter calling him a coward and denouncing him about as vigorously as a good and consistent Christian, that my friend undoubtedly was, could well do. During the night he was constantly grating his teeth and breathing out threatenings as to what he would do. In his saner moods he said he would go into the next battle in such a way as to win promotion and that he would yet prove to this young lady that he was more worthy of her hand than the white livered colonel."[55]

Boswell remained morose for a time, but eventually returned to being his energetic self. Despite his dramatic words at his departure from Glen Welby, he still harbored hope that Sophia would love him; indeed, he had been loving her for so long, he could hardly have hoped otherwise. Ten days after bidding her farewell forever, he was writing to her and hoping for a miracle, and in April he still pined for her "whom I love far more than all the world.... I shall win her yet. My life has no other object. My future happiness I feel depends upon her alone."[56]

But Boswell's was not even the greatest sorrow at Moss Neck. In mid-March, as the campaigning season approached, Jackson prepared to move headquarters upriver to a Mr. Yerby's so as to be closer to Lee. As the staff broke camp and said their good-byes to the Corbins, the scourge of scarlet fever, which had almost claimed Nelly Hotchkiss and had taken four of John Harman's children, came to Moss Neck, seizing three children. Jackson moved on March 16, leaving his friend, little Jane Corbin, on a sickbed. She died the next day. Pendleton was still at Moss Neck, and spent hours comforting the twenty-four-year-old mother, Bertie, his future sister-in-law. She had lost her only child, and, unknown to her at the time, her husband would be killed a few months later. Jackson took the news very hard, and other members of the staff wept as well. She had been, her mother said, "the pet and darling of the whole staff." [57]

Jane Corbin's death became the defining event of the winter at Moss Neck. Jackson's men would always look back with fond remembrances of the simple pleasures of that three-month encampment, but they could not help but feel melancholy in remembering the Corbins' sorrow, Boswell's distraction, and finally, how much the serenity of the place reminded them of the families to which they could not yet return. The more they had made things seem like home, the more they missed their own.

The encampment at Yerby's was less comfortable but more conducive to accomplishing what needed to be done. "It is work, work, all of the time here," Hotchkiss told Sara. [58] He labored hard at maps to accompany the reports of Jackson's battles in 1862. All through the winter, Col. Charles J. Faulkner, [59] who had become Jackson's new chief of staff in November, worked on the reports of the general's campaigns, eventually completing some twenty reports for Jackson's signature, though Jackson apparently did not sign all of them before the campaigning resumed in the spring of 1863. Hotchkiss worked closely with Faulkner, drawing maps to illustrate troop movements and guiding him over the field at Fredericksburg.

But Hotchkiss was distracted from his duties by another episode in his continuing problems with the army bureaucracy. Once again the question of his status at Jackson's headquarters came up. He was a civilian, never having been commissioned in the Confederate service, though he received the pay and benefits of a first lieutenant of engineers. The previous November, Lee had enthusiastically granted permission for Hotchkiss to remain on duty with Jackson, but by February 1863, the picture had clouded. Lee ordered that all civilian employees with the army be enrolled in regiments. Jackson of course wished to keep Hotchkiss at headquarters, but had to comply with orders and directed that Hotchkiss be enrolled. Jackson's intention was to detail Hotchkiss from whatever regiment he joined for duty at headquarters. Hotchkiss, however, frankly did not like the idea of exchanging a lieutenant's pay for that of a private, and he wrote to General Lee's chief of staff seeking a clarification. Lee promptly responded, putting Hotchkiss's worries to rest. "Mr. Hotchkiss having been employed under special authority from these Hd. Qrs. while so employed will be exempt from conscription." [60] It was the last word on Hotchkiss's position on Jackson's staff, but the topographer and some of his commanders would continue efforts to obtain him a commission in the Confederate Engineers.

As the cold days grew fewer and hints of spring tantalized the winter-weary soldiers, Hotchkiss grew restless. "O that I were at home now—I so much enjoy the opening of the year when at home and delight to work in the fresh, cool ground and watch the opening to life of nature's promises for the coming year. Oh when will spring visit this land of gloom, this winter of our sorrow."[61] But even as the dreary, muddy days dragged on, he had good news from home. Brother Nelson had sold the farm. The deal made with the purchaser would allow Sara and the girls to remain where they were in the wooden house at Loch Willow while the new owner took up residence in the large brick mansion on top of the hill. Hotchkiss would only have to pay rent on the house, which, by arrangement, included "one-half of the grapes" grown in the yard. He was very pleased.[62]

Less agreeable, however, was the prospect of another year of debt. The Hotchkisses now had no property and little money. Like countless thousands of others, they had been ruined by the war. Sara had apparently been bothered during the winter by creditors knocking on the door. Hotchkiss was angry and frustrated. "If anyone says I might pay my debts from my salary," he told her, "I can only say that such a person is a heartless wretch—destitute of patriotism and ignorant of what it costs a soldier to serve his country and defend such souless creatures as the set of sharks at home that think only of gain and personal aggrandizement."[63]

But Hotchkiss sought no excuses or relief. He was determined to pay his debts and, he told Sara, pay them soon. "I intend to get out of debt this year if possible. It will require all the place [Loch Willow] brought to pay the debts there and the property is still holden.... I intend to wind it all up, finally, this spring—and end it forever.... I have lists and intend to see that everything is paid and properly accounted for—Out of debt I will be—and if my life is spared will soon be a free man."[64]

One final scene remained to be enacted before that winter came to a close, and it was perhaps the most touching. Jackson's wife and infant daughter arrived at Yerby's for a visit. The baby, Julia, was five months old and had yet to be held by her father. Jackson was filled with joy, not only for the gift of his child but for the health of his wife. The staff stopped by Mrs. Jackson's lodgings one by one or in small groups to pay their respects, all except Hotchkiss, who had fallen victim to an absurd and comical accident. His horse ran off from camp, leaving the topographer immobile. Through three days of rain, Hotchkiss roamed the dripping woods and muddy pastures in search of his animal, finally finding him and returning to camp.[65]

Mrs. Jackson, or the "Lieutenant Generaless," as some of the staff began calling her, stayed at Mr. Yerby's while her husband worked at camp about a mile away. "The General goes down about dark and comes back to breakfast and prayers at 7 a.m.," recorded Hotchkiss, "so is up by daylight ... a pattern for all good soldiers—but one which many of them would be slow to imitate under like circumstances, I imagine."[66] But as Jackson allowed himself little leisure to enjoy the company of his family, the Federals would allow him less. The Northerners across the river began to stir.

Jackson at once sent his wife and child away to safety, then set about determining where the Federals would attempt to cross the river. Lee had been considering the possibilities and had had engineers examining the river fords. Boswell had been sent far upstream to inspect the Confederates earthworks at Banks's and United States fords, both of which would assume importance in the weeks ahead.[67] Clearly the winter sojourn was over, and the war was about to begin again. Hotchkiss was ready. Well rested and in good health, he told Sara he was prepared for anything that might come. "I pray that my life may be spared for my family, but I feel a calm resignation to the will of the Most High, perfectly satisfied that he will do all things well."[68]

*T*HIS EARLY POST-WAR VIEW LESS THAN A MILE FROM THE CROSSROADS OF CHANCELLORSVILLE LOOKS NORTHEAST-WARD ACROSS THE ORANGE PLANK ROAD TOWARD BULLOCK ROAD. AT DUSK ON MAY 2, 1863, JACKSON'S IN-FANTRY REGROUPED NEAR HERE AFTER CRUSHING A FEDERAL FLANK. THE GENERAL LED HIS STAFF MEM-BERS THROUGH THIS INTERSECTION TO RECONNOITRE. IN THE WOODS TO THE RIGHT, THE CONFED-ERACY SUFFERED ONE OF ITS GREATEST TRAGEDIES.

CHAPTER SIX

"DEATH WILL HOLD HIGH CARNIVAL"

B y the spring of 1863, the Federal armies in Virginia had been out-fought, out-marched, and out-thought for two full years. The North was impatient and, in a measure, embarrassed. Clearly the Army of the Potomac had to do better in 1863, or, as incredible as it might have seemed to anyone in the North in 1861, the Union would likely be dissolved. The next twelve months would be crucial.

The Lincoln administration had at last realized over the winter that Burnside was not up to the responsibility of commanding the nation's largest army. In January, Lincoln replaced Burnside with Maj. Gen. Joseph Hooker, a Massachusetts-born professional soldier with a reputation as a hard fighter with a fondness for hard liquor.

Hooker did well in reorganizing his cheerless army, and by April, he was ready to lead it against Lee. Late in the month, he quickly swung most of his army westward and across the Rappahannock on Lee's left flank, leaving a portion of his force at Fredericksburg to distract Lee. Hooker's plan worked beautifully—at first.

On April 30, with Hooker across the river on the Army of Northern Virginia's flank, Lee prepared to meet the threat. He had been caught off balance by the suddenness of Hooker's move, but he reacted quickly, ordering Jackson upriver. On that day, in the absence of orders, Hotchkiss worked on maps. In the evening, Jackson at last

called for him, but only to request more maps, saying "strike off eight maps embracing the region between the Rapidanne and the Rappahannock and reaching back to the Virginia Central Railroad."[1] The Rapidanne (or Rapidan) flows into the Rappahannock from the South. The Federals were already south of the Rappahannock. Jackson apparently was looking beyond the immediate future, thinking perhaps of a movement westward and around to the Federal rear. In any case, the general wished to be prepared should the field of action shift north of the Rapidan.

As Hotchkiss began work, he was summoned again by Jackson about 9 p.m. This time, the general had a more pressing assignment; he wished Hotchkiss to go at once to find a route by which the army could march to Salem Church, whence it could head westward on a major turnpike and intercept the Federals. Hotchkiss set out immediately.

The night was cool and damp, but his way was lighted by a brilliant moon. Hour after hour he rode on the byways and trails west of Fredericksburg, searching for the best route for the corps, the stillness broken only by the sounds of his horse. He did not record what his thoughts were that night, but they surely must have turned toward home. He had written to Sara the day before, expressing apprehension about the imminent battle: "Tomorrow, O! tomorrow, Death will hold high carnival.... I do not expect to be about much in the fight tomorrow, as there are enough to carry orders, unless something should happen to others, when I shall take the place of some of them—but it is somewhat remarkable that not one of Gen. Jackson's staff has ever been wounded seriously—His prayers are a safe shield—and he prays much for his own military family." His words were more portentous than he could have imagined.[2]

The member of the military family perhaps most in need of prayers that night was James Keith Boswell, who still fantasized about a life with the woman who had told him it could never be. He had not surrendered, and, in fact, had vowed that he would win her back, performing with such heroism in the next battle that she could not refuse him. Now, on the eve of that battle, Hotchkiss must have thought of his tent-mate and friend. For weeks, the young man had anxiously awaited the opportunity to prove his courage and his love, and Hotchkiss, who loved Boswell as a brother, worried lest his friend do something rash.

Hotchkiss finally ended his long ride about 4:30 a.m., when he arrived back at headquarters. To his surprise, he found that much of the corps had already moved. Jackson had been unable to wait for Hotchkiss's intelligence, and had set off after Hooker following local guides. Weary from a sleepless night in the saddle, which now appeared to have been for naught, Hotchkiss turned his mount around and headed west again in pursuit of headquarters.

With his movement executed brilliantly, Hooker had every advantage on the morning of May 1, 1863, and seemed ready to strike Lee a hard blow. But suddenly and mysteriously, Hooker seemed to lose his nerve and halted his planned attacks. Some men in the army said Hooker was drunk. Others said Hooker was not drunk, and the deviation from his routine affected his judgment. In either case, the Federal commander had relinquished the initiative—and Lee quickly picked it up.

On the night of May 1, Lee met with Jackson at a woodland crossroads not far from the front lines and Hooker's headquarters which were at a place named Chancellorsville. The two generals pondered the problem faced by the Army of Northern Virginia: it was outnumbered, fragmented, and caught between the two wings of the enemy's army. Lee and Jackson were daring men, sometimes too daring, for their boldness had on occasion brought both close to disaster. Even now, wedged between a rock and a hard place, Lee was thinking offensively. "How can we get at these people?" he asked his lieutenant. The answer did not immediately present itself, and for most of the night the two generals dispatched riders to learn more of the whereabouts of the Federals and the locations and condition of the roads in the vicinity. Boswell and Maj. T. M. R. Talcott, an engineer serving on Lee's staff, made a long and dangerous moonlight reconnaissance of the Federal dispositions in the center, bringing their generals precise information that proved especially valuable in their formation of a plan.

Hotchkiss had caught up with the army in the afternoon and was present at the crossroads with the two generals that night. When he bedded down, he shared a blanket with Jackson, each man covering himself with his overcoat.[3] Hotchkiss must have slept deeply, which might have been expected considering that he had barely slept at all in the preceding thirty-six hours. During the night, Jackson apparently rose and sat again with Lee over a little fire, seeking a solution to their puzzle. The men talked and postulated far into the predawn hours, their staffs sleeping scattered about them in the woods. Some of those young men nearby, awakened momentarily by a chill or the nickering of a horse, blinked back the sleep enough to see the two great generals sitting close to each other on cracker boxes as they had most of the night. It was a sight those officers would remember for the rest of their lives.

By dawn, Lee and Jackson had found a solution. Lee would remain with a portion of the army opposite the Federal front, trying to create the illusion that the entire army still faced Hooker's men. Jackson, taking the rest of the army, by far the larger portion, would march by back roads around the Federal right flank and launch a surprise attack that, given the faulty dispositions of the Federals on that part of the field, held the promise of great success. It was a daring plan, one of the more audacious in military history, and in fact, violated most of the accepted rules of military science. Lee was dividing his small army in the face of a larger and very powerful enemy, gambling that the Federals would delay any attack long enough for Jackson's force of nearly 30,000 men to make a march of more than ten miles. Lee was placing the outcome of the battle, and perhaps the fate of his army, in the hands of Stonewall Jackson.

The march seemed feasible over vaguely known roads, but Jackson was anxious to know the route that would get his column to the Federal flank fastest and in best trim. He called upon Hotchkiss for help. Hotchkiss had spent little time in the region around Chancellorsville, which, because of its dense forests, was known locally as the Wilderness, but he was unusually adept at finding his way through unfamiliar or vaguely familiar country. Jackson had recognized this gift and its value, and had learned to take advantage of it. When the army had to get someplace quickly, Hotchkiss's abilities were invaluable.

"About daylight," Hotchkiss recalled, "General Jackson awakened me and requested that I would at once go to Catherine Furnace, which is quite near … and ascertain if there was any road by which we could secretly pass around Chancellorsville to the vicinity of the old Wilderness Tav-

ern." Hotchkiss left immediately, but he did not know, and Jackson did not reveal, that orders had already gone out and the movement would begin soon regardless of what the topographer found. Hotchkiss understood the letter of his mission, but not the nature of it. He assumed, and believed ever afterward, that that morning he found the route that made Jackson's flank march possible. His assignment was to find any route that might expedite the movement. Hotchkiss's confusion made no difference on May 2, 1863, but led to misunderstandings between Lee and Hotchkiss and some other officers after the war.[4]

Hotchkiss had a map of the area, but it was not very detailed. He arrived at Catherine Furnace and awoke the owner, Mr. Charles B. Wellford, who told Hotchkiss that he had recently opened additional roads through the forest to haul wood and iron ore to his furnace. Hotchkiss marked the location of the roads on his map, seeing that they went toward Jackson's intended destination, and asked Wellford, who owned most of the land Jackson would cross, if he would guide the army, if necessary. Wellford agreed, and Hotchkiss returned to headquarters. Lee and Jackson were still in conference on their cracker boxes, and Hotchkiss placed another box between them and spread out the map, showing them the new roads. As Hotchkiss recalled, the two generals spoke openly: "General Lee then said, 'General Jackson what do you propose to do?' He replied, 'Go around there,' moving his finger over the road which I had indicated upon the map. General Lee said 'What do you propose to make this movement with?' He replied, 'With my whole corps.' General Lee then said, 'What will you leave me?' His reply was 'The two divisions which you now have here.' General Lee at once remarked, 'Well, go on.' "[5]

The march began about daylight, and Jackson sat on his horse by the side of the road for a while watching his men pass by. The troops had orders to move as quietly as possible and did not give their customary cheer when they passed their general. All was silent but for the rhythmic clank of canteens and equipment swaying on the marching hips. The solid road surface allowed the column to make good time with few stragglers. Lt. James Power Smith, Jackson's aide, who had been carrying orders that morning and had to ride the length of the marching column to catch up to Jackson, found that the men in the ranks seemed to be in high spirits. "Slow and tedious is the advance of a mounted officer who has to pass in narrow wood roads, through dense thickets, the packed column of marching infantry, to be recognized all along the line and good-naturedly chaffed by many a gay-spirited fellow: 'Say, here's one of "Old Jack's" little boys, let him by, boys!' in a most patronizing tone. 'Have a good breakfast this morning, sonny?' 'Better hurry up, or you'll catch it for being behind.' 'Tell "Old Jack" we're all comin'.' 'Don't let him begin the fuss till we get thar!' And so on, until about 3 p.m., after a ride of ten miles of tortuous road, I found the general."[6]

Hotchkiss, too, had to ride through that column to find Jackson. After reporting his findings to the generals in the morning, the engineer had remained with Lee as the column moved out, for Lee wanted maps. Only later in the day did Hotchkiss, in company with the Reverend Dr. Lacy, ride off in pursuit. Lacy, whose family lived in the area, knew the roads well and had the previous night helped Jackson and Lee determine that a route to the Federal flank existed. Hotchkiss and Lacy overtook Jackson, and the general immediately asked Hotchkiss to send word back to Lee of the flanking column's whereabouts. Hotchkiss sat in a fence corner, made a sketch map, and sent it by courier to Lee.

Late in the afternoon, with his troops in position and thousands of unsuspecting Northerners resting in their camps a short distance ahead, Jackson gave the order to advance. The attack was swift and sudden and produced spectacular results. The Federal flank collapsed, and tens of thousands of fleeing soldiers filled the woods with chaos. Jackson urged his men onward in the pursuit, driving them through all pockets of resistance and pushing them after the fugitives for nearly three miles in a race with the gathering darkness. Jackson wished to wring every drop of advantage out of the day's success.

About a mile short of the crossroads called Chancellorsville, where Hooker had his headquarters, Jackson's pursuit ground to a halt. Darkness had fallen, and the Confederates were fatigued by the pursuit. Firing continued in places throughout the deepening blackness of the forest. Bodies of troops continued to move through the woods, with caution now, for the enemy was close, but no one knew just where. Officers listened fiercely and peered hard into the shadows.

Jackson, with most of his staff, had reached the front, and the general was impatient to know where the Federals were and in what strength. It seemed obvious that the pursuit could not be continued in the darkness, so Jackson began shoring up his lines, ordering A. P. Hill's division forward to relieve the battle-weary lines disordered by the fight, the pursuit, and the deepening darkness. But Jackson disliked halting the advance, despite the coming of night. He well understood the importance of pursuing a fleeing foe, so though the darkness said he must stop, he still wished to continue. Impatiently and imprudently, Jackson led a few of his staff, together with couriers, and some signalmen off the road and into the woods beyond the Confederate lines. He was anxious to see what lay in the blackness beyond.

Why Jackson thought he must personally obtain more information in the dark woods is a mystery. He was ill-equipped to conduct such a reconnaissance. He was partially deaf, and his eyes had been troubling him for months. He did have with him, however, the keen young senses of members of his staff, including Boswell, and it would have been wiser to have sent one or two of them instead.

The day's success had excited Jackson's men, and the high spirits, along with the normal post-assault confusion and raw nerves, led to some carelessness. As Jackson advanced beyond his battle line, his staff, or Hill's staff, did not inform all the front-line commanders that the general was before them. Hill's men understandably thought only Federals lurked in the woods ahead.

Jackson and his party passed through a marshy hollow and began climbing a gentle rise. Suddenly came a shot, then another, the bullets zipping over the head of Lieutenant Smith. Jackson knew he had found the Federal skirmish line and wheeled about to return to safety. Hotchkiss had been riding with Pendleton some distance to the rear, but they had caught up just as the Federals fired and were with Jackson as he headed back to the Confederate lines.[7]

The fluid, confused Confederate lines through which Jackson had passed had solidified. The shots from the Federals in the dark forest had put A. P. Hill's tense infantrymen on edge, and they peered nervously into the murk. When they saw the body of horsemen riding from the direction of the firing, one of Hill's North Carolina regiments opened fire at close range, knocking two of Jackson's men from their saddles. Jackson and others held up their hands in protest, shouting for the firing to cease, but it was too late. Another volley leapt forth, then another. Jackson, just a few yards in front of the firing troops, took three bullets, one in the right hand, one in the left wrist and forearm, and one shattering the upper bone in his left arm. His horse bolted, running with its stunned and almost helpless rider into thickets. Jackson fell, but was caught by a member of his staff. The firing continued and intensified. No Confederates in the line of battle yet realized the error, and soon the Federals off in the blackness began to respond. Jackson lay on the ground, surrounded by members of his staff,

when A. P. Hill arrived and knelt by the fallen general's head. Capt. R. E. Wilbourn cut away the general's coat sleeve and applied a tourniquet above the arm wound.

Finally, as the Confederate infantrymen realized what had happened, brave stretcher bearers came forward to remove their general just as Federal artillery began sweeping the forest with canister. Hotchkiss, having waited to be certain the general was not killed, reined his horse through the line of battle and set off toward the rear in search of an ambulance and some spirits. The fire from the Federal guns was, Hotchkiss thought, "One of the most terrific storms of such missiles I ever saw—and I was only surprised that every one exposed to it was not destroyed, for it raked the road, which was full of soldiers, artillery, officers on horseback, etc. I hope to never be in such a place again."[8]

The litter bearers lifted Jackson on the stretcher and began moving briskly back to the Confederate lines. Lieutenant Smith, who held one corner of the stretcher, remembered that the Federal artillery was terrifying as "great broadsides thundered over the woods; hissing shells searched the dark thickets through, and shrapnel swept the road."[9]

One of the bearers fell wounded, and so terrific was the storm of Federal artillery that the others put Jackson down in the road and sought protection, but Smith remained with his general. "As the litter-bearers ran to the cover of the trees, I threw myself by the general's side. and held him firmly to the ground as he attempted to rise. Over us swept the rapid fire of shot and shell—grape-shot striking fire on the flinty rock of the road all around us, and sweeping from their feet horses and men of the artillery just moved to the front."[10]

After an interminable few minutes, a lull in the firing permitted Smith to jump up and help Jackson to his feet, then, bearing the general's weight, walk him to the woods. Again he was put on a stretcher, and again a bearer was

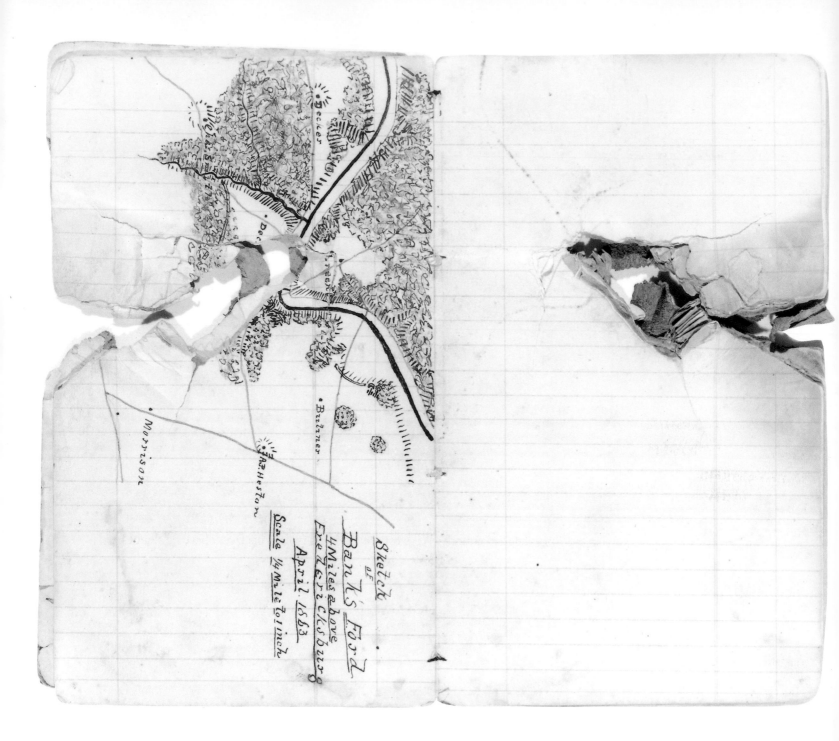

Sketch of Bank's Ford 4 Miles above Fredericksburg April 1863 Scale ¼ Mile to 1 inch

Boswell's bullet-torn notebook shows a sketch the engineer made just days before his death. Hotchkiss removed this book from his friend's body on the afternoon of May 3.

wounded; this time, though, Jackson fell heavily on his wounded arm and cried out in pain. Finally, he was put in an ambulance and sent toward the rear. Dr. McGuire, whom Hotchkiss had found and directed to the scene, arrived and took control, ordering the ambulance to Wilderness Tavern, a few miles west on the turnpike.

Hotchkiss made his way to Wilderness Tavern as well. Finding Jackson in a stupor and McGuire in charge, he returned to his saddle and set off for Lee's headquarters, where, after a four-hour ride, he learned the general already knew of Jackson's wounds. "He was much distressed,"

Hotchkiss wrote, "and said he would rather a thousand times it had been himself. He did not wish to converse about it."[11] The topographer then told Lee as much as he knew of the condition and dispositions of Jackson's troops. While Lee conferred with his chief of staff, Hotchkiss, who had been awake for almost twenty-four hours through high excitement, lay down, exhausted, and slept. It was almost dawn.

After little more than an hour or two of sleep, Hotchkiss was up and taking breakfast with Lee. The general wished him to ride to Jeb Stuart, who had assumed temporary command of Jackson's Corps, to tell him that he must attack vigorously and that Lee would soon come and take command in person. Hotchkiss again rode off over the route he now knew so well, but the excitement, exertions, and lack of sleep had caught up to him. After going several miles, he found himself virtually asleep in the saddle and had to dismount to rest. The battle had long since resumed, making Lee's message to Stuart obsolete, so Hotchkiss decided to attend to a too-long-deferred errand: he went to find Boswell.

He had last seen his friend the previous evening when they followed Jackson into the woods in advance of the battle line. On the return ride, Boswell had been hit by the first volley fired from the North Carolinians. Hotchkiss probably did not realize this at the time, so chaotic and frightening had been the firing and the subsequent wounding of Jackson. But perhaps another member of the staff had seen Boswell fall and mentioned it to Hotchkiss at Wilderness Tavern, where they had watched over Jackson. It is impossible to know whether he knew of Boswell's whereabouts or condition on the afternoon of May 3, but the first place Hotchkiss looked for his missing friend was the woods where Jackson had been knocked down.

"And there I found him," he wrote, "some 20 steps in advance, by the road-side, dead, pierced through the heart by two balls and wounded in the leg. I was completely overcome, although I had expected it from the state of his mind before, expecting him to be killed in this fight."[12] Hotchkiss apparently had not been alone in expecting Boswell's death. Before the battle, Boswell told another friend that he had had a presentiment of his death, much as Hotchkiss had at Fredericksburg. The young engineer, never having recovered from Sophia Carter's rejection, had said that he did not expect to live through the next fight. After the success of Jackson's attack, the unnamed friend congratulated Boswell on his escape. Boswell answered, "Ah, but the battle isn't over yet." Shortly thereafter, he rode forward with Jackson into the black woods beyond the Confederate lines.[13]

Hotchkiss later learned that all through the flank march, "Boswell was constantly seeking for information, regardless of danger all along the enemy's front," still trying to earn the glory or promotion that might win him Sophia's heart. "I found him looking perfectly natural," he wrote to Sara, "a smile on his face. I have no doubt he was instantly killed, for two bullets went through his memorandum book in his side pocket and then through his heart."[14]

Hotchkiss found an ambulance and rode with the body to Wilderness Tavern. Along with the Reverend Dr. Lacy and Howell Brown, he took their friend across the road to Elwood, a large home belonging to Lacy's brother, and there they buried him in the family graveyard. It was Lacy's second trip to the graveyard that day. In the morning, he had buried Stonewall Jackson's left arm, which had been removed during the night. Hotchkiss cared tenderly for Boswell: "I … wrapped his overcoat closely around him,

---

(PAGES 116–117) HOTCHKISS'S PRELIMINARY MAP OF THE CHANCELLORSVILLE BATTLEFIELD IS BASED ON THE DETAILED SURVEY ORDERED BY GENERAL LEE IN MAY 1863.

putting the cape over his head, and buried him thus, in all his martial dress, lowering him to his resting place in a shelter tent I picked up on the field of battle, and then spreading it over him. Mr. Lacy made a noble prayer and we finished our sad duty just as the moon rose over the distant hills of his own loved native country. Mr. Lacy, Mr. Brown and myself and the two men that dug the grave were all that were there, and we freely wept as we left his manly form to await the last trump. He was a Christian and has gained by the exchange of worlds."[15]

After the grave was filled in, Hotchkiss and Brown wearily lay down "on the rich and soft green carpet" near the grave of their friend. They listened to the faint and distant popping of muskets and the contented munching of their horses cropping the fresh new grass, and they slept.

Early on May 4, Mr. Lacy woke Hotchkiss. Jackson was to be moved, and Hotchkiss was needed to guide the ambulance to Guiney's Station, south of Fredericksburg. Jackson was feeling somewhat stronger and was in fair spirits, considering that surgeons had amputated his left arm some thirty hours before. Sharing the ambulance was Col. Stapleton Crutchfield, the Shakespeare-quoting chief of artillery, who had been badly wounded in the leg.

Hotchkiss led the wagon south over dusty roads, passing clusters of wounded soldiers, who cheered the general and shouted good wishes. At the end of the ride, which Jackson bore well, Dr. McGuire moved the general into a small house that served as the plantation office of Thomas Coleman Chandler. The next morning, his horse saddled and ready to return to the battlefield, Hotchkiss called on Jackson to say good-bye. Tired but cheerful, the general told Hotchkiss he hoped to be back with the army soon

and sent his regards to General Lee. Thus Jed Hotchkiss parted with Stonewall Jackson for the last time. Five days later, Jackson was dead.

Neither Hotchkiss nor any of the other members of the staff was surprised when the news came, for they had known their chief was sinking under the effects of pneumonia. But all of them were plunged into a profound grief. Hotchkiss was comforted by the thought that Jackson had lived his life so as to be spiritually ready for death at any time, and now he had moved on to a better place, free of the "constant toil and anxious care for the welfare of those entrusted to him."[16] On the day Jackson died, Hotchkiss wrote to Sara, "Today it is feared that General Jackson has reached his last days, pneumonia has attacked him, debilitated by his wound, and his physicians think the chances for his recovery are very poor—but I do pray Heaven to spare him, unless in the wise counsel of eternity, he has accomplished the end for which he was created."[17] Hotchkiss's greatest sorrow was for those the "Great Chief" had left behind: his family and the South. How could the Confederacy replace him?

Hotchkiss had been absent from the battlefield after Jackson's wounding, missing yet another bloody struggle. The fighting on May 3 had been desperate, and not until late in the day did well-placed Confederate artillery at last force the Federals to abandon their positions and begin their withdrawal. In the next few days, the beaten Federals recrossed the Rappahannock, their ranks thinned by more than 17,000 casualties. Hotchkiss told Sara of the lesson of Hooker's defeat, "The boasted 'fighting Joe' taught that human efforts are unavailing when in a wrong cause."[18] The Confederates held the field, but victory had come at a terrible cost. In addition to Jackson, some 12,800 other

Southerners had fallen, more than one-fifth of Lee's army.

Among Lee's first orders after he was sure Hooker was again across the river was for Hotchkiss to survey and map the battlefield. Hotchkiss, with Howell Brown and some other engineers, began making preparations for the survey, but clearly his heart was not in his work. He did not begin the assignment until three days after Lee had issued the order, and after the work began, he showed uncharacteristic languor, partially because of the unseasonable heat, but mostly because of physical exhaustion and severe depression.

It was in those seven days spent on the field of Chancellorsville that Hotchkiss came close to despair. In the days before and during the battle he had ridden hundreds of miles with little food and less sleep.[19] He had come close to death when riding between the lines with Jackson, had seen his adored commander badly wounded, a horrible shock in itself. On the following night, he had buried his best friend. And now he was to map in detail the fresh field of carnage, revisiting all the scenes of his anguish. He spent seven days riding among the indescribable horrors of a battlefield—the sights, smells, and sounds of the dead and wounded, the burial parties, and the field hospitals. He was sickened by it, and disgusted, and his spirit came as close to breaking as it ever would during the war. Jackson's death on May 10 was a final, crushing blow, and Hotchkiss thought that perhaps he had had enough.

While riding one day, he came upon a woman who told him her story, which at once became both an illustration and a symbol of the suffering and degradation war inflicts on humanity. "I saw a poor woman yesterday," he told Sara, "whom the Yankees had robbed of every thing the third time; she had been in good circumstances; she was mending an old and tattered dress, the only one they had left her, she said, save the poor one she had on—they had taken everything she had laid up to eat—she had prayed, she said, and she hoped it was not a wicked prayer, 'That there might never be another Yankee child born, and that not one of the race might be left on the face of the earth by the first day of next June', and as she spoke the tears ran down her cheeks."[20]

Chancellorsville had shown Hotchkiss with stark clarity how awful was the realm of his existence. The love and joy and nobility of purpose that characterized his life at home were meaningless in this world of hatred and brutality, where only strength mattered and inflicting pain was the ultimate goal. Death did indeed hold "high carnival," as it had for two years, and apparently, as it would for some time. Yet this horrible war and all in it were part of the same world, the same earth, the same universe, as all he loved and cherished. His home, his neighbors, his schoolroom, the mineral samples and botanical collections, the meeting house and Sunday school, all coexisted with the revolting excesses of war. It was all of God's making, all of His creation. And while seeing these horrors from God's hand never shook his faith, it did depress him. No man could have seen and endured what he had at Chancellorsville—the death of dear friends, the wasting of thousands of young lives, the stench and piteous sounds of the battlefield, the desperate and fervent hatred of the penniless old woman—and not have had his perception of reality shaken. The world had lost dignity.

His heart broken, his thoughts disordered, and his mortal source of strength and inspiration gone, Hotchkiss told Sara how much he felt the loss of his hero, Jackson. "We miss him all the time and a void is made here which time can hardly fill. It seems not like our old Hd. Qrs. to any of us, and less to me than to any one else, for my tent mate is gone as well as my General. I do not know whether I shall stay here or not."[21]

Maj. Gen. Richard S. Ewell, successor to Jackson's command, was brave, competent, and extremely considerate of his staff. Ewell made it a point not to expose his officers needlessly to danger, though he frequently went under fire himself. The general prized Hotchkiss and his work and repeatedly praised his topographer in the highest terms. Their cordial friendship lasted for decades.

CHAPTER SEVEN

"JUDGE NOT THE LORD BY FEEBLE SENSE"

The entire Army, indeed, the entire South, felt the loss of Jackson, but none so keenly as the handful of men who had lived with him through months of adventure and hardship. They had lost not merely a great leader, but a friend as well, and every aspect of their lives changed. As Hotchkiss put it, "The singular but good and great man that directed everything and stamped a peculiar character upon it is no longer at his post and everything wears an altered and lonely look, but such is earth and such are earthly things." [1]

After moving together for months and passing in and out of skirmishes and pitched battles without a single death or serious wound among them, the staff members had seen their "charmed circle" shattered with the deaths of Jackson and Boswell and the wounding of Crutchfield, who would lose a leg. Never again would they enter battle strengthened by Jackson's presence or protected by his prayers, and, as the war continued, the death toll among them would increase. [2]

Lee missed Jackson in quite another way; he had lost one of his two chief lieutenants, and finding a suitable replacement to command the Second Corps would be no easy task. The senior general in the corps was A. P. Hill, who had assumed temporary command, but Lee was unsure of whether Hill was capable of permanent command at the corps level.

The irony in Hill's elevation to command of Jackson's corps was that the two men had frequently been at odds, and Jackson had once even had Hill arrested for negligence of duty. Hill, a combative little Virginian from Culpeper, had demanded a court martial so he could clear his name. Lee pigeonholed the entire mess, declaring that the army needed both officers at their posts, and the matter was dropped, but Hill harbored resentment. Although he came to respect Jackson, the relationship remained cool and never extended beyond the purely professional. Now, Hill was in command, and the corps headquarters staff—Jackson's men—believed that they would not be retained by the new commander. He might wish to bring his own staff with him, but more likely, he simply would not wish to serve with the officers who had supported Jackson during the feud.

For their part, the staff respected Hill solely on a military basis, but they bore no affection for him. He was not, and could never be, their general. Hotchkiss, perhaps articulating what many on that extraordinarily devout staff were thinking, put his finger on what they saw as Hill's main failing: "He is not 'a man of God' like Gen. J. and

MAJ. GEN. A. P. HILL, THE COMBATIVE SUBORDINATE WHO HAD FEUDED WITH JACKSON, WAS NOT POPULAR AMONG STONEWALL'S STAFF.

wears not 'the sword of the Lord and of Gideon.' "[3]

By the end of May, Lee had decided that Hill was ready to command a corps—but not Jackson's corps. Lee chose instead to reorganize his army, breaking up Jackson's command and forming a new corps, the Third. Longstreet would continue in command of the First Corps, Hill would command the new Third Corps, and the heart of Jackson's old Second Corps would be led by Gen. Richard Stoddert Ewell.

Dick Ewell was by any standard one of the more peculiar-looking men in the army. Baldheaded and long-beaked with the wiry, droopy whiskers of a Scottish terrier, Old Bald Head was a career soldier, West Point trained and frontier hardened. He was popular among his brother officers and with his men and had fought well through the first year of the war. By May 1863, however, he had been out of the war for nine months after losing a leg at Second Manassas.

Ewell's selection as permanent commander of Jackson's old corps pleased the rank and file as well as the headquarters staff. He was, in a sense, one of them. He and the men he would lead had shared many of the same hardships and had gone into battle together many times—in the Valley Campaign, at Cedar Mountain, and at Second Manassas. They knew he would fight well when the time came, and they felt they could win with him.

Hotchkiss had always liked Ewell, writing to Sara that "we have our wishes gratified here in having Gen. Ewell to command the old army of Gen. Jackson.... much of the 'old army of the Valley' turned out to meet him when he came and seems to be enthused by his presence. An omen of good."[4]

And the appointment of Ewell was an omen of good for Hotchkiss as well, for it came as he was struggling with intense depression of mind and spirit. Had a lesser man or general been promoted to command instead of Ewell, Hotchkiss might have resigned and gone home. But his belief that he could work with the new commander encouraged him. Still, the appointment of a man he respected did not cure him of his despondency. Indeed, no external event could still the turmoil within him. He alone could dispel the agitation of his spirit and return himself to a healthy frame of mind. In his desire to cure himself, he turned more than ever to his greatest source of strength—his faith.

He drew power from reaffirming his beliefs: God was in control of the universe, and all that happened—no matter how horrible it seemed to the human mind—was part of His design. Hotchkiss confessed his ignorance of God's ways and intentions, rededicating himself to serving, not questioning, the Lord. Scripture was balm for Hotchkiss's wounds, and he dwelt on those passages that reassured him of God's ascendancy. He read over and over St. Paul's words in Romans 8:28, "And we know that all things work together for good to them that love God, to them who are the called according to his purpose." For the rest of the war, these words would help him accept and adjust, as would the inspirational verses of what he told Sara was his favorite hymn, "Light Shining out of Darkness," which read, in part:

> Judge not the Lord by feeble sense,
> But trust him for his grace;
> Behind a frowning providence
> He hides a smiling face.

> Blind unbelief is sure to err,
> And scan his work in vain;
> God is his own interpreter,
> And he will make it plain.[5]

Hotchkiss would recover from the loss of Boswell and Jackson, but he would never become inured to the terrible tragedies of war. He came to terms with the carnage through his faith. As the war continued and the slaughter grew ever greater and the destruction and depredations more widespread, his faith in God grew stronger, not because he saw evidence of God's design, but because his view of the world demanded that there be some purpose to the apparent waste of hundreds of thousands of lives and the destruction of the peace and prosperity of so many homes. In the spring of 1864, bracing himself for what he expected would be the bloodiest battle of the war, he told Sara that "the soul, in calm reflection, recoils from the contemplation of the ghastly spectacle. Men cannot become hardened to the horrors of war.... We are to fight it out and leave the issue in the hands of the Dispenser of all events."

For him, the revolting obscenity of war had to be somehow justified, made legitimate or worthwhile. Only the belief that it was God's will could justify the horror.

Despite his army's staggering losses, Lee had good reason to think that the Confederacy's chances for ultimate victory had been improved at Chancellorsville. The Federal army had lost heavily as well, and its morale was probably as low as it ever had been. The Army of Northern Virginia clearly held the upper hand, and Lee intended to make the most of it. He planned once again to take the war into Pennsylvania, where the Northern people would feel the hardships Virginians had been suffering for more than two years. If the invasion went well, Lee could feed his army on Pennsylvania's bounty, destroy or disrupt communication and transportation, and threaten Philadelphia, Baltimore, or Washington. As the warmth of May passed into the edged heat of June, Lee set his army in motion westward and northward, sending Ewell over the Blue Ridge and into the Shenandoah Valley, the corridor of invasion.

The move from the Chancellorsville area was a popular one with the troops. "We were all glad to get away from there," Hotchkiss wrote Sara of the Rappahannock region. "Too many unpleasant memories haunted us there, too many of our noble army had there gallantly met their last enemy. We hope we shall not be obliged to return there, for the feeling of the army was unanimously in favor of a march, anywhere and for any good purpose, in preference to the lazy life of a summer camp."[6] The men of Ewell's Corps were, of course, delighted that "anywhere" happened to be the Valley, which so many of them called home. They did not know their destination at first, but that mattered little once they were again between the mountains near their homes, striding with a swinging step northward on the Valley roads, strong and confident, among the most successful fighters in the world. Morale soared on that march, despite the heat and dust. They considered themselves conquerors and suspected they would soon be closing in for what might be the climactic and decisive battle of the war. And they were ready for it—eager for it. Hotchkiss sensed that the end might be near, telling Sara, "Events crowd on us, and this must be the most important year of the war."[7]

The army crossed into the Valley through beautiful Chester Gap, which Hotchkiss thought was "the finest one I have ever passed through."[8] The topographer and his new commander rolled through the pass southeast of Front Royal in a carriage that Ewell had taken to riding in after the loss of his leg. He would direct battles from horseback, but could no longer endure hours in the saddle during long marches, so he rode, and sometimes conferred with his staff or other subordinates in the relative comfort of his headquarters on wheels.

The land around Front Royal was familiar to Ewell and his men. It had been just fifty-five weeks before that they had stormed through the town and cleared Jackson's flank enroute to Winchester and the decisive victory over Banks. Now they were headed for Winchester again, aiming to drive out the garrison of about 7,000 Federals under Maj. Gen. Robert H. Milroy. Just as Banks had been no match for Jackson, Milroy proved himself unequal to Ewell. The Federals in and around Winchester had made little provision for defense, being content to occupy a number of earthen forts that were more vulnerable than imposing. Ewell sent one division northward through Berryville; then, with two of his divisions, headed northwestward for the final fifteen miles to Winchester. Gen. Robert E. Rodes's division continued northward to Martinsburg to threaten Milroy's line of supply and retreat. Milroy waited.

By June 14, Ewell had troops on three sides of Milroy's position at Winchester, and he opened the attack with his artillery that afternoon. Darkness closed the conflict, with both sides suffering only light casualties. That night, virtually surrounded, Milroy decided to withdraw northward, burning what he could not take with him. But Ewell was ready, and as Milroy reached Stephenson's Depot a few miles north of Winchester, Edward Johnson's Division attacked in the predawn darkness of June 15. The Federal column deteriorated into chaos, and though Milroy himself escaped, about 4,000 of his men fell into Confederate hands, along with 23 pieces of artillery, 300 wagons, an equal number of horses, and a huge amount of matériel. Jubilant, Hotchkiss wrote to Sara while the smoke was still clearing, "This has been one of the most complete successes of the war."[9]

That day, while Ewell's men were mopping up at Winchester, Rodes crossed the Potomac into Maryland, the vanguard of Lee's great invasion. Longstreet moved northward east of the Blue Ridge, and Hill was in motion behind Longstreet. By June 25, all three of Lee's corps were north of the Mason-Dixon Line, and the next day they were roving free in Pennsylvania, the Army of the Potomac far behind. It was an exhilarating but exhausting time for Hotchkiss, who rode with the army during the day and worked far into the night on maps of the entirely unfamiliar terrain.

The Confederates were mildly shocked by the beauty and bounty of southern Pennsylvania. After existing in the poor, worn-out, war-wearied Virginia countryside for two years, where forests had disappeared, where crops and livestock were consumed almost on sight, and where miles of earthworks scarred the raw earth, the Southerners seemed awakened from a bad dream as they were reminded of how a land looked before war's ravage. "The land is full of everything and we have an abundance,"[10] wrote Hotchkiss, telling Sara that Ewell had said "it is like a hole full of blubber to a Greenlander."[11]

The invaders found the people submissive in this land of plenty. The lean, gray hordes had descended on the fat country, "frightening the Dutch out of their senses," Hotchkiss wrote of the German farmers. "They confidently expected us to burn everything and lay waste the country, … It was one of the most amusing sights I ever saw to see the broad-clothed gentry coming in and bringing saddles, bridles, etc., and making a pile of them in the square for the use of the Rebels."[12] Some of the Pennsylvanians took a less grim view of things and showed themselves friendly, joking with the secessionists that they were at last back in the Union.[13]

Ewell's Corps moved north through Greencastle to Shippensburg, where "the people looked sullen" and on to Chambersburg, where Hotchkiss sought out local maps and acquired some engineering supplies. The march continued toward Harrisburg, the state capital, forty miles from the Maryland border. On June 27, the corps stopped at Carlisle and took possession of the U. S. Army barracks, which Hotchkiss thought "a lovely place." Ewell and the other old Army officers could not resist raising the Confederate flag over the installation, and several of the generals issued a few remarks on the occasion, making a small ceremony of it.[14] For Hotchkiss, Carlisle must have brought back melancholy memories, for he had visited there fifteen years earlier on his walk from Harrisburg to Virginia. He went again to look at Dickinson College, where, as a young man, he had whiled away a few pleasant hours chatting with students and professors. Surely he must have envied that carefree young man, that botany student and budding geologist who was so much a product of a peaceful and prosperous world that was gone forever.[15]

The headquarters staff was preparing to move the army toward Harrisburg when word came from Lee at Chambersburg: Ewell must halt his advance and turn southward, converging with Lee and the rest of the army at the town of Gettysburg. Ewell was unhappy, having set his sights on Harrisburg, and Hotchkiss thought him "quite testy and hard to please" because of his disappointment. The general "had every one flying around" and awakened Hotchkiss in the middle of the night for a map.[16] But Ewell followed his orders and turned his corps southward toward Gettysburg.

Lee had recalled the roaming elements of his command because he had learned that the Army of the Potomac was much closer than had been assumed. Moreover, the Federal army had a new commander; Hooker had been replaced by Maj. Gen. George Gordon Meade, a Pennsylvanian, who was respected by the Confederates but was still something of an unknown quantity. Lee wished to bring his army together at once to be prepared for whatever Meade designed to do. The logical place to consolidate was the road hub of Gettysburg.

On the gray, misty morning of July 1, 1863, infantrymen from A. P. Hill's Corps approached Gettysburg from the west and encountered Federal cavalry just outside of the town. Federal infantry came up and soon the engagement became general. At a most opportune time for the Confederates, Rodes's Division of Ewell's Corps arrived on the Federal flank to aid Hill's attacks. Maj. Gen Ewell's corps followed, and throughout the afternoon, the fields west and north of the town were wreathed in powder smoke as the two armies grappled. At one point, Ewell, who had forsaken his carriage on this day of battle, was thrown from his horse when a shell fragment hit the animal on the head.[17] Late in the day, the Federals at last gave way, first on one front, then on the other, until the entire Federal line was in retreat. Thousands of blue-coated men turned and ran through the pasture land toward Gettysburg and the safety of the heights beyond. The Southerners followed closely into the streets of the town, where the chase lost much of its impetus, and the capture of hundreds of fleeing Federals slowed the Confederates further.

The afternoon was well advanced before Ewell's divisions had reformed enough to consider resuming the offensive. Lee sent a message from another part of the field urging Ewell to take the heights if possible, before the Federals had time to anchor their defense there. From where Dick Ewell stood at Second Corps headquarters, such an attack did not seem possible. The Federals held a strong position and appeared to be at work making it stronger. Any assault would be costly, and with night coming on, the attackers might not have enough light to capitalize on any advantage gained. Ewell decided not to order the attack.

According to Henry Kyd Douglas, a former member of Jackson's staff, some of Jackson's former staff officers with Ewell that day, specifically Sandie Pendleton, believed Jackson would have made the attack instantly, without hesitation. The question of whether an attack should have been launched that night became one of the major controversies of the battle and the war. Hotchkiss, however, accepted Ewell's judgment and offered none of his own, as though the question did not even exist: "The pursuit was checked by the lateness of the hour and the position the enemy had secured in a cemetery." [18]

For two more days, Ewell would try to get onto Cemetery Hill, but the Federals were there in great strength and all Confederate efforts to take the hill failed. On July 2, Ewell's attacks on nearby Culp's Hill almost succeeded, as did Longstreet's assaults on the Federal left, but on the morning of July 3, the Federals still stood firm. Lee decided on one more attack, a huge assault on the Federal center. Following an artillery barrage, 12,500 Confederate infantrymen, under the general command of Maj. Gen. George E. Pickett and Brig. Gen J. Johnston Pettigrew, crossed the huge open meadows south of Gettysburg. It

was a thrilling display, but a futile one, for the Federals turned it back handily.

Hotchkiss had seen his countrymen fight "with desperation and great valor," but Confederate losses in the charge had been staggering. That night, he rode over to see the survivors. "I met Pickett's Division, returning after the battle … scattered all along the road; no officers and all protesting that they had been completely cut up." At the same time, Hotchkiss noted that "the unmistakable signs of a retreat were plentiful," with wagons and prisoners moving off. Lee had had enough; the army would return to Virginia.[19] Lee's veterans turned southward with mixed emotions. Hotchkiss gauged the army to be "in fine spirits" still, but he also sensed "a general feeling of despondency … at our great losses, though the battle is regarded as a drawn one." [20]

As Lee's army withdrew, the general realized that the Federals would not immediately pursue. The Southerners reached the Potomac before Meade mounted a full-fledged pursuit. But Lee had much reason for concern. Rain fell in sheets in the days following the battle, and as he rode a glistening and muddy horse southward, Lee knew the Potomac would be high and swift, cutting him off from Virginia. Worse, the Federals came fast once they got started, and Lee concluded that he would not get across the river before Meade caught him. The Virginian decided he would have to turn and meet the enemy's advance until the river dropped and gave his long trains the time they

---

IN THIS UNFINISHED MAP OF THE BATTLEFIELD AT GETTYSBURG, HOTCHKISS PURPOSELY ADDED THE NAMES AT UPPER RIGHT UPSIDE DOWN. THIS WAS THE SECOND CORPS' AREA OF OPERATIONS, AND EWELL AND OTHERS REFERRING TO THIS MAP WOULD HAVE VIEWED IT LOOKING SOUTHWARD, JUST AS THEY HAD LOOKED OVER THE BATTLEFIELD.

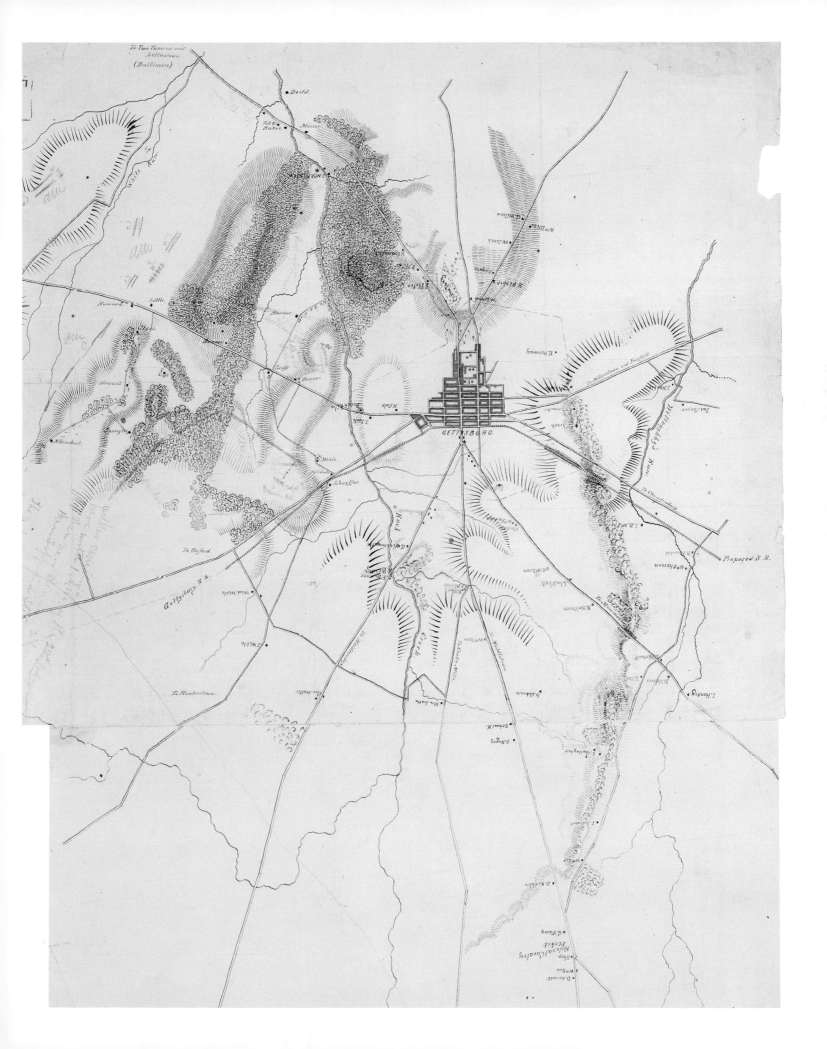

Hd. Qrs. 2nd Corps Orange. C. Ho. Va—
Aug. 15th 1863

My Darling Sara!

I have just returned from an all days ride over the woods & hills along the Rapidan and eaten my frugal dinner of corn, beans, stewed peaches & bread, and now, just as the glorious sun is sinking behind the distant Blue Ridge, looking at me away here in the tented field and at you, away yonder in our quiet home, but lonely, my thoughts follow his setting & I fain would, like Milton's angel, ride up to the Ridge top on one sunbeam & down to you on another, but I will do the next best thing, write you a long letter, especially as I have so long neglected you my Love, so long that you wrote to me first, a kind sweet letter, thus gently chiding me for my long silence since that sweet dream of home, one day in its blissful retreat — but I have been so busy, but that is always the case & I will not bring that as an excuse, though your kind heart will pardon, for you know I have daily thought of writing & as often something has interfered. I got to Staunton in good time the next morning, found William there, my box finished & so was fixed for being off, but I missed my glass, but, thanks to your constant foresight, Maj. Hannam brought it safely a day or two after my return — I found William had a bag of vegetables at Fishersville, Miss Hamilton sitting there as guard with her pleasant, hearty, honest face, that it does one good to get a look at — We got to Gordonsville in good time, a wonder, for a fatality seems to attend my travelling on the cars — I needed to cross. Soon the hills above the river fords near Williamsport, Maryland, were busy with Confederate engineers, including Hotchkiss, surveying the land and laying out lines of defense. By July 12, the construction of an eight-mile-long line of earthworks was almost complete. One Federal officer, an engineer, considered the huge Confederate works most formidable, perhaps the strongest he had ever seen. Meade and his army came upon these defenses just as they were being finished, and the Federals prepared for an assault. The well-prepared Confederates braced for the battle. But it did not come. The confrontation failed to reach its climax, for Meade hesitated. Soon thereafter, the river began to drop, and Lee began his crossing. By the morning of July 14, his army was once again in Virginia.[21]

The great invasion had failed. Pennsylvania, Philadelphia, Baltimore, Washington—all were secure for the Union. Lee had subsisted on Pennsylvanian forage and livestock for little more than a week, and now his hungry and footsore army returned to the depleted fields of Virginia. The climactic battle they had hoped for had been fought, but it had climaxed only the campaign, not the war. The fighting would continue, and the end that had seemed so close three weeks earlier was now no longer even in sight. Less than two weeks after the battle, Hotchkiss felt disposed to put the campaign in perspective, and revealed much about the army's state of mind. The defeat, he wrote, lacked significance: "A few pawns lost on the chess board of war—We did not take the heights at Gettysburg for they had already cost us too many lives, but came away from there at our own pleasure and today the army of Northern

HOTCHKISS USUALLY WROTE TO HIS WIFE AT LEAST ONCE A WEEK. HIS LETTERS NOT ONLY ALLAYED HER FEARS AND KEPT HER INFORMED BUT SERVED AS HIS LINK TO HIS FAMILY AND HOME, WHICH HE GREATLY MISSED.

Va. stands, as it has always stood, the sure defense of the heart of the Confederacy, and though disaster may befall our arms elsewhere it has not as yet befallen them here, and, by God's blessing, we hope never may. We have lost many men, but they died bravely on the field of honor, not in inglorious retreat, and their living companions only left the gory field until they had so crippled the foe that he was powerless to do them harm."[22]

Four days later, Meade's army was recrossing the Potomac into Virginia.

The tempest that had whirled through Virginia and across the Mason-Dixon line in the spring and early summer seemed to have exhausted the two armies that now sat glowering at each other in northern Virginia. For the next two months, the combatants would content themselves to rest and reorganize, probe and skirmish—and plan the next move.

Hotchkiss, as usual, used the quiet period to catch up on some work. His situation at headquarters had changed somewhat in that Ewell had no desire to use the topographer as Jackson had. Hotchkiss would not guide troops into position for Ewell, nor would he take the general into the field to show him troop positions and significant features of the terrain. Ewell had a different, more sedentary role in mind for Hotchkiss. The general had younger men to carry orders and direct troop movements, but he had few who could turn the information gathered by scouts into maps. "I … am not as much exposed to danger as I used to be," he told Sara, "Gen E. confining me to my special duties and not asking me often to do any others."[23] Ewell did not care to risk losing Hotchkiss's talents, and planned to take few unnecessary chances with him. Of course those "special duties" included surveying, so Hotchkiss would still spend much time in the saddle.

Hotchkiss was now more able than ever to concentrate on fulfilling the Second Corps's cartographic needs, not only because of Ewell's perception of the topographer's role, but because Hotchkiss had help. Sampson B. Robinson of the 7th Louisiana Regiment had been detailed during the Pennsylvania Campaign to work at headquarters with Hotchkiss as a topographical assistant. Robinson was a genial and companionable Englishman who was skillful as a draftsman, which pleased the talkative and demanding Hotchkiss. Still more to the topographer's liking was that Robinson, perhaps as a result of his residence amid the culinary delights of Louisiana, was a talented chef. Few men in that army appreciated a good meal as well as did Hotchkiss. His letters home were filled with descriptions of the tasty, but simple, fare he managed to acquire at headquarters. He was especially fond of pickles, butter, bread, and fruit. Long after the war, Hotchkiss met and talked with the Reverend Dr. Lacy, who messed with Hotchkiss, Robinson, McGuire, and others, and one of the recollections most treasured by Lacy was of the "delicious beefsteaks" Robinson would somehow produce from the tough army-issue meat.[24] Small pleasures meant much in the army, and a talented comrade like Robinson was sure to be popular and treasured. Hotchkiss and the "little Englishman" grew very close.[25]

The season of rest, the arrival of Robinson, and pleasant employment in solitary surveys of the countryside boosted Hotchkiss's spirits higher than they had been in months, and as always when his heart was light, he thought of home. He had been able to interrupt one of his surveys to spend a single day there, and since his return to camp he had seemed to miss Sara more than usual. One hot August evening he penned a sweet and melancholy declaration of love and longing: "I have just returned from an all day's ride over the roads and hills along the Rapidan and eaten my frugal dinner of corn and beans, stewed peaches and bread, and now, just as the glorious sun is sinking behind the distant Blue Ridge, looking at me away here in the tented field and at you, away yonder in our quiet home, but lonely, my thoughts follow his setting and I fain would like Milton's Angel, ride up to the Ridge top on one sunbeam and down to you on another, but I will do the next best thing, write you a long letter. " And he continued the letter in the morning: "5 $^{1}/_{2}$ a.m. I resume it now in the cool of this pleasant Sabbath morning, sitting on my blanket in my night garments; early for me to be up, yet at home, when there is some one to caress and fill the morning hours with delight, but here when rested one feels like leaving his hard pallet. The General spends his nights away from camp, his wife being in town and it has really made the old fellow look young again having taken away much of his former roughness of manner, in short, in his case, as in all other men's it is true that marriage is the natural condition of man, the one in which there is the fullest development of his whole nature and the greatest amount of earthly bliss to be attained when the parties thus joined are determined and willing to enjoy it and only smile at the few clouds that will flit over any summer sky." [26]

As strong a proponent of marriage as he was, Hotchkiss disliked the presence at headquarters of General Ewell's wife, whom the general had married just months before during his convalescence. Few officers saw the presence of wives as beneficial, and Hotchkiss claimed that "all are much opposed to having women in camp, as officers neglect their duties to attend to their wives." [27] The general still called the widow "Mrs. Brown," and was apparently quite attentive to her. But the effect was not good on the staff, and they almost unanimously thought she should go home, except perhaps her son, Campbell Brown, who had been appointed to his stepfather's suite.[28] Mrs. Brown was so strong a figure and wielded such influence over the general that officers and men joked about her fitness for command—and began to wonder about his. Dr. Lacy recalled that on one occasion he visited the outlying camp of Gen. Robert E. Rodes's Division. The good-natured Rodes playfully inquired about affairs at headquarters, asking "who commanded the Second Corps, whether Mrs. Ewell, General Ewell, or Sandy Pendleton, hoping it was the last."[29]

Meade was determined to leave Lee's army alone through the beastly hot weather of August, and the condition of the Army of Northern Virginia improved markedly as a result. The ranks swelled and morale climbed. Hotchkiss wrote to Nelson, "Our men are being nicely clothed and shod and will soon present a nice appearance; a uniformed army. The Commissariat of our army is in fine condition too and today the soldiers had roasting ears issued to them, a barrel to the hundred men, and that much is to be issued daily while the roasting ears season lasts. There is enough to eat."[30] And the spiritual health of the army improved as well. "Every one seems to have been impressed with a proper sense of the importance of humbling ourselves before God, confessing our sins and imploring his aid in the time of our extremity," wrote a pleased Hotchkiss. The setback at Gettysburg had not been considered a defeat, but still some in that army wondered what had happened. They had thought themselves invincible, and were puzzled when they found they were not. The quiet weeks of August provided time for reflection and for coming to terms with the "reason" for their "reverse."

"Mr. Lacy preached, at our Hd. Qrs.," Sara learned, "to some 1,500—among them Gens. Lee, Johnson, Rodes, etc.… He said though we had suffered a few reverses they were only needed to check our pride—and in the only way it could be checked. David had 3 alternatives offered him for the punishment of his pride and he chose to fall into the hands of God. We had vainly thought we could do anything by our own might and had arrogated the glory to ourselves, but God had restrained us and it might prove our salvation."[31]

And so the heat of the summer passed away, and all looked to the more temperate days of autumn as the time when "the work of blood must be resumed." Lee's army was rested, was growing stronger in body and spirit, and was confident.[32]

Hotchkiss continued to make good use of the time remaining before campaigning began again. He made long surveys through the Valley, into the western mountains, and across the Piedmont east of the Blue Ridge. When he was ill for a time in September, Dr. McGuire ordered him home to rest. He continued his examinations of the country after rejoining the army, but put the mapping projects aside in October when the armies finally stirred. Elements clashed at Bristoe Station, not far from Manassas, and though Hotchkiss was present, his role was insignificant, as most of the fighting was done by A. P. Hill's Corps.

The autumn, too, began passing away, and the big battle all expected had not yet come off. Skirmishing was continuous, and Meade attempted to draw Lee into a major engagement in November at Mine Run, but finally, the fair weather passed, the rains and frosts came, and the roads turned too soft for the passage of armies. Both armies went into winter quarters, and the war in Virginia froze.

And so it remained until spring. Hotchkiss, Robinson, and another draughtsman now on Hotchkiss's staff, C. W. Oltmanns, worked on maps most of the winter, supplying a near-constant and insatiable demand for drawings. The three men labored in relative comfort away from the armies in a rented office in Staunton. This was Hotchkiss's headquarters and would remain so for many months. He now had a place to retire to when he was not needed in camp and when the cartographic demands of his job exceeded those of scouting and surveying.[33]

But the winter was not to be spent entirely at the drafting board in a warm office. In January of the new year, Maj. Gen. Jubal A. Early, who was commanding the Valley District, gave Hotchkiss a major assignment. The general ordered Hotchkiss to survey the mountains southwest of Staunton and west of Lexington, paying special attention to strong defensive positions. The order apparently originated with Lee, who was trying to anticipate what the warm campaigning weather would bring from the Federals. The Federals might well try again to occupy the Valley, and the Confederates needed to prepare for that contingency. Lee's army, especially Jackson's old corps, knew the lower Valley well, but the upper Valley, south of Staunton, had yet to feel the tread of the armies and, to a great degree, remained unknown territory. Lee wanted the region mapped.

On January 25, Hotchkiss saddled his horse and headed into the mountains. He took one companion, a cavalryman assigned to him as a messenger, because, as he explained to Early, "It expedites my observations much to have someone to send to ascertain names of houses, etc., while I am taking notes and sketching topography, etc."[34] The survey was the most difficult and most prolonged of Hotchkiss's military career. For the better part of two months he would be in the saddle almost continuously, occasionally stopping at home or at the office in Staunton or taking refuge elsewhere during periods of foul weather. He had to endure wind, snow, freezing rains, slippery roads, frosts, and dense fog, all in addition to the physically taxing duty of riding perhaps twenty miles a day. And he had adventures as well; suspicious local militia officers pursued and questioned him, as they had on virtually every long reconnaissance. It was hard service, but almost two years of campaigning had inured him to hardship. Finally, in

March, he wearily returned to Staunton to begin putting his notes together so he and his assistants could produce the desired map. It took more than a month to draw, though he worked on other maps in the interim, but by late April, it was finished—just in time to be packed away with the other maps that had provided him and his two draughtsmen with winter employment. The roads were drying and the armies would soon be moving. It was time to return to headquarters.

The cartographers rejoined Lee's army east of the mountains, and on May 1, Hotchkiss wrote to Sara of the atmosphere of apprehension in camp. "Everything indicates that in less than 48 hours we may have the bloodiest battle of the war fought on this very ground, and the fresh green shores of the Rapidan be stained by the life blood of thousands."[35]

The words were prophetic. The Federals moved just days later, converging in the dense, almost impenetrable forests of the Wilderness. It was on the eastern edge of the Wilderness that Jackson had been wounded and Boswell killed. Now 118,000 Federals moved through the seventy-two-square-mile forest, led by a new commander, a tough and successful fighter named Ulysses S. Grant.

Lee had just 62,000 men to meet the advance, but was prepared and greeted the Federals with Ewell's Corps. Hotchkiss was not with Ewell as the battle began on May 4. He and his staff, Robinson and Oltmanns, were to the rear working on maps. He rejoined Ewell on the fifth, and despite Ewell's previously expressed intention to keep Hotchkiss out of the fighting, the topographer was immediately put to work carrying orders and scouting along the flanks of the enemy, twice taking messages to Lee.

On the 6th, he was up early—3 a.m.—in time to witness a dawn attack in which the Federals advanced to within forty yards of the Confederate lines. But the Southerners turned back the assault. "We discomfited them," wrote Hotchkiss offhandedly, "completely."[36]

Throughout that hot, momentous day, the fighting surged through the forests, troops firing blindly into the murk and smoke, battle lines breaking, reforming and breaking again in the confusion of noise, death, and chaos in close quarters. In many places, the woods caught fire from the discharge of rifles, and wounded men were trapped and burned by the consuming flames. Hotchkiss rode about the battlefield making sketches, carrying orders and reconnoitering. At one point, he came as close to death as he ever would on a battlefield. A bullet smashed into the binoculars that hung from his neck over his breast. The glasses were destroyed, but his skin was barely bruised.[37] At last, in the evening, the Southerners launched a final counterthrust. The attack might have proved decisive, but darkness prevented the Southern infantrymen from pressing their advantage, and the killing stopped.

The carnage had been awful. Grant lost 18,000 men, about fifteen percent of his force. Lee lost more than seventeen percent—combat veterans of long experience who could not easily be replaced. In less than three days of fighting, the two armies lost more than 28,000 men. But the fighting was not yet over.

For almost three years, Federal armies in Virginia had withdrawn to regroup after suffering high casualties in battle. But on the morning of May 7, under Grant, for the first time and to the surprise and delight of soldiers in the ranks, the Army of the Potomac did not pull back to lick its wounds, but prepared to move south toward Richmond, forcing Lee's army to follow and fight.

And Lee did both. For the next two weeks, the armies would battle in the fields and forests around Spotsylvania Court House. The Confederates constructed long lines of earthworks, and some of the more desperate fighting of

the war raged on those breastworks as Federals attacked en masse. "Grant fights stubbornly," assessed Hotchkiss, "and keeps butting his head against our breastworks, and is getting it badly bruised."[38] A Federal predawn assault on May 12, however, showed promise of success when it breached the Confederate line and captured about 3,000 men of Ewell's Second Corps. But the break was repaired and Lee's men held on. Hotchkiss admitted to Sara that he had never seen anything on any battlefield to match the fury of the fighting at Spotsylvania.[39]

While the savagery continued at Spotsylvania, fighting elsewhere claimed another of Hotchkiss's friends. He was "saddened, deeply saddened, by the death of Gen. J. E. B. Stuart,—one of the noblest spirits in the Confederacy." Stuart, the sly and jovial banterer so popular throughout the army, and Hotchkiss's coconspirator in the scheme to get poor, dead Boswell behind enemy lines to see his sweetheart, had fallen in battle at Yellow Tavern, Virginia. It was a great loss to Lee and the army.[40]

Grant broke off the engagement at Spotsylvania and again pushed his army southward, demanding that Lee react. The two armies would clash almost continuously for the next month, and their casualty figures reached shocking heights. By mid-June, Grant had pushed Lee's army to the outskirts of Richmond. Lee was forced to extend his defensive lines far to the south and east of the city to protect the vital railhead at Petersburg. Grant had grabbed the initiative from Lee and pushed the Virginian to the very gates of Richmond. Lee's army was in a difficult position, and it would get even more difficult.

As Lee fell back upon Richmond and Petersburg, the viability of his army came to depend on the railroads that entered the cities from the south and west. The rails became a lifeline connecting the army and the capital of the Confederacy with the rest of the South. In mid-June, a strong Federal column threatened the city of Lynchburg, a supply hub and a main hospital center in south-central Virginia, and a junction on three railroads: the Virginia and Tennessee, the Orange and Alexandria, and the South Side, which carried supplies to Petersburg. The Federals, commanded by Maj. Gen. David Hunter, had brought destruction to much of the Valley, burning barns, mills, homes, crops, and in Jackson's Lexington, the Virginia Military Institute. Hotchkiss heard of the wholesale destruction, and like so many other husbands, fathers, sons, and brothers in the army, worried about loved ones in the Valley. Hunter did damage Staunton, but Loch Willow escaped unharmed.[41]

Lee disapproved of Hunter's terror and flame tactics and wished to dispose of him, but the crux of the issue was Lynchburg: it was too important to the Confederacy to lose to the torch. Lee quickly decided, once again, to divide his force in the face of a larger enemy. He would send the Second Corps to defend Lynchburg.

Hotchkiss was pleased to be returning to the Valley. He was full of hope, as always, that the end was near. "Be of good cheer," he told Sara. "I hope this campaign will end the war and in God's good providence bring me to remain in my quiet home and bear my portion of its cares,—and free from the double load of duty imposed by these cruel times."[42]

THIS WILDERNESS BATTLEFIELD MAP WAS DRAWN BY S. B. ROBINSON, A DRAUGHTSMAN WHO WORKED FOR HOTCHKISS. AFTER HOTCHKISS COMPLETED A SURVEY AND DREW HIS MAP, ROBINSON MADE COPIES. THE DUPLICATES, LIKE THIS ONE, WERE ALMOST IDENTICAL TO HOTCHKISS'S ORIGINALS. (PAGES 136–137) THIS MAP OF THE BATTLEFIELD AT SPOTSYLVANIA COURT HOUSE IS ONE OF HOTCHKISS'S FINEST. IT TOOK CAREFUL PLANNING AND A STEADY HAND TO CONVEY SO MUCH TOPOGRAPHICAL INFORMATION AND STILL CLEARLY SHOW TROOP POSITIONS.

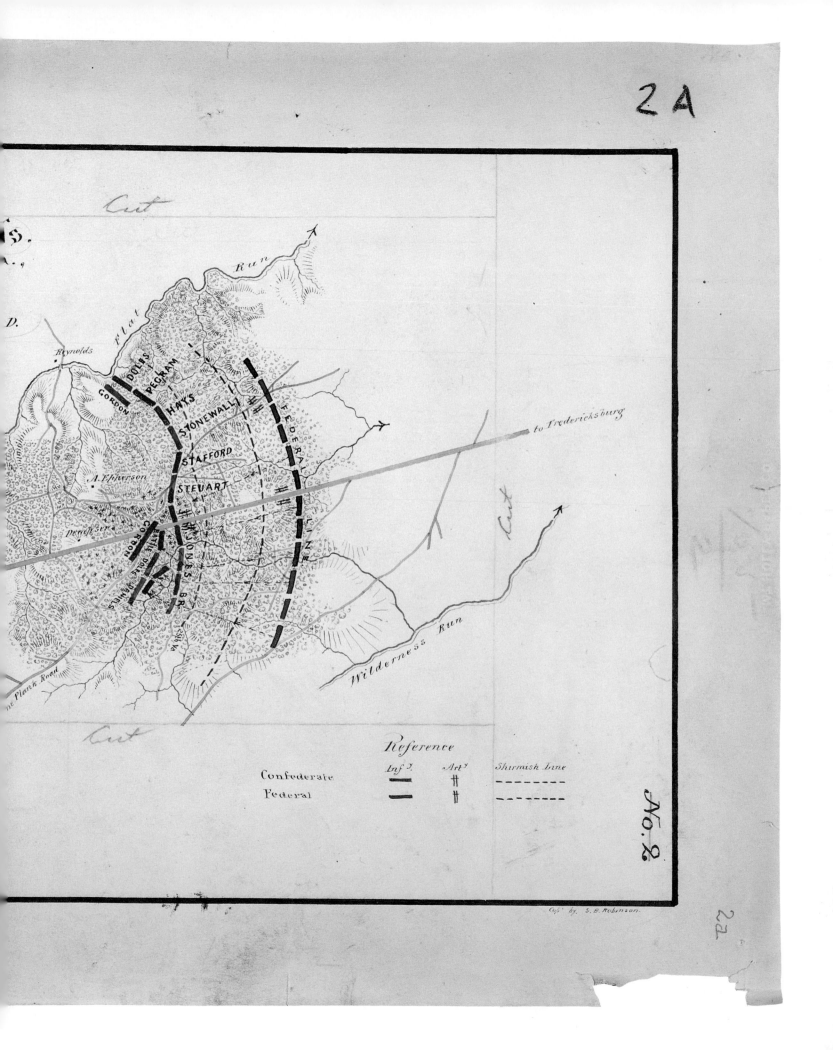

Cut

Run

Flat

Run

Reynolds

DOLES

PEGRAM

GORDON

HAYS

STONEWALL

STAFFORD

STEUART

A. Efferson

Pegust Ser

GORDON

M. JONES BR.

55th Va

Wilderness Run

FEDERAL LINE

to Fredericksburg

Cut

Plank Road

Cut

Reference

	Inf.ᵈ	Art.ʸ	Skirmish lnne
Confederate			
Federal			

Cop. by. S. B. Robinson.

2a

Sketch showing Positions and Entrenchments of the
SECOND CORPS A.N.V. during
the Battles of Spotsylvania C.H.
from May 9th to May 21st 1864.

Scale 1 : 40.000.

Reference

	Inf.	Art.	Ent.
Confed	=	╫	▬
Federal	=	╫	

Peyton

Baxter

To Fredericksbg

Mrs. Alsop

Pendleton

Harris

Capt. Alsop

Gayle

Beverly

F. Beverly

Anderson

Icolar

Barn   Dabney

Spotsylvania C.H.

Gayle

J. Coleman

Mrs. Clark

L t. Gen. Jubal A. Early did much with little when the armies struggled for the Shenandoah Valley in 1864. Badly overmatched, Early tried to make good use of all his resources, including his topographer, who knew the region intimately. The general's aggressive campaign kept Hotchkiss in the saddle and at the drafting table for long hours.

CHAPTER EIGHT
"ALL THINGS WORK TOGETHER FOR GOOD"

The men of the Second Corps of the Army of Northern Virginia were on the road toward Lynchburg by 3 a.m. on June 13, but they moved under the guidance of a new hand. In the fighting at Spotsylvania, General Ewell's frail health had worsened and, after the fighting on the North Anna, he was incapable of immediately resuming command of the corps. Lee had not been entirely pleased with Ewell's performance as a corps commander, so he took this opportunity to replace him. Hotchkiss had grown quite fond of Ewell, and later learned that the general reciprocated this high regard. For his report of the 1864 campaigns, Ewell wrote: "I wish to express in the strongest manner my appreciation of the services rendered by Maj. Jed. Hotchkiss Topographical Officer of the Corps—probably one of the very best officers of that branch of (the) service. I never regretted the confidence I always placed in his zeal & judgment and his activity & energy were incomparable." [1]

In Ewell's place, Lee appointed a man whom he hoped could make better use of the fighters of Jackson's old Second Corps. On May 31, 1864, Jubal A. Early was promoted to lieutenant general and given command of the corps.

As Ewell had been, Early was well known to the men of the Second Corps, for he had been marching and fighting with them for many months. A gray and crotch-ety forty-seven years old, Early was a truculent and aggressive leader. He had been graduated from West Point but had turned to law and was engaged in that profession at the outbreak of the war. A contented bachelor who was polite to but impatient of women, Early seemed to feel most comfortable amid the brandy and cigar smoke of male company. There was little of the courtly Virginia gentleman about the general; he was all hardy masculinity. He liked to speak freely and cared little for decorum. One subordinate wrote diplomatically after the war that Early had "a pungent style of commenting on things he did not like," [2] but the truth was that the general was often loud and profane. One of Jackson's staff remembered hunting through the cold black woods for Early's headquarters after the Battle of Fredericksburg. He finally found him by following the stream of profanity ringing through the forest to where couriers were trying with little success to light a fire for the general. [3]

Now Early commanded Jackson's old Second Corps, and aside from their fondness for terse speech, Jackson and Early had little in common. Jackson neither drank nor swore; Early enjoyed doing both, though apparently only the latter to excess. Jackson was devout and attributed all his accomplishments to God's blessing; Early could be vain and bad tempered. Jackson was generally good-natured, but his sense of humor was heavy and ponderous. Early was caustic, cynical, and witty—and he was not impressed or intimidated easily. On one march, Jackson, who was obsessive about maintaining good discipline during movements, sent Early a note asking why he had seen so many men straggling behind Early's division. Early brushed aside what many commanders would have taken as a reprimand and wryly responded that the general had seen so many stragglers because he had ridden at the rear of the column.

But the two men had one thing in common: neither was afraid to fight, and indeed, both seemed anxious to close with the enemy at every favorable opportunity. Early, however, was perhaps too anxious, and sometimes joined battle recklessly. He was not as attentive to details or as inspired as Jackson had been, but few generals were. Early's over-aggressiveness could get him into a scrape now and then, but he knew how to get himself and his men out, and as a rule, Lee was more prone to encourage aggressiveness than excessive prudence. Early had Lee's confidence and had earned it through three years of solid service.

Hotchkiss, like the rest of the holdovers from Jackson's staff, saw that Early was neither the man nor the general Jackson had been, but the topographer was among the many who thought well of Early, probably agreeing with one general's assessment that whatever the general's personal faults, he "had a good heart." [4]

The Second Corps's topographical engineer was invited to remain at corps headquarters—still as a civilian employee—but he was not immediately able to continue in his duties. Hotchkiss was again ill and began the trip to Lynchburg in an ambulance,[5] but by the time the column reached the threatened city, Hotchkiss was again fit for duty and busied himself in making maps.

The swift and dramatic march to save Lynchburg, however, ended in anticlimax. At Early's approach, Hunter altered his plans and fled westward to the mountains. So

precipitate was his flight, and so closely did Early pursue, that many of Hunter's Federals collapsed from exhaustion, and many who did not remembered it as the hardest march they ever made.

Hunter's timidness was an unexpected boon to the Confederate cause, for it left the Valley free of any large Federal force and the door to Maryland and Pennsylvania open and unattended. Early, with orders from Lee, immediately moved north, hoping that an invasion of Maryland, and the consequent threat to Washington, would cause General Grant to divert some of his force to defend his capital, thus easing the pressure on Lee.

Early's little army crossed into Maryland on July 5 and 6.[6] Hotchkiss shared the enthusiasm of the troops as they crossed the Potomac for the third time in the war, but the thrilling spectacles and high hopes that had characterized the first two invasions, in September 1862 and June 1863, were notably absent in July 1864. Hotchkiss the optimist believed some good would come of this foray into the Free State, but he was realistic enough to know that it was little more than a raid, a gambit by which Lee hoped to buy some time.

The Federals offered little resistance to Early's troops, and spirits rose in the Confederate ranks as the columns headed eastward through Maryland toward Washington. Finally, on the sunny morning of July 9, the Confederates came upon the Federals just east of Frederick. Skirmishers obstructed roads, and blockhouses and artillery pieces guarded the bridges over the Monocacy River. The Southerners, outnumbering their foes by almost two-to-one,

HOTCHKISS'S MAP OF THE ENGAGEMENT AT MONOCACY, MARYLAND, WAS DRAWN IN DECEMBER 1864, PROBABLY IN HIS STAUNTON OFFICE, AND WAS BASED ON SURVEY DATA COLLECTED ON THE FIELD JULY 10, 1864, THE DAY AFTER THE BATTLE.

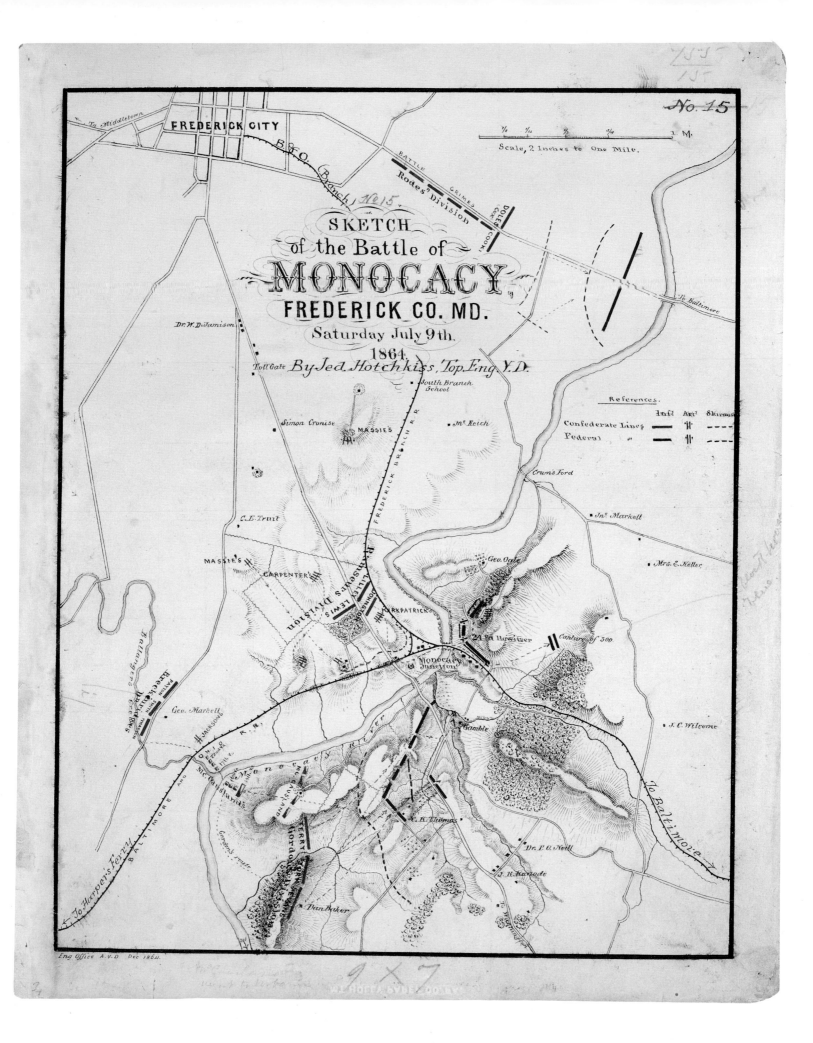

FREDERICK CITY

To Middletown

BATTLE GRIMES

Rodes' Division

DOLE'S COX COOK

To Baltimore

Scale, 2 Inches to One Mile.

SKETCH
of the Battle of
MONOCACY,
FREDERICK CO. MD.
Saturday July 9th.
1864.
By Jed. Hotchkiss, Top. Eng. V.D.

Toll Gate

Dr. W. D. Jamison

South Branch School

Simon Cronise

MASSIE'S

Jn° Keich

References.

Inf. Art. Skirmis.

Confederate Lines

Federal

Crum's Ford

C. E. Truit

Jn° Markell

MASSIE'S

Geo. Cole

Mrs. E. Keller

CARPENTER'S

RAMSEUR'S DIVISION

LILLEY

LEWIS SIMS

JOHNSON

KIRKPATRICK

24 Pd Howitzer

Capture of 300

Monocacy Junction

Gamble

J. C. Wileome

RICKETTS' DIVISION

Geo. Markell

JACKSONS

McCausland's

EVANS

Monocacy River

C. K. Thomas

TERRY GORDON'S DIVISION

Dr. F. O. Neill

J. R. Farrade

Gordon's route

To Harper's Ferry

BALTIMORE AND OHIO R.R.

Dan Baker

To Baltimore

Eng. Office A.V.D. Dec 1864.

THE BRAVE AND CONTENTIOUS MAJ. GEN. JOHN BROWN GORDON WAS CONSIDERED BY HOTCHKISS TO BE A HERO WITH FEW PEERS AS A FIGHTER.

turned into a map. He had no time to linger on the project, however, for Early was pushing on toward Washington.[8]

As the invaders neared the enemy capital, the weary troops began to falter in the killing heat and choking dust. Early tried to buoy them, riding among the columns and telling the marchers he would take them into Washington that very day. But the men had reached their limit and could not be pushed. They arrived outside the defenses of Washington exhausted. Early did not push them into an immediate attack, and the delay permitted troops sent north by Grant to strengthen the capital city's garrison. Early recognized that his opportunity had passed and wisely relinquished any hope of a determined attack. He withdrew on the hot night of July 12, having failed to enter Washington, but having succeeded in drawing off some troops from Lee's front—an accomplishment of only temporary benefit.

The tired Confederates marched better now that they were on the way home, and foragers had enough energy to commandeer large numbers of cattle and horses. Hotchkiss had obtained a few prizes of war as well; under orders from Early, he took maps from the home of Montgomery Blair, postmaster general of the United States. Other Confederates, without orders from Early, also invaded Blair's home, looted it, and eventually burned it.[9]

On July 14, the dusty column reached the river and began to cross into Virginia. The Federals did not vigorously pursue, and the Confederates crossed without haste, the troops undoubtedly finding the cool waters a needed relief from the brutal heat.[10] Hotchkiss told Sara, "I never experienced warmer weather," but otherwise managed, as usual, to cast a golden light on events. "We have been over 3/4 of the state of Maryland," he wrote in his assessment of the campaign, "scared 'Old Abe' so that he has ordered a good portion of his force away from Richmond. Captured thousands of horses and cattle, whipped the enemy in a

forced their way to and finally across the river, driving the Northerners from their positions with heavy casualties. Early had won the field, and a tactical victory, but his march had been delayed by a full day, a fact whose full consequences would not become apparent for another forty-eight hours.

Hotchkiss was jubilant. The invasion was exhausting for him as he marched with the army during the day and worked on maps at night. The victory at Monocacy rejuvenated and refreshed him, and his exultation was clear in his journal, where he noted that the routed Federals had been chased for more than two miles.[7] He quickly rode around the battlefield and made sketches that he later regular battle and with small loss, returned safely to a position that threatens Washington and Pa. at the same time, and are ready to move in any direction.—By all odds the most successful expedition we have ever made into the enemy's country." [11]

But the reality of the situation was less promising for the Confederacy. The "good portion" of Grant's army ordered to turn back Early was now free to pursue the Confederates or return to the Richmond-Petersburg front. The Confederates had stirred up a political hornet's nest in Washington. Now the Lincoln administration and Grant decided that the Valley must once and for all be secured, and a separate command was formed to undertake the assignment. At its head was Maj. Gen. Philip H. Sheridan, an energetic and effective leader. The stage was set for a showdown in the Shenandoah.

Early's return to Virginia initiated a season of skirmishing and movement in which elements of the two armies clashed in minor combat several times. The Confederates recrossed the Potomac on a raid in late July, and Hotchkiss went along, reporting that they took "150 horses, 2,000 bush. of corn, a large lot of leather, etc." before returning to Virginia. [12] In one skirmish back in Virginia, Hotchkiss had the opportunity to witness the bravery of a man he had long admired on professional grounds: Maj. Gen. John B. Gordon, a hard, thin, fierce-looking man who had become one of the army's best fighters. At Sharpsburg, Gordon had been wounded five times, including one bullet in the face, but had not left the field until he had been carried off. Swarthy, clear-eyed, and erect of carriage, Gordon looked and acted like a soldier and was widely admired throughout the army. Hotchkiss saw why: "Gen. Gordon was struck by a glancing ball, in the forehead, and bled profusely," he told Sara, "but was not much hurt.—He did not get off his horse or stop to have his wound dressed, but pressed on after the enemy, all

sprinkled with blood,—the very personification of a hero." Hotchkiss came to know and like Gordon even more in the weeks and months ahead and teamed with him in developing one of the more brilliant and dramatic episodes of the war. [13]

Early handled his army well in those waning days of summer, and Hotchkiss, for one, was impressed. "The country owes much to Gen. Early, and his vigilance, I think, will keep this Valley safe from incursions of the enemy." But as usual, Hotchkiss was being overly optimistic, weighting Early's mild successes too heavily and Lee's difficulties—enduring a siege at Petersburg—too lightly. He was realistic enough, however, to join other Confederates in realizing that whatever hope the Confederacy had for independence rested in a large measure on the result of the November election in the North. "The signs are brightening," he wrote Sara late in August, "and I still confidently look for a conclusion of hostilities with the ending of 'Old Abe's' reign.'" [14]

Hotchkiss would have been less optimistic had he known the ferocity with which Sheridan would seek to regain control of the Valley. After just a few weeks of command, the Federal general had maneuvered the Confederates out of the lower Valley. But Early gave ground reluctantly and was quick to reclaim it when he could. The sparring and maneuvering finally came to an end on September 19. Early and his little army lay near Winchester, and Sheridan launched a full-scale assault. The resulting fight came to be known as the Third Battle of Winchester. Early's men fought well, but tactical errors cost the Confederates dearly, and the Federals pushed the Southerners through the streets of the town and into the meadows to the south. Third Winchester was the only one of the three battles around that town that ended in Confederate defeat, and it was the only one at which Hotchkiss was not present.

MAJ. GEN. ROBERT E. RODES WAS A MUCH-RESPECTED VETERAN OF LONG SERVICE UNDER JACKSON, LEE, AND OTHERS. HOTCHKISS VIEWED HIS DEATH AS A CALAMITY FOR THE CONFEDERACY.

Early's topographer had received permission to go to Staunton and Churchville for a few days to attend to some business. He was returning, riding northward along the Valley Pike, when he heard the news of the fight at Winchester. "When I got to New Market [I] heard that we had had a disastrous battle and General Rodes had been killed," he wrote in his journal, referring to the brave and energetic division commander Robert E. Rodes. A little later, he met Rodes's staff bearing their slain general "to his afflicted wife." Hotchkiss watched the body pass with a keen regret, and shared the sorrow of Rodes's men, some

of whom stood along the road lamenting their loss.[15] "We have never suffered a greater loss save in the Great Jackson," Hotchkiss told Sara. "Rodes was the best Division Commander in the Army of Northern Virginia—and was worthy of and capable for any position in it."[16]

At Third Winchester, Early lost 3,900 irreplaceable men, including the incomparable Rodes. But the worst was to come just three days later at Fisher's Hill, an eminence athwart the Valley between Massanutten Mountain and Little North Mountain just south of Strasburg and some twenty miles south of Winchester. It was a strong position, and the Confederates had fortified it with earthworks during an earlier visit. But as Early's veterans filed into the old trenches, the commanding general realized that the long defensive line across the hill required more men than he had remaining to him. He compounded the problem by improperly placing his cavalry, which, as events soon revealed, were unequal to defending the flanks of the little army. Sheridan came upon Early at Fisher's Hill on September 21. The Federals spent the day maneuvering, and by the next day, they were ready to attack. Maj. Gen. George Crook's divisions crashed upon Early's left, scattering the cavalry and slamming into the unprepared infantry. Years later, General Gordon stated that the battle, "or, to speak more accurately, the bout at Fisher's Hill, was so quickly ended that it may be described in a few words. Indeed, to all experienced soldiers the whole story is told in one word—'flanked.' "[17]

Hotchkiss was in the midst of the fighting and was slightly wounded in the hand by a spent shell fragment. His horse was more seriously wounded. He attempted to lead reinforcements forward, but the chaos was too great. In the gathering autumn dusk, as men and horses swept by him to the rear, Hotchkiss turned against the tide of panic and joined Col. Sandie Pendleton in rallying a few infantrymen and posting them along a fence on a knoll along with two field guns. The makeshift rearguard slowed the Federal advance for a few moments, but then gave way. It was here that Sandie Pendleton was mortally wounded in the abdomen. He had been a favorite of Jackson's and had been treasured by all his commanders for his efficiency and energy. He was, more than any other, somehow symbolic of the remarkable and highly educated young gentlemen with whom Jackson surrounded himself. He died the next day, five days before his twenty-fourth birthday. His new wife, Kate Corbin Pendleton, formerly of Moss Neck, was pregnant with their first child. "I am truly sorry for his young wife," wrote Hotchkiss to Sara. "He was one of the best officers in the army and it will be difficult to fill his place." [18]

But Hotchkiss could spare no time to assist his fallen friend, for the army was in grave peril. The bridges over the creeks in the army's rear were insubstantial structures, and Hotchkiss thought they might not bear up during the flight. If they collapsed, the army would be trapped. He left the knoll, rode quickly to the bridges, and managed to get the frantic teamsters in the wagon train, which "was fairly flying," to slow down before they crossed the spans. Most of Early's shattered army escaped, but the losses of men, arms, animals, and equipment at Fisher's Hill made the battle a disaster of huge proportions.

Thrashed soundly twice in one week, Early had no choice but to abandon the lower Valley and seek refuge farther south. He moved by way of Staunton, where citizens were preparing to evacuate the town, to Port Republic and on to Brown's Gap, where Jackson had camped two years earlier. To this safe haven Sheridan probably would not follow, giving the Southerners time to lick their wounds and wonder what to do next.

Lee was chagrined by Early's defeats, but the commanding general was not yet ready to abandon the Valley. Despite being badly outnumbered at Petersburg, Lee sent reinforcements to Early in a desperate attempt to hold the Valley and protect the Virginia Central Railroad. Maj. Gen. Joseph B. Kershaw's division entered the Valley through Swift Run Gap, and Early sent Hotchkiss to meet the newcomers and guide them to the army's encampment. [19] The effect these reinforcements had on Early's army went far beyond the mere swelling of numbers. Here, for the weary veterans of the Valley, were new comrades, new muskets, and a new lease on life. Kershaw's command represented a vote of confidence from Lee. Where the men of Early's command had been beaten and depressed, now they were buoyed up and game to try the Federals one more time. "The news of Kershaw's approach," wrote one observer, "ran along the sleeping ranks, and aroused them as if an electric battery had been sending its stimulating current through their weary bodies. Cheer after cheer came from their husky throats and rolled along the mountain cliffs, the harbinger of coming victory." [20]

But the reinforcements notwithstanding, Early's army still needed rest and reorganization and could not resume the offensive yet. The Federals had followed the Confederates up the Valley and probed and skirmished for several days before retiring. In one of these little fights, Hotchkiss had his second brush with death in less than a week when his horse was killed beneath him. [21]

As Early's battered army rested, Sheridan, apparently believing the Confederates at Brown's Gap were no longer a threat, began withdrawing toward the lower Valley. As he went, however, he began carrying out Grant's orders to destroy anything that could aid the Confederates in the Valley. Sheridan's troopers were armed with torches and ordered to burn all that might sustain a Confederate army. "So," wrote John B. Gordon after the war, "he [Sheridan] decided upon a season of burning, instead of battling; of assaults with matches and torches upon barns and haystacks, instead of upon armed men who were lined up in front of him." [22] Early's defeated legion was impotent to interfere.

By day the skies of the Valley were soiled with black smoke, and by night the heavens were lighted by the orange glow of hundreds of burning barns and haystacks. [23] War had at last come to the great Valley in its most modern and debased form. The devastation of crops and farmland was total, and the region became a charred and desolate wasteland.

By the end of the first week in October, Sheridan's burners had finished their work in that part of the Valley and began retiring toward Winchester. Somewhat rested, Early's army followed. [24] Hotchkiss was active in assisting the movement, supervising parties repairing bridges and telegraph lines while continuing oversight of his cartographers. [25] He was, as usual, optimistic about the state of things around him. "Everything here wears a cheerful aspect," he told Sara in one letter, and later in the week he wrote that he thought "the prospect seems bright in every quarter." It is a measure of his intense cheerful faith and positive outlook that at this time, in mid-October, 1864, when things looked gloomy indeed for the Confederacy—Lee under siege at Petersburg and Richmond, Atlanta lost, and the Federals under Maj. Gen. William T. Sherman preparing to march through Georgia virtually unopposed, Gen. John B. Hood's Army of Tennessee wrecked beyond repair, and Early's bruised army so weak it had to stand by and watch Sheridan torch the Valley—that he could see things in a promising light. Early's tentative pursuit of Sheridan and a movement by Hood into Sherman's rear in Tennessee seemed to Hotchkiss omens of good. "In fact," he wrote, "we have always gained by taking bold measures; and if Sherman is compelled to leave Georgia there will be a great revulsion of feeling in the North and peace sentiments will be in fashion again." [26] And, of course, to Hotchkiss and many others in the Confederacy, the No-

vember election in the North continued to shine as the South's greatest hope. All would be well for the Confederacy, they thought, if every son of the South rose up at this crucial time and fought with enough renewed vigor to convince the Northern voters that they would not succumb. If the Confederate armies could hold on, the peace party candidate—Gen. George McClellan—might win the election, and the South would have its independence. [27] "The next 6 weeks determine our fate," Hotchkiss told Sara, "and every man must come out for that time and do his duty. The enemy is determined to do all that numbers can do this year and we must, shall and will meet him with even numbers—not even, as figures tell it, but even as moral courage and unconquerable will tell it." [28]

Sheridan halted his army at Middletown and established an encampment south of town on the banks of Cedar Creek. There the Federals rested, sated in victory and confident that the Valley was theirs. The Federal high command shared this confidence and turned to deciding how Sheridan's force could best be put to use now that the Valley was secure. Sheridan left the army at Cedar Creek and traveled to Washington for a conference.

But the Valley, blackened and desolate as it was, had not yet been surrendered by Jubal Early. The Confederate general had led his troops northward in Sheridan's wake and again put his men into their old positions at Fisher's Hill. Old Jube, as the men called him, then began looking for a way to strike the complacent Federals.

On October 17, Early sent a party of men to the summit of Massanutten Mountain, which towered almost 2,000 feet above the creek and offered a commanding view of much of the Valley. The Confederates had long ago established a signal station on a spur of the mountain—called Signal Knob—and the Federals were content to allow their foes to watch them from this superb vantage. Early was grateful for this advantage, and sent four intelligent and

experienced men up the mountain: Maj. Gen. John B. Gordon, Brig. Gen. Clement A. Evans, Maj. Robert W. Hunter (Gordon's chief of staff), and Jed Hotchkiss. The climb up the rugged and densely wooded slopes, across screes of tumbled sandstone, over fallen trees, and along narrow ridge lines consumed hours and demanded stamina. Finally, the foursome reached the knob and beheld a view both magnificent and terrible. The gorgeous Valley, clear and green-gold in the bright autumn sun, offered, Gordon thought, "an inspiring panorama. With strong field-glasses, every road and habitation and hill and stream could be seen and noted." [29]

But the natural beauty was marred by the presence on the Valley floor of the two armies in their earthworks,

THE DISTINCTIVE PROFILE OF MASSANUTTEN LOOMS ABOVE THE VALLEY NEAR THE VILLAGE OF STRASBURG. THIS 1884 VIEW SHOWS THE SUMMIT WHERE HOTCHKISS, GORDON, AND OTHERS STUDIED FEDERAL TROOP POSITIONS IN THE VALLEY BELOW.

which ran like jagged red scars across the green fields. It was the Federal army, of course, that the climbers wished to see, and of it they saw almost all. "Not only the general outlines of Sheridan's breastworks," wrote Gordon of what they saw, "but every parapet where his heavy guns were mounted, and every piece of artillery, every wagon and tent and supporting line of troops, were in easy range of our vision. I could count, and did count, the number of his

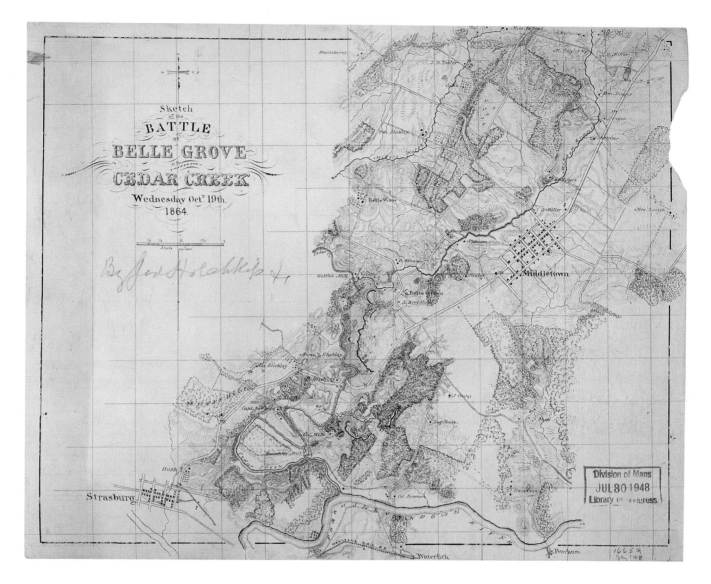

To complete this map of Federal entrenchments south of Middletown which were visible from Massanutten's signal station (just off the bottom of the map), Hotchkiss probably used sketches made on the mountain. General Gordon crossed the Shenandoah River near Colonel Bowman's.

---

guns. I could see distinctly the three colors of trimmings on the jackets respectively of infantry, artillery, and cavalry, and locate each."[30]

The observers took their time and made careful note of Sheridan's dispositions. Hotchkiss made a sketch map, and he discussed with Gordon the terrain at the foot of the mountain. The fall of the sun toward the mountains in the west forced the four men to begin their descent in time to reach the bottom before dark, but what they had seen from the height had excited them. They had seen an opportunity of getting at the Federals, and Gordon and Hotchkiss had formed a plan of attack, the details of which they discussed and pondered on the long walk down the mountain. It was dark before they arrived at camp, and Hotchkiss stayed to dinner at Gordon's mess, continuing to debate the problems and advantages of their plan. Late at night, Hotchkiss returned to Early's headquarters and made a preliminary report to the general. Gordon would present the complete plan the next day.[31]

Gordon's party had seen from the mountain that Sheridan had been careless in siting his defensive lines, and the Federal left, just below Massanutten, was especially weak. Gordon thought the weakness of the flank was due to a faulty assumption by Sheridan or Sheridan's engineers. "It was unmistakably evident that General Sheridan concurred in the universally accepted opinion that it was impractical for the Confederates to pass or march along the rugged and almost perpendicular face of Massanutten Mountain and assail his left."[32] Gordon was mistaken in his use of the word "universally," for Jed Hotchkiss knew that it was quite practical to move past the base of Massanutten between the face of the mountain and the North Fork of the Shenandoah. In a remarkable coincidence, exactly two years earlier—to the day—Hotchkiss had surveyed the foot of Massanutten between the hamlet of Buckton, the principal ford on the river, and the town of Strasburg. He therefore knew positively that a way could be found to move a large body of troops to the fords on Cedar Creek and the North Fork, where they could cross and assail Sheridan's poorly placed flank.

Hotchkiss possessed the knowledge he did because of Stonewall Jackson's foresight. In the early spring of 1862, Jackson had commissioned Hotchkiss to make a map of the Valley because he suspected the region would be the scene of fighting. In the autumn of 1862, Jackson had already completed one major operation in the Valley, but the map was still incomplete. The general still thought the map would be valuable, for the Valley would almost certainly see more fighting. He desired that Hotchkiss finish the map, and, in Hotchkiss's words, "approved fully of my plan of [surveying] operations … and told me to continue to use, diligently, as heretofore, the good weather and make up my notes of as much of the country as possible."[33] It is

at least partly because of Jackson's use of Hotchkiss's abilities, then, that Jubal Early was able to attack Sheridan at Cedar Creek.

Hotchkiss, who had outlined the plan for Early on the night of October 17, presented a fuller version on the 18th, superseding General Gordon, who had planned to brief Early. Hotchkiss acted quickly because he feared Early was coming under the influence of another officer who proposed another plan. While Gordon's party was on Massanutten, Brig. Gen. John Pegram had made a reconnaissance of a different part of Sheridan's line and later urged that Early attack there. Hotchkiss, of course, knew Pegram from their service together in the mountains of western Virginia in July 1861. It was Pegram who vacillated and delayed in the evacuation of Camp Garnett and who eventually surrendered most of his troops. Only those who followed Hotchkiss escaped. "Professor" Hotchkiss had thought the behavior of the West Pointer disgraceful and considered him to be personally "arrogant" and "selfish." Pegram had shown enough merit in the succeeding three years to rise to the rank of brigadier—but Hotchkiss had apparently not changed his opinion of him.[34] He wanted Gordon's plan adopted because it was sounder, but he also disliked Pegram's plan because he disliked its author.

Hotchkiss wrote in his journal that he did not wish Early's judgment "to be forestalled" by Pegram. In the presence of both officers, he indicated on a map how the attack on the Federal left could be effected. Early called a conference and discussed the plan with his officers, finally giving his approval. Pegram, however, remained unconvinced, at least according to Hotchkiss, who recorded that the young general himself climbed Massanutten and came back with a report quite different from Gordon's and Hotchkiss's. Pegram went to Early, Hotchkiss wrote, "to report some new works that he thought he had discovered from the mountain on the enemy's left, and he rather opposed the movement." Considering his feelings toward Pegram, and considering that Pegram's trip up Massanutten was clearly made to find evidence that Gordon and the topographer were wrong, it must have been with some satisfaction that Hotchkiss wrote that Pegram failed in his efforts to sway the commanding general: "General Early held firm." The attack was to be made by Gordon's route on the morning of October 19.[35]

On the afternoon of the eighteenth, Hotchkiss rode with Gordon and Maj. Gen. Stephen Dodson Ramseur to see the route the attacking force would take past Massanutten. Gordon described it as a "a dim and narrow pathway … along which but one man could pass at a time."[36] Satisfied, the men returned to camp in the afternoon, but Hotchkiss immediately set out again for the pathway, this time with pioneers—experienced laborers—from Rodes's Division to clear out small trees and build makeshift bridges or walkways over marshy spots. The eve of the battle was dark by the time Hotchkiss and his tired crew finished their work. The trail was ready.[37]

As Hotchkiss rode back to camp, he expected to meet the head of Gordon's column advancing along the trail, but he found the general, his officers, and all their troops waiting in camp—for General Pegram, who was not with his command. Still not convinced of the merit in Gordon's and Hotchkiss's plan, Pegram was again appealing to Early to allow him to attack another part of the Federal line. Early refused, and Pegram at last returned to his men. With his column now complete, Gordon began his secret march at 8 p.m.[38]

They moved silently through the dark forests, stripped of the canteens and loose equipment that gave a marching column its gentle tinkling and clanking music. Couriers had been placed along the route to ensure the marchers made no wrong turns where forks or byways intersected the trail. Gordon was proud of his marching veterans, all of whom felt the solemnity of their work. "With every man, from the commanders of divisions to the brave privates under them, impressed with the gravity of our enterprise, speaking only when necessary and then in whispers, and striving to suppress every sound, the long gray line like a serpent glided noiselessly along the pathway above the precipice."[39]

By another route, Hotchkiss led Kershaw's Division into position at Bowman's Ford on Cedar Creek, just upstream from where Gordon was crossing the North Fork of the Shenandoah. It was 5 a.m., and the topographer's work was done. The affair was now in the hands of the infantrymen. As the Confederates waited in the cold blackness of the woods, they heard a few bugles sound a languid reveille in some of the still-dark Federal camps. A light mist hung over the creek.

At the appointed time, the Southerners splashed into the deep, numbing waters of Cedar Creek and out again into the chilly autumn air on the other bank. Suddenly, the attack was sprung, and the wet Confederates burst forward. Hotchkiss, now a spectator, seemed surprised himself at how easily Kershaw had his men going through the Federals. "In almost a moment he was going up the hill and over the breastworks. A few flashes of musketry, a few shots of artillery, and he had the works, guns and all."[40]

The result of the night march around the Federal flank was stunning. All through the morning, the Confederates pushed the off-balance Northerners from position after position. "Our men," Hotchkiss told Sara, "swept over the works and … cleaned them out completely from their camps, captured twenty pieces of artillery, ambulances, wagons, all the tents of the two corps, in fact gained one of the most complete victories I ever witnessed."[41] The spectacle must have been thrilling to Southern eyes—Early's ragged legions, so badly mauled and embarrassed just a month earlier, now advancing with vigor and vengeance

HOTCHKISS THOUGHT BRIG. GEN. JOHN PEGRAM HAUGHTY AND OVERBEARING IN 1861, AND THE TOPOGRAPHER DID NOT CHANGE HIS OPINION IN 1864.

out of the morning mists, driving their abusers pell mell. "A more splendidly conceived and executed movement I never saw," wrote Hotchkiss.[42]

But these surging Confederates were not the same men, either in body or spirit, who had followed Jackson in the Valley more than two years earlier. Their clothes and shoes were worn out, leaving them ill-protected from the cold autumn air, and their bellies—almost always empty—were tight with hunger. Understandably, many of these men stopped, some for only a few moments, as their lines of battle swept through the riches strewn about the abandoned Federal camps. They grabbed some bacon or biscuits here, some coffee there, dry socks or a clean shirt wherever they could find them. But as more and more men fell out of the ranks, the attack lost impetus.

Sometime before noon, the Confederates had to halt near Middletown to reform lines. Hotchkiss believed that the plan was to continue the assault, but, he told Sara, "so many of our troops had left the ranks to plunder the Yankee camps that it was a long time before it could be done."[43] Hour after hour passed as officers tried to gather their men. Early seemed indisposed to press forward, perhaps thinking the Federals had been defeated and the day won. Gordon, however, pleaded to be allowed to continue the attack, stating that the battle still hung in the balance. The situation remained little changed throughout the afternoon. "Thus we lay until 4 p.m.," wrote Hotchkiss, "making a few efforts to get off the immense captures we had made of artillery and everything else."[44] The delay would prove fatal.

In one of the more dramatic episodes of the war, Sheridan, returning from his conference in Washington, heard the sounds of the battle and rode at a gallop up the Valley Pike from Winchester. He rejoined his army in the late morning, rallied his men, and launched a counterattack. The Federal cavalry swept in on Early's flanks, proving once again that it was superior to Early's horsemen. The Federal infantry showed its mettle and advanced in force, and the combined weight of the Federal attack first cracked, then demolished the Southern brigades that had been victorious just hours before. The Confederate left, Hotchkiss recorded, "was seized with a sudden, unexpected, and unnecessary panic, and gave way, and the whole line did the same thing."[45]

Now it was Early's turn to be stunned as he saw his fast-disintegrating army streaming to the rear, firmly gripped by panic. They ran for miles, the Federal cavalry at their heels. Hundreds of Southerners fell prisoner, but even those who escaped were through with fighting for a while. "We retired over Cedar Creek," Hotchkiss grimly remarked, "more like a mob than an army."[46]

Early was appalled and tried to salvage the situation by setting up a rearguard of cavalry and sending Hotchkiss south to Edinburg to stop the tide of fugitives from the ranks. But the damage was done; his army was effectively destroyed, and at last, the Valley was lost.

In the days following the Battle of Cedar Creek, Early ungenerously blamed the disaster on the men who fell out to plunder rather than on himself and his officers. Hotchkiss recognized that the privates had hurt the cause, but knew as well that the commanding general is responsible for everything that happens in his army. Early had failed at Cedar Creek. "We had the greatest victory of the war in the morning and one of the greatest losses in the evening—and needlessly,"[47] wrote Hotchkiss, who blamed the "disgraceful defeat" on "the delay in pressing the enemy after we got to Middletown." Perhaps suggesting that the magnitude of their success might have startled and confused the oft-beaten Confederates of the Valley District, Early succinctly summed up the battle, "The Yankees got whipped and we got scared."[48]

On the third day after the battle, Hotchkiss boarded a stage for Richmond, having been selected by Early to carry news of the fight to Lee.[49] Early, recognizing at last his own failure on the day of battle, ordered his messenger "not to tell General Lee that we ought to have advanced in the morning at Middletown, for, said he, we ought to have done so."[50]

The Battle of Cedar Creek marked the end of Confederate viability in the Valley and signaled that the days of the fledgling nation were numbered. Lee could not indefinitely hold Richmond and Petersburg now that his supply lines from the Valley and the west were exposed. The Army of Northern Virginia would sometime soon—perhaps in weeks, perhaps months—be forced to evacuate Richmond, and then it would be only a matter of time before the legions of Federals closed in from all directions to bring Lee's army to bay. It was a bleak prospect for devotees of the dream of Southern independence.

Hotchkiss, however, kept his spirits up, and tried to keep up Sara's as well, by filling his letters with optimism, but it is difficult to know where his natural buoyancy ended and his efforts to cheer Sara began. If genuine, his hopefulness seemed to be fully realized self-delusion. Less than two weeks after the disaster at Cedar Creek, he told Sara that "all things wear a cheerful aspect,"[51] and later wrote, "I still think all 'Things work together for good' to indicate a speedy conclusion of the war and if we are able to keep, as heretofore, to the end of this campaign. We shall not be troubled by them another year."[52] He accepted the reality that the Federal successes had done much to bolster Lincoln's chances of reelection and that the hope of a negotiated peace with a new administration was fading. "I do not see that any good can come to us from this Yankee election," Hotchkiss wrote on the day of the vote, "and yet I long to know how it has gone; to know if the majority of the people have approved the course of 'Old Abe' for the last four years and desire a continuance of the same."[53] But he could not bring himself to believe that the Northern people supported the policies of Lincoln, and he convinced himself that if Lincoln won it would be dishonestly. "I do not think there will be a real election," Hotchkiss wrote. "So many have been sent from the army and from government employ to use the influence, patronage and means of corruption at their disposal that they will carry the election by fraud, if no other way."[54]

Hotchkiss's self-delusion is understandable. He, along with most Confederates, was wrestling with the ever-growing likelihood of defeat and the death of hopes and dreams of more than three years. Southerners had believed so firmly that God was on their side that they had always

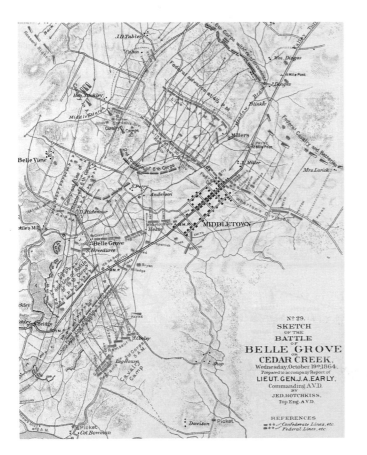

THE U.S. WAR DEPARTMENT BORROWED MANY OF HOTCHKISS'S MAPS AFTER THE WAR AND MADE LITHOGRAPHS FOR THE *Official Records Atlas*. IN THE PROCESS, AN ARTIST COPIED THE MAPS ONTO A STONE USING WAX OR GREASE PENCILS. A NEW YORK CONTRACT LITHOGRAPHER HANDLED MOST OF THE HOTCHKISS MAPS, INCLUDING THIS DETAIL OF THE BATTLE OF CEDAR CREEK. THUS THE *Atlas* ONLY INDICATES HOTCHKISS'S ABILITIES AS A SURVEYOR AND TOPOGRAPHER, NOT AS A CARTOGRAPHER.

Hotchkiss stopped in Georgetown to call on his aged friend the Rev. Beverly Tucker Lacy, who had been chaplain on Jackson's staff for the final four or five months of the general's life. It had been Lacy who had ridden with Hotchkiss through the forests of Chancellorsville as Jackson made his flank march, and it had been Lacy who had helped bury Boswell. The chaplain had continued to serve at Second Corps headquarters after Jackson's death, and

Hotchkiss came to value him as a close friend, especially admiring Lacy's abilities as a sermonist. Now old and partially paralyzed, Lacy was, according to Hotchkiss, delighted to see his old friend, and the two spent an hour recalling comrades and the adventures of their service together. Lacy pleased Hotchkiss by telling of a conversation he had had with Jackson shortly after joining the staff in December 1862. The general spoke of each member of the staff, describing for the chaplain the characteristics and qualifications of the men he thought composed "the best and most efficient staff in the army." Lacy remembered that Jackson had especially commended "Hawks, his Commissary, Harman, his Quartermaster, Pendleton, his Adjutant General and Hotchkiss his Topographical Engineer. Of the last named he remarked that his skill in acquiring and communicating a knowledge of the topography of the country was very remarkable, surpassing that of anyone he had ever known; he also commented on his unceasing diligence and energy in discharging the duties of his office and in the execution of difficult duties entrusted to him."[3] Despite its being thirty years old and coming to him second hand, this compliment from the great Jackson, probably the man he admired most in all his life, obviously thrilled Hotchkiss. He knew Jackson had approved of his work, but the reticent general was sparing with personal compliments, and Hotchkiss could never know that the general admired and appreciated his abilities so much that he would drop his piety to boast of his topographer to a newcomer.

Hotchkiss's plan to write history almost suffered a fatal blow soon after the war, when the U.S. war department demanded that he relinquish his map collection. He protested that the charts were private property and that he would not surrender them, though he would gladly allow them to be copied for the sake of history. The government persisted in its claim to what they considered Confederate documents, and Hotchkiss decided to go to the top with his case. He took his maps to Washington and met with General Grant, whom the Virginian found cooperative. The two men soon came to an agreement: Hotchkiss would keep his maps and copy for a fee several that Grant selected as being of especial value. The government would bother Hotchkiss no more, and would, in fact, seek his help in future projects to record the history of the war. A large excerpt from his journal for the period covering the 1864 Valley Campaign was printed in *The War of the Rebellion, Official Records of the Union and Confederate Armies*, the government's documentary history of the conflict.[4]

Hotchkiss organized the letters, official reports, newspaper clippings, and copious notes he compiled so they could be found when needed. He created what he called his "War Book," a large, bound scrapbook full of correspondence and recollections, all catalogued for easy reference. Still not satisfied with the state of his raw materials, he had almost all of his correspondence about the war, including the scores of letters he had written to Sara, typed, which could not have been an easy or inexpensive task in the 1880s or 1890s. He supervised the typing and corrected the proofs, signing letters as he finished them.

But the struggle to stay financially afloat took up most of the time that might have been devoted to writing his great book. In 1897, he told a friend "The prolonged stagnation in business here has made it very difficult for me to give attention to anything but caring for my mineral properties and striving, but so far with little success, for their development. In my business experience of 50 years I have never known such unfavorable conditions as we have had for the past 4 or 5 years. Soon as a change comes I hope to take up the memoirs that I have so long had in mind."[5] But the book was never far from his mind. When a friend asked how the volume was progressing, Hotchkiss wrote, " 'The cares of the world and the deceitfulness of riches' have interfered very seriously with my intentions but not with my garnering, constantly, a large amount of information that I can well work into such a book."[6]

The demands of business notwithstanding, Hotchkiss was by the late 1890s deeply involved in a historical project that consumed much free time. Col. G. F. R. Henderson, a British army officer, was engaged in writing a biography of Jackson. Through a roundabout route of mutual acquaintances, Henderson came into correspondence with Hotchkiss. The colonel was seeking the assistance of knowledgeable men who could read and comment with authority on his manuscript. Hotchkiss, ever agreeable and willing to help, was keenly interested in seeing that his friend and former commander be served well, and he agreed to assist Henderson. So began a long and painstaking correspondence that has been invaluable to historians for decades.

As Henderson finished writing each chapter, he sent it to Hotchkiss, who read it and made notes and criticisms by inserting a number by a word or sentence on the manuscript and then writing his comments out on a separate sheet, keyed to the manuscript by the inserted number. An excerpt from his comments on Henderson's chapter on the 1862 Maryland Campaign illustrates that Hotchkiss spared no energy nor let pass any ambiguity in his review of the manuscript: "(58) As a rule all the slopes ascending from the Antietam in both directions are very steep. The roads approach that stream by ravines cutting these slopes. (59) Sharpsburg was a very old town on a very important highway leading to the West and it was as well known to the postal authorities of the United States as to those of Maryland. I would say east of the hamlet rather than above although mainly on a ridge, but not entirely so. Lee's stand was on a limestone rock a natural outcrop. There was no granite there. (60) The Dunkard church was a brick building either painted or whitewashed I am not certain which. Be sure and spell it Dunkard. There was no large copse standing in a field of waving maize. I would revise these statements by the correct map which I recently sent you. …(62) The stone bridges were very substantially built and could not have been destroyed without special preparations with drilling tools, etc., and there was no time for that. The only practicable ford was one some distance below the Burnside bridge by which Burnside's flanking party turned the Confederate right late in the afternoon of the 17th. (63) It is hardly correct to say that Lee's right rested on the Antietam as he had a cavalry force some distance south of the force that defended the Burnside bridge. I do not know what point you mean when you say that east of these woods was a commanding knoll. I have underscored here some words for attention."[7]

And even when Hotchkiss was through raking over each chapter, he was still not satisfied that history—which was for him absolute, incontrovertible fact—had been completely served. He often sent chapters to Dr. Hunter McGuire for comment and occasionally to Dr. James Power Smith. He checked the details with Dr. Robert Louis Dabney, then living in Texas, and Col. Thomas Munford, who served in Jackson's cavalry. He wrote to Confederate generals Lafayette McLaws, John B. Gordon, Fitzhugh Lee, and Federal general John Gibbon, who had been with Jackson at West Point. No detail was too small to be checked. Henderson well appreciated what Hotchkiss could contribute to the quality of his book, and wrote that to him, "whatever of value these volumes may contain is largely due. Not only did he correct the topographical descriptions, but he investigated most carefully many disputed points; and in procuring the evidence of eyewitnesses, and thus enabling me to check and amplify the statements of previous writers, he was indefatigable."[8]

So strong was Hotchkiss's respect for absolute accuracy that he openly locked horns with former colleagues when he found reason to question their remembrances.

One especially interesting disagreement came about when Henderson began receiving help from Henry Kyd Douglas, a Marylander who had served for a time on Jackson's staff. When Douglas had joined the headquarters staff, he was barely into his twenties and filled with the enthusiasm and energy of youth. The men at headquarters grew fond of him, including Hotchkiss, who, in April 1862, described him to Sara as "one of your wide awake smart young men—I like him."[9]

But by the 1890s, some of Jackson's men had changed their minds. Hotchkiss wrote to a friend in 1896 that "Douglas was a brave and gallant soldier full of ambition and I never heard anything to his discredit in connection with any duty assigned to him and … I would not say anything derogatory to his character," but added that "since the war he has made himself liable to criticism by writing numerous articles full of romance particularly in reference to his own deeds claiming that his statements are reliable history when plenty of witnesses can be found to question these statements, as some of them have done for the sake of the truth of history."[10] Jubal Early wrote to Hotchkiss that "from what I have heard about Kyd Douglas, he is one of those men who is disposed to claim a great deal for himself."[11] Hunter McGuire was less diplomatic in his letters to Hotchkiss and clearly considered the Marylander a humbug when it came to writing history. When Hotchkiss contested one of Douglas's claims about his duties in the Maryland Campaign, the latter became indignant and "stoutly contended, as usual, that he knew what he was writing about." Hotchkiss gracefully let the matter drop, but he was on firm ground in his argument, for a document contradicting Douglas's story had been published in the *Official Records*. The engineer finally alerted Henderson to the need for extra care when using anything from the Marylander's pen. "Pardon me for again warning you about quoting from Douglas," he cautioned. "He shoots with a long bow and generally misses the mark."[12] The episode with Douglas saddened Hotchkiss, for he still thought well of the man, writing to a friend, "I not only have no dislike of him, except for his bombastic ways, [but] our relations have always been of a friendly character."[13]

Hotchkiss was no less honest about other veterans, regardless of their rank, and he freely passed judgment on the service and postwar claims of fellow Confederates. He spoke well of Early and Ewell, but was harsh in his criticism of A. P. Hill, with whom, of course, Jackson had feuded. Gen. James Longstreet, who had also directed barbed words toward Jackson during the war, published his memoirs long after the war and loosed a torrent of criticism at Jackson, Lee, and other former comrades. Hotchkiss and McGuire were quick to come to the defense of their commander's reputation, and both men were among the strongest critics of Longstreet's bitter book.

But Hotchkiss did not enjoy the infighting after the war. He much preferred to talk over old memories with friends with whom he had served closely and was not in disagreement. He also realized that a great many people would like to hear his own recollections, and he went on the lecture circuit. He spoke on the war all over the eastern part of the country, delighting audiences from Boston to New Orleans. "The Valley Campaign of 1862," "Topography in War," and "The Battle of the Wilderness" were among his subjects, and all his talks were illustrated with map sketches made extemporaneously on a portable blackboard he carried with him. Everywhere, whether at Harvard, Princeton, Washington, D.C., or Lexington, Virginia, his listeners gave him high praise for both his content and his relaxed style, polished smooth by decades in the classroom. He enjoyed the talking immensely, as he always had, never having been able to correct what Jackson had considered his "great fault."

When Confederate veterans began organizing frater-

COLONEL THOMAS MUNFORD SERVED IN MANY CAMPAIGNS WITH HOTCHKISS. AFTER THE WAR, THE TWO OLD SOLDIERS KEPT UP A LONG AND SENTIMENTAL CORRESPONDENCE.

nal groups to support each other and perpetuate the memory of their fallen comrades, Hotchkiss was in the forefront, forming, with others, the Stonewall Jackson Camp of the United Confederate Veterans in Staunton. He was known as "Major Hotchkiss." He had never been commissioned in the Confederate army, and his wartime rank of captain had been temporary and largely honorary. But most old soldiers of that war were "promoted" after the close of hostilities by their comrades or respectful neighbors, and Hotchkiss was no different.

As Hotchkiss passed into his late sixties, he began spending more and more time trying to pin down details of those brilliant and exciting times three decades earlier when he rode beside one of the great figures in military history. Many of the events and images had faded and become muddled in his memory, yet others remained sharp and clear. His friend, Col. Tom Munford, knew the experience, telling Hotchkiss that war scenes were still so vivid to him that "some of them haunt me whenever the Valley is mentioned." But it was the blurred memories that troubled Hotchkiss, and he devoted much of his energy in his last years to trying to unmuddy the waters. "The time is so long past, and the scenes so far off," wrote Munford, "it is important, when you and I discuss these old scenes, that we have on our thinking caps."[14] The long, lingering glances over his shoulder as he neared the end of his journey brought him bittersweet memories of old times with McGuire and Smith and Munford, who once told Hotchkiss that writing about the Army of Northern Virginia was "writing family matters. We all belong to the same family."[15]

In June 1897, Hotchkiss was far from well, but he still had the energy and enthusiasm to want to write. Progress on his memoirs was slow. "I have hitherto done nothing more than at times to dictate my remembrances of certain battles and marches, etc.," he told Henderson in March 1897.[16] But that month he embarked upon a most ambitious attempt to write "family matters." Gen. Clement Evans, one of the three officers with whom Hotchkiss had climbed Massanutten Mountain prior to the Battle of Cedar Creek, was editor of a series of publications called *Confederate Military History*. Each volume in the series laid out aspects of the wartime history of a single Confederate state. Evans signed Hotchkiss to a contract to write the volume for Virginia, which would be perhaps the most significant volume in the series, considering the great amount of fighting concentrated there. Hotchkiss was to complete this volume—40,000 to 60,000 words—by the close of December 1897, a period of seven months. He

went to the project with a will and wrote furiously, but not surprisingly, he missed the deadline. What is surprising is that he and Evans ever thought that an undertaking of that size could be completed in such a short time. Hotchkiss was still at it a year after his initial deadline, and was revising the manuscript up until his final illness. He did not live to see the book published.[17]

In his final year, Hotchkiss was at last restricted in his travel by illness. He spent much of his time in The Oaks, corresponding with old Confederates, sharing with them the emotions only they could understand. With much regret, he declined the invitation of one group of Valley Army veterans, who planned a commemoration for the thirty-sixth anniversary of the Battle of McDowell because he was too infirm to travel to their mountain meeting place. But he assured them of his good will and fond wishes, writing, "My comrades, surviving to brighter days but glorying in even sad memories, … believe me yours, ever faithful to the bonds of 1861-1865, even as we are now faithful in the cause of our common country."[18]

Hotchkiss's health declined steadily through the latter part of 1898, and in January 1899, he took to his bed. If he saw the end of his life approaching, the contemplation of death engendered neither terror nor regret. He had consciously lived his entire adult life in preparation for his death, and looked forward to its coming not with trepidation but with joy. "We are much accustomed to look upon death as an enemy, and not as a friend," he once wrote, "we do not consider that he alone can open for us the gates of heaven." He believed death was sorrowful if the departing spirit was unprepared to meet judgment, but if one lived his life ever mindful that he would be called into account, if he honored the word of God and endeavored to create, as

Hotchkiss had once put it, "a mortal life … fit for putting on an immortal being,"[19] then death was not an end, but a beginning. In an essay written at Mossy Creek in 1849, when he was twenty years old, Hotchkiss articulated the philosophy that would give his life focus and purpose, a life not dominated by apprehension, but by a vigorous pursuit of eternal happiness. "We should not fear death, but strive to have boldness of heart that at his coming we may welcome him and exclaim, 'O death where is thy victory, O Grave where is thy sting.'" He asked the Lord for strength, praying "that I may spend the time allotted to me … on earth so that when the final hour shall come, when thy summons bids my soul to attend the judgment seat, O may I meet it with joy! may I meet it prepared! and having a well grounded hope of a life of endless felicity in thy kingdom."[20] He died at 11 p.m., January 17, 1899, just a month and a half past his seventieth birthday.[21]

Dr. James Power Smith, Jackson's former aide, said the words of benediction at Hotchkiss's funeral. It was most fitting that a member of Jackson's military family paid tribute to the man who had done so much to help secure Stonewall's success in war and reputation in peace. History would show that Jackson would have been a different general without Hotchkiss, and the war would have been a different war had Jackson advanced less surely in all his movements.

But on that January day, as Dr. Smith spoke above the grave of his friend on a hillside in Staunton, such earthly concerns as war and fame mattered little. Now it was just Jed Hotchkiss, husband, father, and Christian. He had walked with some of the foremost men of his age and had not only earned their respect and trust but had been an indispensable element in their achievements. For many men, that fleeting fame would have been the defining accomplishment of their lives, but it is the measure of Jed Hotchkiss that his professional achievements were little

more than temporal baubles to him. Though gratifying, whatever success he had enjoyed in his earthly endeavors was, as General Jackson had often reminded him, due to the benevolence of a kind Providence.

Hotchkiss left an impressive record of professional achievement, but just as noteworthy, and perhaps even more remarkable, are his personal attainments. His extraordinary strength of spirit—his energy and faith and self-discipline—had supported him through the most difficult time in the nation's history. He had survived when others had succumbed, many simply surrendering the will to continue struggling against the adversity of the war. And it is pleasant to believe, as Hotchkiss did, that it was God's will that he had lived, perhaps to touch more young lives, to help rebuild his state, to pass on to new generations the stories of courage and suffering and to enlighten more spirits with his confident optimism.

Rooted deep in his faith that God was in control, Hotchkiss's positive attitude, his utter refusal to be dominated by worries or negative thoughts, was his greatest strength. He knew that all one needed to be happy was the desire to be happy; that one had only to believe that all would be well to make it so. "We are the arbiters of our own conditions more than is usually supposed," he wrote to Sara, "we are happy or miserable, and we make those around us happy or miserable, at our own will or pleasure."[22] Misery, fear, and the horror of countless battlefields were powerless against him because, in the end, he denied them power.

And when death finally came, Jed Hotchkiss embraced it, confident that it was his reward for a life of duty and service. He had lived to some purpose. He, like the trees and plants of the earth that he had studied so intently and loved so well, had given life and sustenance to other living things and, with the passing of his season, left the earth richer, stronger, and more beautiful.

ENDNOTES

NOTES TO CHAPTER ONE

1. Journal, March 24, 26, 1862, Jedediah Hotchkiss Papers, Manuscript Division, Library of Congress. See also "Campaigns of 1861, '62," in Box 1, Hotchkiss Papers.
2. Recollections of Judge Charles S. Bundy, originally published in *The Echo* (Windsor, Broome County, New York), quoted in Charles H. Osterhout, *Stonewall Jackson's Map-Maker (Jed Hotchkiss)*, 1978, 89.
3. Jedediah Hotchkiss, "The Tuscarora Indians," *The Echo* (December 1894).
4. Journal, various entries, July-September 1845, Hotchkiss Papers, microfilm reel 1, frames 2-13.
5. Ibid.
6. Ibid., 1846-47, Hotchkiss Papers.
7. Ibid., April 29, 1848.
8. 1850 U.S. Population Census, Augusta County, Virginia, National Archives, 934-225. The census returns for Augusta County show nine Forrers age eighteen or under. Seventeen people, including Hotchkiss, were counted as officially part of the Forrer household, but some of these, judging by their ages, may have been employees at the ironworks.
9. Journal, March 21, 1848, Hotchkiss Papers.
10. Ibid., May 24, 1848.
11. Ibid., March 28, 1848.
12. Miscellaneous entries in Journal, May 1850.
13. The name on Hotchkiss's daughter's headstone is spelled "Nellie," but at least in her early years, Hotchkiss invariably spelled his daughter's name "Nelly." Hotchkiss's spelling is used here throughout.
14. Journal, March 20, 1862, Hotchkiss Papers.
15. 1860 U.S. Population Census, Augusta County, Virginia, National Archives, 1333:941.
16. Hotchkiss Papers, 50:433. The lecture "Live for Some Purpose" was delivered in October 1860 at Branch Meeting House for the Union Presbyterian Church Sunday school.
17. Journal, January 2, 1865, Hotchkiss Papers. See also Jedediah Hotchkiss, *Make Me a Map of the Valley*, ed.

Archie P. McDonald (Dallas, Texas: SMU Press, 1973), xxii, xxviii, 318.
18. Eighth Census of the United States (1860).
19. Joseph A. Waddell, *Annals of Augusta County, Virginia, from 1726 to 1871* (Staunton, Virginia: 1902), 455.
20. Letter printed in Jedediah Hotchkiss, *Confederate Military History*, vol. 3, *Virginia* (Atlanta, Georgia: 1899), 38. (Hereafter Hotchkiss, *Virginia*).
21. Ibid.
22. Waddell, *Annals*, 456.
23. Jedediah Hotchkiss to his wife, Sara, August 11, 1861, Hotchkiss Papers, 4:724.

NOTES TO CHAPTER TWO

1. Hotchkiss to Sara, June 27, 1862, Hotchkiss Papers, 4:717.
2. A macadamized road was a thoroughfare, usually a highway or turnpike, with an all-weather surface of broken (crushed or chipped) stone and provisions made for drainage. The stone would be laid on the road loosely and liberally so that over time, with the passage of traffic, the surface would be compressed and become solid and impervious to water. The process drew its name from its inventor, Scottish surveyor John Loudin McAdam (1756-1836). The Valley Turnpike in the Shenandoah Valley was macadamized and became one of the more important and heavily traveled roads in Virginia. See *The Dictionary of National Biography* (Oxford University Press), 12:395-97.
3. Hotchkiss to Sara, July 5, 1861, Hotchkiss Papers, 4:718.
4. Ibid.
5. For excellent discussions of the tools and practices of military topography in the age before aerial mapping, see Herbert M. Wilson, *Topographic Surveying* (New York: John Wiley & Sons, 1905), 395-403; H.A. Musham, *The Technique of the Terrain* (New York: Reinhold Publishing Corp, 1944), 7-9, 22-23, 62-63, 82-83, 94-99, 165-79; Robert C. Matson, *Elements of Mapping* (Houghton, Michigan: Michigan College of Mining and Engineering, 1940), 15-20.

6. Hotchkiss to Sara, October 2, 1864, Hotchkiss Papers, 4:792.
7. Ibid., July 30, 1861, 4:723.
8. Ibid., July 7, 1861, 4:719.
9. Ibid., July 5, 1861, 4:718.
10. Ibid., July 7, 1861, 4:719.
11. Ibid.
12. Ibid.
13. Ibid.
14. Ibid., August 4, 1861, 4:724.
15. Ibid., August 16, 1861, 4:725.
16. Ibid., August 4, 1861, 4:724.
17. Ibid., August 11, 1861, 4:725.
18. Ibid., September 3, 1861, 4:727.
19. Ibid., August 11, 1861, 4:725.
20. *The War of the Rebellion: Official Records of the Union and Confederate Armies* (Washington, D.C.: 1880-1901) series I, vol. 2, 261-64. (Hereafter OR).
21. Hotchkiss, *Virginia*, 50.
22. Musham, *Technique of the Terrain*, 178.
23. Lilley rose to the rank of brigadier general in the Confederate army, and he and Hotchkiss served in close proximity throughout the war. Lilley was wounded three times in an engagement near Winchester, Virginia, in July 1864, and lost an arm.
24. OR, I, 2, 266
25. Ibid., 261-64.
26. Ibid.
27. Hotchkiss to Sara, July 15, 1861, Hotchkiss Papers, 4:719.
28. OR, I, 2, 261-64.
29. Despite his performance at Rich Mountain, Pegram rose steadily through the Confederate Army to the rank of brigadier general. He was killed in battle two months before Lee's surrender in 1865.
30. Hotchkiss to Sara, July 18, 1861, Hotchkiss Papers, 4:720.
31. Hotchkiss to Sara, July 18, 1861, Hotchkiss Papers, 4:720.
32. Hotchkiss Papers, 49:133.
33. For an excellent discussion of the accomplishments of Crozet, Boye, Wood, and other pioneers of Virginian cartography, see E. M. Sanchez-Saavedra, *A Description of the Country* (Richmond: The Virginia State Library, 1975).
34. Hotchkiss to Sara, July 30, 1861, Hotchkiss Papers, 4:722.
35. Ibid., 4:723.
36. Ibid.

37. Hotchkiss to Fitz Lee, October 22, 1891, Hotchkiss Papers, 49:355.
38. Hotchkiss, *Virginia*, 3:156.
39. Hotchkiss to Fitz Lee, October 22, 1891, Hotchkiss Papers, 49:354-55.
40. Hotchkiss to Sara, August 11, 1861, Hotchkiss Papers, 4:725.
41. Hotchkiss to Fitz Lee, October 22, 1891, Hotchkiss Papers, 49:355.
42. Hotchkiss to Sara, August 16, 1861, Hotchkiss Papers, 4:726.
43. Hotchkiss to Fitz Lee, October 22, 1891, Hotchkiss Papers, 49:357-58.
44. Ibid.
45. Ibid.
46. Hotchkiss to Sara, September 3, 1861, Hotchkiss Papers, 4:727.
47. Hotchkiss to his brother Nelson, September 18, 1861, Hotchkiss Papers, 4:851.
48. Ibid.

NOTES TO CHAPTER THREE

1. Richard Taylor, *Destruction and Reconstruction: Personal Experiences of the Late War*, ed. Richard Harwell (New York: Longmans, Green, and Co., 1955), 45.
2. Journal, March 17, 1862, Hotchkiss Papers.
3. Hotchkiss to Sara, March 21, 1862, Hotchkiss Papers, 4:729.
4. Hotchkiss Papers, 39:244ff; Hotchkiss to Sara, April 14, 1862, Hotchkiss Papers 4:736.
5. Hotchkiss to Sara, March 21, 1862, Hotchkiss Papers, 4:729.
6. "Reminiscence of General John Gibbon," Hotchkiss Papers, 39:199.
7. "Testimonial of J. R. Graham," Hotchkiss Papers, 49:231.
8. Journal, May 13, 1863, Hotchkiss Papers. This incident parallels an act by Gen. George S. Patton in the Second World War, for which he was severely censured. Patton was a devoted student of Jackson's career and declared he modeled some of his campaigns after Jackson's.
9. OR, I, 5, 1053.
10. William Allan, *History of the Campaign of Gen. T. J. (Stonewall) Jackson in the Shenandoah Valley of Virginia* (Philadelphia: J. B. Lippincott & Co., 1880), 46.
11. Ibid., 45, 47.
12. Journal, March 24, 1862, Hotchkiss Papers.

13. Hotchkiss to Sara, March 25, 1862, Hotchkiss Papers, 4:730.
14. Ibid., March 26, 1862, 4:731.
15. Journal, March 26, 1862, Hotchkiss Papers
16. Ibid.
17. Ibid. The teamster assigned to Hotchkiss was William Humphreys, who would drive the topographical wagon for almost the entire war.
18. Journal, March 28, 1862, Hotchkiss Papers.
19. Hotchkiss to Sara, March 30, 1862, Hotchkiss Papers, 4:733.
20. Ibid., April 4, 1862, 4:734.
21. Ibid.
22. Hotchkiss to William L. Chase, March 28, 1892, general correspondence, folder on Gen. Thomas J. Jackson, Hotchkiss Papers, 51:518.
23. Hotchkiss to Sara, April 14, 1862, Hotchkiss Papers, 4:736.
24. Journal, April 1, 1862, Hotchkiss Papers.
25. Ibid., August 17, 1862.
26. After the war, Hotchkiss compiled a substantial portfolio on Jackson's staff, including detailed biographical sketches of most of the principal members. See Hotchkiss Papers, 39:370ff.
27. Hotchkiss to Sara, April 4, 1862, Hotchkiss Papers, 4:736.
28. William G. Bean, *Stonewall's Man: Sandie Pendleton* (Chapel Hill: University of North Carolina Press, 1959), 7-11, 20, 35-36, 45.
29. "Biographical Sketch by Dr. Stuart McGuire" (Hunter H. McGuire's son), Hotchkiss Papers, 39:263ff.
30. Hunter H. McGuire to Hotchkiss, May 19, 1896, Hotchkiss Papers, 34:111.
31. Hotchkiss to Sara, April 14, April 4, 1862, Hotchkiss Papers, 4:736.
32. William G. Bean, "Captain James Keith Boswell," *Virginia Cavalcade* (Winter 1970): 30-35.
33. Hotchkiss to Sara, April 14, 1862, Hotchkiss Papers, 4:736-37; copy of fragment from diary of James Keith Boswell, February 9, 1863, Hotchkiss Papers, 51:374.
34. Bean, *Stonewall's Man*, 84.
35. Henry Kyd Douglas, *I Rode With Stonewall*, ed. Fletcher M. Green (Chapel Hill: University of North Carolina Press, 1940), 52.
36. John A. Harman to his brother, May 15, 1862, Hotchkiss Papers, 39:270?

(number illegible). The conversation Harman relates took place following the army's move to McDowell.
37. Hotchkiss to Sara, April 14, 1862, Hotchkiss Papers, 4:736.
38. Journal, April 14, 1862, Hotchkiss Papers.
39. Hotchkiss Papers, 39:274-76, 39:298.
40. Hotchkiss to Sara, April 4, 14, 1862, Hotchkiss Papers, 4:736.
41. "Maj. A. M. Garber's Anecdotes," Hotchkiss Papers, 39:274.
42. Harman to his brother, May 15, 1862, Hotchkiss Papers, 39:270? (number illegible).
43. "Garber's Anecdotes," Hotchkiss Papers, 39:274.
44. "Recollection of A. Hawks," Hotchkiss Papers, 39:366.
45. "Garber's Anecdotes," Hotchkiss Papers, 39:274.
46. Ibid., 39:275.
47. Harman to his brother, April 18, 1862, Hotchkiss Papers, 39:270? (number illegible).
48. Hotchkiss to Sara, April 24, 1862, Hotchkiss Papers, 39:739.
49. Ibid., April 20, 1862, 4:737.
50. Ibid., 4:738.
51. Dabney letters quoted in Howard McKnight Wilson, *The Tinkling Spring, Headwater of Freedom: A Study of the Church and Her People, 1732-1952* (Fishersville, Virginia: Tinkling Spring and Hermitage Presbyterian Churches, 1954), 283.
52. Ibid., January 15, 1851, 284-85.
53. Hotchkiss Papers, 49:468-69.
54. Journal, April 30, 1862, Hotchkiss Papers.
55. Hotchkiss Papers, 49:468-69; Journal, April 30, 1862.
56. Diary of Lt. John W. Mauk, Company K, 10th Virginia Infantry, in Harry M. Strickler, *A Short History of Page County, Virginia* (Richmond, Virginia: Dietz Press, 1952), 177.
57. Journal, May 8, 1862, Hotchkiss Papers.
58. Hotchkiss Papers, 49:180.
59. Mark M. Boatner III, *The Civil War Dictionary* (New York: David McKay, 1959) 532.
60. Hotchkiss Papers, 49:180.
61. Hotchkiss to Sara, May 9, 1862, Hotchkiss Papers, 4:741.
62. Hotchkiss Papers, 49:179-80.
63. Ibid., 49:180.
64. Allan, *Shenandoah Valley*, 80.

65. Ibid.
66. Journal, May 20, 1862, Hotchkiss Papers.
67. Hotchkiss to Sara, May 26, 1862, Hotchkiss Papers, 4:742.
68. Ibid.
69. Mauk diary, Strickler, *Page County*, 179.
70. Hotchkiss to Sara, May 26, 1862, Hotchkiss Papers, 4:742.
71. OR I, 12, pt. 1, 708.
72. Ibid., 720.
73. Ibid., 708.
74. Hotchkiss Papers, 39:366.
75. Journal, May 31, 1862, Hotchkiss Papers.
76. Hotchkiss Papers, 49:180ff.
77. Ibid.
78. Hotchkiss to S. J. C. Moore, September 8, 1896, Hotchkiss Papers, 34:212.
79. Harman to his brother, June 5, 1862, Hotchkiss Papers, 39:270? (number illegible).
80. Hotchkiss to Nelson, June 4, 1862, Hotchkiss Papers, 4:798.
81. Journal, June 6, 1862, Hotchkiss Papers.
82. Ibid., June 8, 1862.
83. Ibid., June 9, 1862.
84. Allan, *Shenandoah Valley*, 165-66.

NOTES TO CHAPTER FOUR

1. Hotchkiss to Chase, March 28, 1892, Jackson folder, Hotchkiss Papers, 51:518.
2. Ibid.
3. Boswell to Hotchkiss, July 11, 1862, Hotchkiss Papers, 4:438.
4. Journal, July 14-15, 1862, Hotchkiss Papers.
5. Hotchkiss to R. L. Dabney, April 6, 1896, Hotchkiss Papers, 34:50.
6. Hotchkiss to Sara, July 22, 1862, Hotchkiss Papers, 4:744.
7. Ibid., August 3, 1862, 4:745.
8. Ibid., August 9, 1862, 4:746.
9. Hotchkiss to Nelson, August 14, 1862, Hotchkiss Papers, 4:800.
10. Journal, August 10, 1862, Hotchkiss Papers.
11. Hotchkiss to Nelson, August 14, 1862, Hotchkiss Papers, 4:801.
12. Hotchkiss to Chase, March 28, 1892, Jackson folder, Hotchkiss Papers, 51:518.
13. Journal, August 13, 1862, Hotchkiss Papers.
14. Hotchkiss to Chase, March 28, 1892, Jackson folder, Hotchkiss Papers, 51:518.

15. Hotchkiss to Sara, August 16, 1862, Hotchkiss Papers, 4:746.
16. Ibid., September 8, 1862, 4:747.
17. Hotchkiss to Nelson, September 8, 1862, Hotchkiss Papers, 4:747.
18. Hotchkiss to Sara, September 21, 1862, Hotchkiss Papers, 4:749.
19. Ibid., September 8, 1862, 4:747.
20. Journal, September 5, 1862, Hotchkiss Papers.
21. Hotchkiss to Sara, September 8, 1862, Hotchkiss Papers, 4:747.
22. Journal, September 6, 1862, Hotchkiss Papers.
23. Hotchkiss to Sara, September 8, 1862, Hotchkiss Papers, 4:748.
24. Hotchkiss to Hunter H. McGuire, January 25, 1897; Journal, December 9, 1862, Hotchkiss Papers. This hat had shielded Jackson's brow all through the Valley Campaign and the other fights in Virginia. Hotchkiss was later uncertain as to whether he bought the new hat in Frederick or Martinsburg, but he was certain that Jackson wore it until December 1862, when Mrs. Jackson gave her husband a new cap. On December 9, 1862, Hotchkiss wrote in his journal that Jackson had remembered the cap and had asked for it. "I took it to him and he put it on, remarking that it fitted him better than any other cap he had ever had, but it was no longer fit to wear and he thought of having another one made like it. I told him if he was going to have it cut up I wanted a button from it as a souvenir of what it had seen. We then conversed awhile on other topics. When I rose to depart he said: 'I reckon you may have the cap.' I thanked him for it and took it to my tent where S. Howell Brown … begged earnestly for one of the buttons that fastened on the strap, and I gave him one."
25. Hotchkiss Papers, 39:248-52. George Junkin became a captain in Company E, 25th Virginia Cavalry, was wounded twice, and survived the war to become a judge and the father of twelve children.
26. Hotchkiss to Sara, September 8, 1862, Hotchkiss Papers, 4:748.
27. Ibid., September 17, 1862, 4:748.
28. Ibid.
29. Journal, September 17, 1862, Hotchkiss Papers.
30. G. F. R. Henderson, *Stonewall Jackson*

and the American Civil War, (New York: Grosset and Dunlap, 1943), 524.
31. Journal, September 19, 1862, Hotchkiss Papers. The canal Hotchkiss mentions is the Chesapeake and Ohio Canal on the Maryland side of the Potomac.
32. Hotchkiss to Sara, September 21, 1862, Hotchkiss Papers, 4:748.
33. Hotchkiss to Nelson, September 28, 1862, Hotchkiss Papers, 4:805.
34. Ibid., 4:804.

NOTES TO CHAPTER FIVE

1. Journal, October 8, 1862, Hotchkiss Papers.
2. Ibid., September 29, 1862.
3. Hotchkiss Papers, 49:136.
4. Journal, September 29, 1862, Hotchkiss Papers.
5. Allan to Hotchkiss, November 20, 1866, Hotchkiss Papers, 49:210.
6. Various letters to Sara, Hotchkiss Papers, 4:749-50.
7. Hotchkiss to Sara, October 26, 1862, Hotchkiss Papers, 4:750.
8. Journal, November 20, 1862, Hotchkiss Papers. A small irony in the incident is that Macon Jordan was the intoxicated officer who so completely lost control of his men on a bridge-burning expedition led by Hotchkiss during the Valley Campaign.
9. Hotchkiss to Nelson, September 28, 1862, Hotchkiss Papers, 4:803; Journal, October 19, 25, 1862; Hotchkiss to Nelson, November 19, 1862, 4:805.
10. Hotchkiss thought he might have been mustered into Confederate service with the Augusta County militia on March 23, 1862, but he could not clearly recall the facts after the war. Whether he was technically a private is not clear; Jackson officially treated him as a civilian.
11. Journal, November 2, 1862, Hotchkiss Papers.
12. Hotchkiss to Sara, November 12, 1862, Hotchkiss Papers, 4:751.
13. Archie P. McDonald, "The Illusive Commission of 'Major' Jedediah Hotchkiss," *The Virginia Magazine of History and Biography*, vol. 75, no. 2:183.
14. Journal, November 6, 1862, Hotchkiss Papers.
15. Hotchkiss to Sara, November 12, 1862, Hotchkiss Papers, 4:751.

16. Ibid., November 16, 1862, 4:752.
17. Journal, November 15, 1862, Hotchkiss Papers.
18. Ibid., November 16, 1862.
19. Ibid., November 28, 1862.
20. Ibid., November 29, 1862.
21. Ibid., December 5, 1862.
22. Hotchkiss to Sara, March 1, 1863, Hotchkiss Papers, 4:759.
23. Journal, December 12, 1862, Hotchkiss Papers.
24. James Power Smith, "With Stonewall Jackson," (Gaithersburg, Maryland: Zullo and Van Sickle Books, 1982): 29. Reprinted from article of same name in *Southern Historical Society Papers* vol. 5 (1920), New Series. Smith's "fancy sketch" of Jackson's appearance that day struck Hotchkiss as inaccurate. He wore, said Hotchkiss, the soft hat the topographer had purchased for him in Maryland three months earlier. No one could see what uniform the general wore, Hotchkiss wrote to Henderson, because "I am quite sure that his big army overcoat was buttoned up, from top to bottom, all day." As for the dramatic ride along the lines, Hotchkiss again disagreed with his friend Smith: "He did very little, if any, 'galloping.'" See Hotchkiss to G. F. R. Henderson, Hotchkiss Papers, 51:505.
25. Hotchkiss to Sara, December 13, 1862, Hotchkiss Papers, 4:753.
26. Journal, December 13, 1862, Hotchkiss Papers.
27. Smith, "With Stonewall," 29.
28. Hotchkiss places this field "just on the western slope of the spur back from Walker's batteries, and not far from Hamilton's Crossing." See Hotchkiss to Henderson, Hotchkiss Papers, 51:505.
29. McGuire to Hotchkiss, May 19, 1896, Hotchkiss Papers.
30. Hotchkiss to Sara, January 21, 1863, Hotchkiss Papers, 5:757. Jackson's staff took up a private collection, raising $850 among themselves, and donated it to the people of Fredericksburg. See Hotchkiss Papers, 4:456.
31. Journal, December 16, 1862, Hotchkiss Papers.
32. Smith, "With Stonewall," 39.
33. Hotchkiss to Sara, December 17, 1862, Hotchkiss Papers, 4:754.
34. Ibid.
35. Smith, "With Stonewall," 41.

36. Hotchkiss to Sara, January 11, 1863, Hotchkiss Papers, 4:756.
37. Journal, December 23, 1862, Hotchkiss Papers.
38. "Confederate War Items by Mrs. Kinsolving formerly Mrs. Corbin," Hotchkiss Papers, 49:380.
39. Hotchkiss to Sara, March 15, 1863, Hotchkiss Papers, 4:760.
40. Ibid., January 11, 1863, 4:756.
41. Bean, *Stonewall's Man*, 111.
42. "Confederate War Items," Hotchkiss Papers, 49:382.
43. Ibid.
44. Hotchkiss to Sara, December 4, 1862, Hotchkiss Papers, 4:752.
45. Boswell diary, February 25, 1863, Hotchkiss Papers, 51:375.
46. Hotchkiss Papers, 51:379.
47. Ibid.
48. Hotchkiss to Sara, January 21, 1863, Hotchkiss Papers, 4:757.
49. Boswell diary, January 14, 1863, Hotchkiss Papers, 51:372.
50. Hotchkiss to Sara, January 21, 1863, Hotchkiss Papers, 5:757.
51. Boswell diary, January 19, 1863, Hotchkiss Papers, 51:372.
52. Ibid., January 21, 1863.
53. Ibid.
54. Ibid., January 27, 1863.
55. Hotchkiss Papers, 51:379. Others shared Boswell's opinion, for Welby Carter was variously described as "fat," "greasy," and "a coward." See Robert K. Krick, *Lee's Colonels* (Dayton, Ohio: Morningside House, 1991), 85. Boswell's assessment of Carter's courage was apparently accurate, for Carter was dismissed from the service for cowardice at the Battle of Tom's Brook, October 9, 1864. He married Sophia deButts Carter in 1867.
56. Boswell diary, February 8, April 4, 1863, Hotchkiss Papers, 51:374, 51:377.
57. "Confederate War Items," Hotchkiss Papers, 49:382. 58. Hotchkiss to Sara, April 13, 1863, Hotchkiss Papers, 4:763.
58. Hotchkiss to Sara, April 13, 1863, Hotchkiss Papers 4:763.
59. 39:335 (number illegible), Hotchkiss Papers. Faulkner was another of the remarkable men on Jackson's staff. Before the war, he served in the Virginia legislature and was a congressman for eight years before becoming United States minister to France. When Virginia seceded, Faulkner resigned his post and returned to the

United States, only to be imprisoned by Federal authorities. After his release, he joined Jackson's staff, originally as a volunteer.
60. Hotchkiss Papers, 49:139.
61. Hotchkiss to Sara, April 8, 1863, Hotchkiss Papers, 4:763.
62. Ibid., March 27, 1863, Hotchkiss Papers, 4:761.
63. Ibid., December 17, 1862, Hotchkiss Papers, 4:754.
64. Ibid., April 13, 1863, Hotchkiss Papers, 4:763.
65. Ibid., April 24, 1863, Hotchkiss Papers, 4:764.
66. Ibid.
67. Boswell diary, April 8, 1863, Hotchkiss Papers, 51:378.
68. Hotchkiss to Sara, April 8, 1863, Hotchkiss Papers, 4:763.

NOTES TO CHAPTER SIX

1. Journal, April 30, 1863, Hotchkiss Papers.
2. Hotchkiss to Sara, April 29, 1863, Hotchkiss Papers, 4:764.
3. Journal, May 1, 1863, Hotchkiss Papers.
4. See T. M. R. Talcott, "General Lee's Strategy at the Battle of Chancellorsville," *Southern Historical Society Paper* 34 (1906): 5-27. Hotchkiss's account of what transpired between Lee and Jackson on the night of May 1 and the morning of May 2 differs from accounts by other officers involved, and in some particulars, is not supported by other facts, such as the times orders were issued and received and the hour at which certain troops moved. In his recollections of events, Hotchkiss somewhat exaggerates Jackson's contributions that night, and by association, his own, although this was almost certainly not done intentionally and is probably merely a result of incomplete information, fatigue, and grief, given the events of the next forty-eight hours. Though his conclusions seem to be erroneous (see Talcott), his account of events is not in the least contrived and can easily be reconciled with other accounts to arrive at a comprehensive view of what probably happened. Such a hybrid account is presented here.
5. Hotchkiss to Chase, March 28, 1892, Jackson folder, Hotchkiss Papers,

51:518. Hotchkiss always understood this to be the moment when Jackson conceived the idea of the flank march. The discussion also makes sense, however, as a reaffirmation by Jackson of a plan already agreed upon, the information from Hotchkiss confirming that the movement could be made one way or another. Jackson did not use the Welford road as his main route and perhaps did not use it at all.

6. Smith, "With Stonewall," 47.

7. Hotchkiss to Sara, May 19, 1863, Hotchkiss Papers, 4:766. Many of those with Jackson that night left accounts of what happened, and all vary in details. Bean, in *Stonewall's Man*, states that Pendleton was not with Jackson when he fell and that it was Pendleton who later found Dr. McGuire. Bean's source, apparently, was McGuire's "Account of the Wounding and Death of Stonewall Jackson," in McGuire and George Christian's *The Confederate Cause and Conduct in the War Between the States* (Richmond, Virginia: L. H. Jenkins, 1907). Hotchkiss states that he was with Pendleton and they had joined Jackson by the time he was wounded, immediately after which Hotchkiss "found Dr. McGuire and sent him forward" (Journal, May 2, 1863, Hotchkiss Papers). The account given here of the incident relies on Hotchkiss's recollections, except for events he did not witness, in which cases Smith's long-accepted account is the source.

8. Hotchkiss to Sara, May 19, 1863, Hotchkiss Papers 4:766.

9. Smith, "With Stonewall," 52.

10. Ibid.

11. Journal, May 2, 1863, Hotchkiss Papers.

12. Journal, May 3, 1863, Hotchkiss Papers.

13. Bean, "Boswell," 35.

14. Hotchkiss to Sara, May 19, 1863, Hotchkiss Papers, 4:766.

15. Ibid.

16. Ibid.

17. Ibid., May 10, 1863, 4:765.

18. Ibid., May 6, 1863, 4:764.

19. Hotchkiss slept perhaps thirteen hours between April 29 and May 4, twice in that time going about thirty-six hours without sleep.

20. Hotchkiss to Sara, May 19, 1863, Hotchkiss Papers, 4:766.

21. Ibid.

NOTES TO CHAPTER SEVEN

1. Hotchkiss to Nelson, May 20, 1863, Hotchkiss Papers, 4:814.

2. Hotchkiss to Sara, May 10, 1863, Hotchkiss Papers, 4:765.

3. Ibid., May 19, 1863, 4:766. Hotchkiss hardened his views toward Hill later, during and after the war. In 1892, he wrote, "I do not [write] for the purpose of disparaging the courage or the military skill of Gen. A. P. Hill, but to show that he was very careless in his manner of obeying orders, and was by no means the vigilant soldier that he should have been … Hill did not seem to have the proper appreciation of the element of time in military affairs, and then he had a very hot-headed and badly disciplined temper." See microfilm reel 49, Hotchkiss Papers.

4. Hotchkiss to Sara, May 31, 1863, Hotchkiss Papers, 4:766.

5. This hymn is still popular in Presbyterian and Methodist worship, although now it is known by the title "God Moves in a Mysterious Way." The words were written by the English poet William Cowper (1731-1800), allegedly after he emerged from a period of depression so severe that he had attempted suicide. See John Julian, ed., *A Dictionary of Hymnology*, (1892; reprint, New York: Dover Publications, 1957), vol. 1, 433.

6. Hotchkiss to Sara, June 6, 1863, Hotchkiss Papers, 4:767.

7. Ibid.

8. Ibid., November 12, 1862, 4:751.

9. Ibid., June 15, 1863, 4:767.

10. Journal, June 26, 1863, Hotchkiss Papers.

11. Hotchkiss to Sara, June 25, 1863, Hotchkiss Papers, 4:767.

12. Ibid.

13. Journal, June 26, 1863, Hotchkiss Papers.

14. Ibid., June 28, 1863.

15. Hotchkiss to Sara, June 28, 1863, Hotchkiss Papers, 4:768.

16. Journal, June 29, 1863, Hotchkiss Papers.

17. Ibid., July 1, 1863.

18. Ibid. As will be discussed in the epilogue, Hotchkiss considered Douglas an unreliable witness on matters relating to the war, claiming he was prone to exaggeration. Douglas wrote his memoirs after the war, and though

entertaining, they clearly show the influence of hindsight. Pendleton was not living when the memoir was published, so Douglas's statements concerning what happened at Ewell's headquarters on the evening of July 1, 1863, having now been called into question, remain unsubstantiated.

19. Journal, July 3, 1863.

20. Ibid., July 3, 1863; Hotchkiss to Sara, July 5, 1863, Hotchkiss Papers, 4:769.

21. Edwin B. Coddington, *The Gettysburg Campaign: A Study in Command* (New York: Charles Scribner's Sons, 1968), 565-66.

22. Hotchkiss to Sara, July 14, 1863, Hotchkiss Papers, 4:769.

23. Ibid., July 5, 1863.

24. Hotchkiss Papers, 39:282.

25. Hotchkiss to Sara, July 14, 1863, Hotchkiss Papers, 4:769.

26. Ibid., August 15, 1863, 4:771.

27. Ibid., November 22, 1863, 4:778.

28. Ibid., August 30, 1863, 4:773.

29. Hotchkiss Papers, 39:282.

30. Hotchkiss to Nelson, August 21, 1863, Hotchkiss Papers, 4:818.

31. Hotchkiss to Sara, August 21, 1863, Hotchkiss Papers, 4:773.

32. Ibid., August 15, 1863, 4:771.

33. "I have an office in Staunton; Breeze Johnson's old office. If you can come over come there for the night. My men will be there if I am not." See Hotchkiss to Nelson, January 21, 1864, Hotchkiss Papers, 4:824.

34. Hotchkiss dispatch to Early, January 21, 1864, Hotchkiss Papers, 49:401.

35. Hotchkiss to Sara, May 1, 1864, Hotchkiss Papers, 4:781.

36. Journal, May 6, 1864, Hotchkiss Papers.

37. Hotchkiss obituary, *The Confederate Veteran* 7, (1899): 271.

38. Hotchkiss to Sara, May 11, 1864, Hotchkiss Papers, 4:782.

39. Ibid., May 13, 1864, 4:782.

40. Ibid., May 15, 1864, 4:782.

41. Ibid., June 16, 1864, 4:783.

42. Ibid., June 28, 1864, 4:785.

NOTES TO CHAPTER EIGHT

1. Hotchkiss Papers, 41:147. Ewell explained to Hotchkiss after the war that he had inadvertently left this paragraph out of his report to General Lee.

2. John B. Gordon, *Reminiscences of the*

Civil War (New York: Charles Scribner's Sons, 1903), 318-19.

3. Smith, "With Stonewall," 33.
4. Gordon, *Reminiscences*, 319.
5. Journal, June 15, 1864, Hotchkiss Papers.
6. Ibid., July 5, 1864.
7. Ibid., July 9, 1864.
8. Ibid., July 10, 1864.
9. Ibid., July 11, July 13, 1864.
10. Ibid., July 14, 1864.
11. Hotchkiss to Sara, July 15, 1864, Hotchkiss Papers, 4:786.
12. Ibid., August 10, 1864, 4:787.
13. Ibid., August 26, 1864, 4:789.
14. Ibid.
15. Journal, September 20, 1864, Hotchkiss Papers.
16. Hotchkiss to Sara, September 21, 1864, Hotchkiss Papers, 4:791.
17. Gordon, *Reminiscences*, 326.
18. Hotchkiss to Sara, September 23, 1864, Hotchkiss Papers, 4:792.
19. Journal, September 26, 1864, Hotchkiss Papers.
20. Gordon, *Reminiscences*, 331.
21. Journal, September 26, 1864, Hotchkiss Papers.
22. Gordon, *Reminiscences*, 328.
23. Journal, September 29, 1864 and following, Hotchkiss Papers.
24. Ibid., October 6, 1864.
25. Ibid., October 10, 11, 1864.
26. Hotchkiss to Sara, October 15, 1864, Hotchkiss Papers, 4:794.
27. The Confederates based their hope on McClellan's well-known popularity with his former troops. Hotchkiss told Sara in September: "I suppose McClellan will be elected, as nearly all the Army of the Potomac goes for him." See Hotchkiss to Sara, September 3, 1864, Hotchkiss Papers, 4:791.
28. Ibid., October 11, 1864, 4:793.
29. Gordon, *Reminiscences*, 333.
30. Ibid., 334.
31. Journal, October 17, 1864, Hotchkiss Papers.
32. Gordon, *Reminiscences*, 335.
33. Hotchkiss to Sara, November 16, 1862, Hotchkiss Papers, 4:752.
34. For a discussion of Pegram and his rank in 1864-65, see Mark Mayo Boatner, *The Civil War Dictionary* (New York: David McKay, 1959), 629-30.
35. Journal, October 18, 1864, Hotchkiss Papers.

36. Gordon, *Reminiscences*, 336.
37. Journal, October 18, 1864, Hotchkiss Papers.
38. Ibid.
39. Gordon, *Reminiscences*, 336.
40. Journal, October 19, 1864, Hotchkiss Papers.
41. Hotchkiss to Sara, October 21, 1864, Hotchkiss Papers, 4:794.
42. Ibid.
43. Ibid., October 21, 1864, 4:794.
44. Journal, October 19, 1864, Hotchkiss Papers.
45. Ibid.
46. Hotchkiss to Sara, October 21, 1864, Hotchkiss Papers, 4:794.
47. Ibid., November 14, 1864, Hotchkiss Papers, 4:829.
48. Journal, October 19, 1864, Hotchkiss Papers.
49. Ibid., October 22, 1864.
50. Ibid., October 23, 1864. Gordon ever afterward believed Early lost the battle of Cedar Creek by refusing to push onward after the broken Federals in the afternoon, and Hotchkiss recorded in his journal on October 29 that the disagreement had already gone public. "A contention between Generals Gordon and Early about the Battle of Cedar Creek, &c." See Journal, October 29, 1864, Hotchkiss Papers.
51. Hotchkiss to Sara, October 31, 1864, Hotchkiss Papers, 4:795.
52. Ibid., November 5, 1864, 4:795.
53. Ibid., November 8, 1864, 4:796.
54. Ibid.
55. Ibid., November 5, 1864, 4:795.
56. Ibid. Hotchkiss was at this time told once again that he could not be commissioned as an engineer because he was a Virginian. See McDonald, "Commission," 185.
57. Hotchkiss to Sara, November 14, 1864, Hotchkiss Papers, 4:797.
58. Journal, March 2, 1865, Hotchkiss Papers.
59. On May 30, 1862, a lone Federal trooper chased Hotchkiss for several miles before giving up. See journal for that date.
60. Journal, March 2, 1865, Hotchkiss Papers.
61. Ibid., March 26, 1862.
62. Ibid., April 9, 1865.
63. Ibid., April 13-15, 1865.
64. Ibid., May 9, 1865.

NOTES TO EPILOGUE

1. Hotchkiss to Chase, March 28, 1892, Jackson folder, Hotchkiss Papers, 51:518.
2. Hotchkiss to Sara, November 1862, Hotchkiss Papers, 4:778.
3. Hotchkiss Papers, 39:282.
4. McDonald, *Make Me A Map of the Valley*, xxxi.
5. Hotchkiss to Henderson, April 20, 1897, Hotchkiss Papers, 34:331.
6. Ibid., March 6, 1897, 34:293.
7. Hotchkiss Papers, 34:272.
8. Henderson, *Stonewall*, xvii.
9. Hotchkiss to Sara, April 14, 1862, Hotchkiss Papers, 4:737.
10. Hotchkiss to Col. W. F. Mason McCarty, October 1, 1896, Hotchkiss Papers, 34:226.
11. Ibid., 34:225. Hotchkiss quotes directly from an Early letter that could not be found.
12. Hotchkiss to Henderson, January 27, 1897, Hotchkiss Papers, 34:264.
13. Hotchkiss to McCarty, October 1, 1896, Hotchkiss Papers, 34:226. Douglas's memoirs, *I Rode with Stonewall*, were published in book form in the 1940s and included many of the "romance" stories that Hotchkiss and McGuire found offensive. Douglas's book had been widely respected until recently, when the criticisms of Hotchkiss and McGuire became known. See Dennis E. Fry, "Riding with Stonewall," *Civil War* 9, no. 5 (1991): 40-46.
14. Munford to Hotchkiss, Hotchkiss Papers, 49:242.
15. Ibid., 49:247.
16. Hotchkiss to Henderson, March 6, 1897, Hotchkiss Papers, 34:293.
17. Hotchkiss's book is considered by many to be the best volume in the *Confederate Military History* series, and it remains a superb overview of operations in the Old Dominion from the Confederate point of view.
18. Hotchkiss to Comrades of V.V., A.N.Va., May 6, 1898, Hotchkiss Papers, 34:498.
19. Hotchkiss Papers, 50:433.
20. "Death," Hotchkiss Papers, 5:124.
21. Hotchkiss obituary, *The Confederate Veteran* 7 (1899), 270-271.
22. Hotchkiss to Sara, September 6, 1863, Hotchkiss Papers, 4:774.

BIBLIOGRAPHIC ESSAY

Presented with a wealth of primary and secondary materials about Hotchkiss, Jackson, and the general's staff and campaigns, I wanted to avoid a dependence on sources familiar to students of the Civil War. I wished to take advantage of the plethora of information, yet did not wish to simply rehash the Jackson literature. I wanted to present new material, and, moreover, my goal was to present a portrait of Hotchkiss, the man and the soldier, not merely to relate a history of his service. I chose, therefore, to make Hotchkiss's own papers the foundation of my research. All other references then became "secondary," in that they were not central to my purpose. I did rely on several other firsthand accounts to fill in gaps in the story, but I was extremely selective in my use of these sources.

The Jedediah Hotchkiss Papers in the Manuscript Division of the Library of Congress, Washington, D.C., contains approximately 20,000 items and occupies more than thirty-two feet of shelf space. The collection has been microfilmed (sixty-one reels), and researchers can borrow reels through interlibrary loan. The twenty-three-page guide to the collection prepared by the library staff in 1978 is indispensable. Aside from Hotchkiss's diaries on reels 1 and 2 and his letters to his wife and brother on reel 4, the most interesting items relating to his war service are included in what he called his "War Book," which includes manuscript copies of correspondence with G. F. R. Henderson and many others from 1896 to 1898, concerning Jackson and his campaigns and battles. An index can be found on microfilm reel 34, frame 3. Related family materials can be found in the Hotchkiss-McCullough Papers in the Alderman Library, University of Virginia, Charlottesville.

Hotchkiss's large personal collection of maps, which includes his own maps as well as those drawn by other cartographers, is now part of the collections of the Geography and Map Division in the Library of Congress. I found Richard W. Stephenson's *Civil War Maps: An Annotated List of Maps and Atlases in Map Collections of the Library of Congress* (Washington, D.C.: Library of Congress, 1961) and *The Hotchkiss Map Collection: A List of Manuscript Maps* (Falls Church, Va.: Sterling Press, 1977), published by the Library of Congress and compiled by Clara E. LeGear, especially valuable in exploring the map collection.

Any study of Jed Hotchkiss must include a careful reading of *Make Me A Map of the Valley* (Dallas, Tx.: Southern Methodist University Press, 1973), the published version of his war diary edited by Archie P. McDonald. Dr. McDonald included a long introduction and extensive annotations that will provide any interested student with a basic understanding of Hotchkiss and his war service. Dr. McDonald also wrote an enlightening article—"The Illusive Commission of 'Major' Jedediah Hotchkiss," *Virginia Magazine of History and Biography* (April 1967, 181-85), which discusses Hotchkiss's military status during the war.

A Hotchkiss descendent, Charles Hotchkiss Osterhout, privately published *Stonewall Jackson's Map-Maker (Jed Hotchkiss)* in 1977. The book apparently was printed in a limited edition and is now hard to find, though the Geography and Map Division in the Library of Congress has a copy. Mr. Osterhout's book consists mainly of excerpts from Hotchkiss's letters and papers arranged thematically. Though useful to a degree, the work contains some errors, many unsubstantiated statements, and no citations, which severely limits its value. Mr. Osterhout also published an article on his ancestor, "A Johnny Reb from Windsor, New York," *Courier Magazine* (January 1950).

Peter W. Roper's interesting article, "The 'Discovery' of the Hotchkiss Maps and Papers," *Winchester-Frederick County Historical Society Journal* (4(1989):1-27) discusses how the Hotchkiss Papers came to the Library of Congress. Mr. Roper is also the author of a biography titled *Jedediah Hotchkiss, Rebel Mapmaker and Virginia Businessman* (Shippensburg, Pa.: White Mane Publishing Co., 1992), which I have not read due to its appearance too late to be of use in preparing my study of Hotchkiss.

Other articles that illuminated aspects of Hotchkiss and his career include Lillian Craig's "Agents of Peace and Progress," *Virginia Cavalcade* (Spring 1965); "Major Jed. Hotchkiss," an obituary in *The Confederate Veteran* (7:270-71); Dennis E. Frye's "Riding With Stonewall," *Civil War Magazine* (9(1991), no. 5:40-46); Hotchkiss's own essay "The Tuscarora Indians" in *The Echo* (Windsor, N.Y., December, 1894); and a small booklet given me in Hotchkiss's former hometown titled *History of Loch Willow Presbyterian Church, Churchville, Va.* (Centennial Committee, 1966). I learned a great deal about life in the Valley from the *Historical Atlas of Augusta County Virginia* (Chicago: Waterman, Watkins & Co., 1885), which was co-authored by James A. Waddell and Hotchkiss, whose contribution was apparently limited to drawing the maps.

I gained insight into the fascinating subject of military topography by looking at old textbooks written by or for military engineers in the early part of this century, still before the widespread use of aerial cartography. I was surprised and delighted to learn that the tools and methods of surveying had not changed appreciably between the Civil War and World War I or later. Gerald Maxwell's *The Military Map: Elements of Modern Topography* (London: MacMillan & Co., 1918) was very helpful, as were Herbert M. Wilson's *Topographic Surveying, Including Geographic, Exploratory, and Military Mapping* (New York: John Wiley & Sons, 1905) and Harry A. Musham's *The Technique of the Terrain: Maps and Their Use in the Field in Peace and War* (New York: Reinhold Publishing Corp., 1944). Wilson's work was especially valuable for its discussion of engineer-ing instruments and their uses. Musham's book explains many of the problems encountered by military surveyors and proposes solutions.

Two works by James L. Nichols cast light on the trials faced by engineers trying to work within the Confederate war machine. "Confederate Map Supply" in *The Military Engineer* (January-February 1954) and "The Confederate Engineers" in *The Military Engineer* (September-October 1930) were most informative about the methods and means of the Confederate Engineer Bureau.

Robert C. Matson's *Elements of Mapping* (Houghton, Mich.: Michigan College of Mining and Technology, 1940) and E. A. Reeves's *Maps and Map-Making* (London: The Royal Geographical Society, 1910) helped clarify cartographic processes in the age before aerial photography.

One cannot possibly understand Hotchkiss's value to his commanders without knowing how poorly surveyors and cartographers had served Virginia in the nineteenth century. E. M. Sanchez-Saavedra's *Description of the Country: Virginia Cartographers and Their Maps 1607-1881* (Richmond: Virginia State Library, 1975) provides an excellent description of the state of topography in the Old Dominion at the outbreak of the war. Any researcher interested in cartography and surveying in the Civil War era would do well to tap the library of the United States Geological Survey in Reston, Virginia. Among the USGS holdings are textbooks, journals, and guidebooks relevant to nineteenth-century surveying and mapping, many relating directly to Civil War campaigns. The library also holds more than two dozen articles and pamphlets written by Hotchkiss regarding the mineral deposits of various parts of the commonwealth after the war. Many of these articles appear in Hotchkiss's respected journal *The Virginias*, of which the library holds a set.

Hotchkiss's faith was a dominant force and is thus a major theme of this book. Three general references provided insight into the Presbyterianism practiced by Hotchkiss and Jackson: *Encyclopaedia of Religion and Ethics*, vol. 10., edited by James Hastings (New York: Charles Scribner's Sons, 1956); *The Encyclopedia of Religion*, vol. 11., edited by Mircea Elliade (New York: Macmillan Publishing Co.); and *A Dictionary of Hymnology*, vol. 1., edited by John Julian (New York: Dover Publications, Inc.).

Studies of Jackson and his campaigns are legion. Most of what I relate about Jackson and his character is based on my readings of essays on and recollections of the general in the Hotchkiss Papers. Hotchkiss assiduously gathered such items on Jackson, and most of them have remained unpublished and untapped. Of the general and biographical works published on Jackson, I found the following to be the most helpful: Lenoir Chambers's, *Stonewall Jackson*, 2 vols. (New York: Morrow 1959) and Frank E. Vandiver's *Mighty Stonewall* (New York, 1957). Other useful biographies include G. F. R. Henderson's *Stonewall Jackson and the American Civil War* (London, New York: 1898), in the publication of which Hotchkiss played such a large role; and Robert Louis Dabney's *Life and Campaigns of Lieut. Gen. Thomas J. Jackson* (New York, 1866). Dabney was Jackson's chief of staff, and this biography is full of personal insight and anecdote. Dabney was also one of Jackson's chief admirers, so this book is tainted by favorable bias.

Douglas Southall Freeman's *Lee's Lieutenants*, 3 vols. (New York: Charles Scribner's Sons) is a standard and highly readable reference on the general's campaigns. Robert G. Tanner's *Stonewall in the Valley* (Doubleday, 1976) is an entertaining study of the 1862 spring campaign, but the most serviceable history, and the one upon which I based my chapter on the Valley Campaign, is that of Jackson's ordnance chief, William Allan, *History of the Campaign of Gen. T. J. (Stonewall) Jackson in the Shenandoah Valley of Virginia* (reprinted by Morningside Bookshop, 1987). Allan

cooperated with Hotchkiss on this book, and the result of their collaboration should be any scholar's starting place for a study of that operation. The two also worked together on *The Battlefields of Virginia: Chancellorsville* (New York: 1867), which remains valuable despite some errors of assumption. Allan also wrote the very fine *The Army of Northern Virginia in 1862* (Cambridge, Mass.: Riverside Press, 1892, reprinted by Morningside Bookshop, 1984), which is valuable for its coverage of Robert E. Lee's campaigns in that year. Hotchkiss's own *Virginia*, vol. 3 in *Confederate Military History*, edited by Clement A. Evans (Atlanta, Ga., 1899), is an excellent Southern perspective on the war in Virginia and provides the superb detail and insight that could only be offered by an eyewitness. Jeffry D. Wert's *From Winchester to Cedar Creek: The Shenandoah Campaign of 1864* (Carlisle, Pa.: South Mountain Press, Inc., 1987) was very helpful in clarifying Hotchkiss's role in that campaign.

Stonewall Jackson's Way: Route, Method, Achievement (Verona, Va.: McClure, 1969) by local authority John Wayland is a rare and precious book rich in fact and lore about Jackson and the places he slept, fought, or merely passed while in the Valley. Mr. Wayland's *Twenty-Five Chapters on the Shenandoah Valley* (C. J. Carriter Co., 1976) offers other significant background on the region.

Many of the men who marched with Jackson and Hotchkiss related their stories after the war. Among those I found most enlightening are Richard Taylor's *Destruction and Reconstruction* (New York, 1879); John O. Casler's classic *Four Years in the Stonewall Brigade* (Guthrie, Ok., 1893), later editions of which were revised by Hotchkiss; William T. Poague's *Gunner With Stonewall*, edited by Monroe F. Cockrell (Jackson, Tenn., 1957); and John H. Worsham's *One of Jackson's Foot Cavalry* (New York, 1912, reissued by McCowan-Mercer, 1964). Portions of the diary of infantryman John W. Mauk are published in Harry M. Strickler's *A Short History of Page County, Virginia* (Richmond, Va., 1952; reprinted by C. J. Carrier Co., Harrisonburg, Va., 1974). The events on the confusing night of May 1-2, 1863, at Chancellorsville are set forth by T. M. R. Talcott, one of Lee's engineers, in "General Lee's Strategy at the Battle of Chancellorsville," *Southern Historical Society Papers* (34(1906): 1-27). James I. Robertson, Jr.'s *The Stonewall Brigade* (Baton Rouge: Louisiana State University Press, 1963) is an excellent study of one of the general's finer fighting units.

I came to know some of the fascinating men of Jackson's headquarters and personal staff through a number of primary and secondary sources. Hotchkiss's friend and tent-mate J. K. Boswell kept a diary, and portions of it are preserved in the Hotchkiss Papers. It has been published under the title, "The Diary of a Confederate Staff Officer," *Civil War Times Illustrated* (October 1983). Adele Mitchell published "James Keith Boswell: Jackson's Engineer" in *Civil War Times Illustrated* (June 1968), and W. G. Bean related the unhappy story of Boswell's tragic obsession with Sophia deButts Carter in "Captain James Keith Boswell," *Virginia Cavalcade* (Winter 1970). Miscellaneous personal and official papers of both Robert Louis Dabney and John Harman rest in the Hotchkiss Papers. Howard McKnight Wilson's *Tinkling Spring, Headwater of Freedom: A Study of the Church and Her People, 1732-1952* (Fishersville, Va.: The Tinkling Spring and Hermitage Presbyterian Churches, 1954) contains interesting insights on former pastor Dabney. Henry Kyd Douglas's *I Rode with Stonewall* (Chapel Hill: University of North Carolina Press, 1940) is an entertaining memoir by one of Jackson's staff officers and has long been treasured by students of Lee's army. Hotchkiss and others believed Douglas had a higher regard for a good story than he did for the truth, so the reliability of Douglas's account is now in question. Still the book has value and will undoubtedly remain a favorite of students and buffs. James Power Smith, Jackson's aide-de-camp, wrote a long and entertaining recollection of his service called "With Stonewall Jackson in the Army of Northern Virginia," *Southern Historical Society Papers* (vol. 5 (New Series): 1920, reprinted by Zullo and Van Sickle Books, Gaithersburg, Md., 1982). Finally, W. G. Bean's fine biography *Stonewall's Man: Sandie Pendleton* (Chapel Hill: University of North Carolina Press, 1959) not only paints a clear portrait of Jackson's young and superbly efficient staff officer, but also provides a glimpse of what life was like at Second Corps headquarters.

I found several biographies and articles provided an adequate background for understanding Hotchkiss's contributions to the campaigns and battles of his commanders subsequent to Jackson. James I. Robertson, Jr.'s *General A. P. Hill: The Story of a Confederate Warrior* (New York: Random House, 1987) is the best study of the Second Corps's interim commander, and Richard S. Ewell's letters in *The Making of A Soldier: Letters of General Richard S. Ewell,* edited by Percy Hamlin (Richmond, Va.: Whittet & Shepperson, 1935) provided insight into the character of that officer. Jubal A. Early's *Memoir of the Last Year of the War for Independence in the Confederate States of America* (Lynchburg, Va., 1867) was helpful, if not too detailed, as was J. C. Featherston's "Gen. Jubal Anderson Early," *Confederate Veteran* (26:432). John B. Gordon's *Reminiscences of the Civil War* (New York: Charles Scribner's Sons, 1903) was indispensable in determining Hotchkiss's part at the Battle of Cedar Creek.

Among the general reference works that proved helpful are Robert K. Krick's *Lee's Colonels* (3rd edition, Dayton, Oh.: Morningside House, 1991); Ezra Warner's volumes *Generals in Gray* (Baton Rouge: Louisiana State University Press, 1959) and *Generals in Blue* (Baton Rouge: Louisiana State University Press, 1964); and Lee A. Wallace Jr's. *A Guide to Virginia Military Organizations 1861-1865* (Lynchburg, Va.: H. E. Howard, Inc. 1986).

INDEX

A

"All things work together for good" 123, 153
Allan, William 56, 88, 92, 156
Allegheny Mountains 45, 52, 53
Allen, L. V. 18
Antietam Creek 88, 89
Antietam, Battle of (see Battle of Sharpsburg)
Appomattox Court House 154
Army of Northern Virginia 78, 82, 88, 89, 94, 109, 110, 131, 144, 152, 154, 161; crosses Potomac River, 82–83
Army of Tennessee 146
Army of the Potomac 45, 79, 87, 93, 109, 124, 125, 133, 167
Ashby, Turner 55, 62, 63, 71, 73, 74
Augusta County Militia Battalion 51, 52, 165
Augusta County, Virginia 15, 18, 19, 26, 35, 46, 52, 58, 63, 64, 77, 155; public schools 155
Augusta Female Seminary, Staunton, Virginia 155
Augusta Lee Rifles (of 25th Virginia Infantry) 35, 36, 37

B

Baltimore, Maryland 123, 129
Banks's Ford, Rappahannock River 107
Banks, Nathaniel P. 50, 51, 63, 64, 66, 68, 69, 71–72, 73, 79, 124
Battle of Cedar Creek 146–147, 148, 149–152, 157, 161, 168
Battle of Cedar Mountain (or Cedar Run) 79, 80, 81, 91, 122
Battle of Chancellorsville 108, 109–115, 116–117, 118–119
Battle of Chantilly 82
Battle of First Manassas 45, 47, 55
Battle of Fisher's Hill 144–145, 146
Battle of Fredericksburg 94–95, 96–97, 98, 139
Battle of Gettysburg 125–126, 127
Battle of McDowell 40–42, 66–68, 161
Battle of Monocacy 140, 141, 142
Battle of Second Manassas 81–82, 122
Battle of Second Winchester 71–72
Battle of Sharpsburg 88–89, 92
Battle of Spotsylvania 133, 136–137, 139
Battle of The Wilderness 132–133, 134–135
Battle of Third Winchester 143–144
Battle of Waterloo 57
Battle of Waynesboro 153
Baylor, William S. 11, 46, 47, 52, 71, 82
Bell, John 19

Berryville, Virginia 92, 124
Beverly, Virginia 24, 33, 34, 36
Blair, Montgomery 142
Blue Ridge Mountains 24, 50, 61, 62, 64, 66, 69, 79, 123, 130, 131
Boonsboro, Maryland 83
Boswell, James Keith 57–58, 69, 74, 78, 81, 93, 101, 102, 103–106, 107, 110, 113, 115, 121, 123, 132, 133, 157, 166; diary of 114
Bowman's Ford, Cedar Creek 150
Boye, Henry 37, 38, 163
Breckenridge, John C. 19
Bridgeford, D. B. 56
Bridgewater, Virginia 69
Bristoe Station, Virginia 131
Broome County, New York 18
Brown's Gap, Virginia 66, 145
Brown, Campbell 130
Brown, S. Howell 54, 68, 115, 116, 118, 165
Buckton, Virginia 149
Buffalo Gap, Virginia 66
Bull Pasture Mountain 67
Bull Pasture River 40
Bull Run 45, 82
Burnside, Ambrose E. 93, 94, 109, 159

C

Camp Garnett, Virginia 24, 25, 26, 27, 33–37, 149
Carlisle Barracks 14, 125
Carlisle, Pennsylvania 14, 125
Carter, R. Welby 105, 166
Carter, Sophia deButts 102, 103, 105, 115, 166
Cartography (see mapping)
Catherine Furnace 111
Catoctin Mountains 83
Cedar Creek 146, 148, 149, 150, 151, 152, 157
Chambersburg, Pennsylvania 125
Champagne 72
Chandler's Plantation (at Guiney's Station)
Cheat Mountain, Virginia 36, 41, 43, 91
Chester Gap, Virginia 124
Chickahominy River 78
Church music 63
Churchville Cavalry (of 14th Virginia Cavalry) 24
Churchville, Virginia 18, 24, 43, 68, 144
Confederate Engineer Corps 26, 27, 41, 57, 91, 93, 100, 153
Confederate Military History 161, 168
Confederate War Department 49, 93
Congress, United States 45, 94, 156

Conrad's Store, Virginia 62, 74
Corbin, Jane 101, 106
Corbin, Kate 101, 145
Corbin, Richard 99, 101
Corbin, Roberta "Bertie" 100, 106
Crook, George 144
Crozet, Claudius 37, 163
Crutchfield, Stapleton 58, 74, 116, 121
Culpeper County, Virginia 93
Custer, George A. 153

D

Dabney, Rev. Dr. Robert Louis 56, 63, 159
Davis, Jefferson 24, 41, 75
Dayton, Virginia 92
Dickinson College, Carlisle, Pennsylvania 125
Douglas, Henry Kyd 56, 126, 159, 160, 167, 168
Dry River Gap, Virginia 68

E

Early, Jubal A. 7, 132, 138, 139, 140, 142, 143, 144, 145, 146, 147, 148, 149, 150, 151, 152, 153, 154, 159, 160, 168; invades Maryland 140–142
Edinburg, Virginia 52, 152
Elkton, Virginia (see Conrad's Store, Virginia)
"Elwood" 115
Emancipation Proclamation 94
Evans, Clement A. 147, 161
Ewell's Corps 122, 123, 125–126, 132, 133
Ewell, Richard S. 7, 8, 63, 66, 69, 71–72, 74, 120, 123, 124, 125, 129, 130, 131, 132, 139, 160, 167; at Gettysburg 125–126; Hotchkiss's opinion of 122; in command of Jackson's Corps 122; wife of 130–131

F

Faulkner, Charles J. 106, 156, 166
Fauquier County, Virginia 57–58, 102, 104
Forrer, Daniel 15, 16, 163
Forrer, Henry 15
Fort Sumter, South Carolina 19
Franklin, Virginia 68
Frederick, Maryland 83, 84, 140
Fredericksburg, Virginia 94, 98, 100, 101, 106, 109; destruction of (see also Battle of Fredericksburg) 95, 96–97, 98
Frémont, John C. 63, 66–68, 69, 73, 74, 75
Front Royal, Virginia 69, 70, 71, 72, 73, 124

G

Garnett, Robert S. 24, 26, 33, 36, 40
Gearing, William 19
Gettysburg, Confederate rationale for defeat at 129
Gettysburg, Pennsylvania (see also Battle of Gettysburg) 88, 125–126, **127**, 131
Gibbon, John 159
"Glen Welby," 103, 105
Gordon, John B. **142**, 143, 144, 145, 147, 148, 149, 150, 151, 159, 168;
   Hotchkiss's opinion of 143
Gordonsville, Virginia 78, 79, 81
Grant, Ulysses, S. 132, 133, 140, 142, 145, 154, 158
Greencastle, Pennsylvania 125
Griggs, Emily 18
Grinnan, O. M. 18, 21
Guiney's Station, Virginia 116

H

Hampden-Sydney College, Virginia 63
Harman, John A. 58–60, 61, 72, 74, 75, 106, 155, 157, 164
Harpers Ferry, Virginia 13, 45, 50, 52, 73, 83, 84, **85**, 86–**87**, 88, 89
Harrisburg, Pennsylvania 13, 83, 125
Harrisonburg, Virginia 61, 63, 64, 66, 68, 69, 73, 74
Hawks, Wells J. **56**, 60, 72, 157
Heck, Jonathan 24, 26, 27, 30, 33–37
Henderson, G. F. R. 158, 159, 161, 166
Hill, A. P. 88, 89, 112, 113, **122**, 125, 131, 160, 167;
   Hotchkiss's opinion of 121–122, 167;
   succeeds Jackson 121–122
Hood, John B. 146
Hooker, Joseph 109, 110, 111, 112, 119, 125
Hotchkiss, Anne 17, **20**
Hotchkiss, Harriet 18
Hotchkiss, Jed
   and battlefield scenes 30, 31, 67, 71, 79, 81–82, 98, 117–119, 123
   appointed First Military Assistant Engineer 153
   as a Confederate historian 156–159, 161
   as a student 14
   at Fisher's Hill 144–45
   barricades mountain gaps 68
   begins mapping 16
   birth of 12
   boyhood 12–13
   bridge burning 62–63
   buries Boswell 115
   buys Jackson a hat 83, 165
   cartographic techniques 29–30, 59
   cheerfulness 13, 83, 146

corresponds with G. F. R. Henderson 158–159
death of 162
depressed 117–119
devises bridge 69
devotion to family 31, 52, 53, 99
diet 30, 130
dislike of drink 42, 93
dislike of Fredericksburg region 101
duties as a topographer 27, 40, 53, 64, 69, 73, 75, 77–78, 81–82, 85, 87–89, 92, 94, 101, 106, 109, 110, 129, 131, 132, 142
enters Confederate service 23
faith 13, 122–123, 162
familiarity with Valley 54
hatred of war 53, 74, 82, 99, 100, 101, 123, 134
helps Boswell 102–103, 105
hired by T. J. Jackson 52
hired by W. W Loring 41
horses 88, 107, 144, 145
illnesses 40, 43, 74, 94, 131, 140, 161, 162
in retreat from Gettysburg 129
intellectual habits 14
leads retreat from Camp Garnett 34–36
lectures 160
living quarters 30, 42
loquacity 91–92
loses surveying equipment 36–37, 153
love of history 12
marries S. A. Comfort 17
meets T. J. Jackson 17
methods of survey 27–28, 132
mission to Signal Knob 147–148
mission to the Peak 64
obtains Nine-Sheet Map 37
office in Staunton 131
on Early at Cedar Creek 152
on Ewell at Gettysburg 129
on teaching 15–16
opinion of A. Lincoln 94, 98, 152
opinion of A. P. Hill 121–122, 160, 170n
opinion of H. K. Douglas 159–160, 170n
opinion of J. Longstreet 160
opinion of J. Pegram 33, 149
opinion of J. A. Early 138, 140
opinion of J. B. Gordon 143
opinion of J. E. B. Stuart 100
opinion of R. E. Lee 42, 93
opinion of R. E. Rodes 144
opinion of R. S. Ewell 120, 122, 130
opinion of T. J. Jackson 47, 50, 59, 72, 91

opinion of U. S. Grant 133, 157
opinion of W. W. Loring 42
optimism 83, 143, 146, 152–153, 162
personal finances 31, 33, 100
photographs of **10**, **20**, **56**
plans memoirs 156, 158, 161
postwar writings 156, 161
presentiment of death 96–97
"promoted" to major 160
receives exemption from Lee 106
returns home after war 154
role at Cedar Creek 149–151
role at Chancellorsville 110–112, 114–115, 166–167
self-delusion 152–153
self-education 16
sense of duty 12–13, 21, 42, 82, 83, 146
temporary appointment as engineer 93
value to Jackson 54, 162
views on marriage 130
views on slavery 19
views on states' rights 19–20
working conditions 42
wounded 144
Hotchkiss, Lydia 12
Hotchkiss, Nelly 17, **20**, 52, 53, 59, 106, 163
Hotchkiss, Nelson 17, 18, 31, 43, 74, 80, 89, 100, 131, 155;
   sells Loch Willow 100, 107
Hotchkiss, Sara Ann Comfort 16, 17, 18, **20**, 21, 29–31, 37, 40, 42, 43, 47, 51–52, 53, 57, 59, 61, 62, 68, 72, 77, 79, 81, 82, 83, 84, 89, 92, 93, 94, 96, 98, 99, 100, 101, 103, 106, 107, 109, 115, 118, 119, 122, 123, 124, 125, **128**, 129, 131, 132, 134, 142, 143, 144, 145, 146, 151, 152, 153, 156, 158, 159, 162
Hotchkiss, Stiles 12
Humphreys, William 164
Hunter, David 134, 140
Hunter, Robert W. 147

J

Jackson, Anna Morrison 48, 107, 165
Jackson, Elinor Junkin 48, 84
Jackson, Julia 107
Jackson, Thomas J. 11, **44**, 46, 47, 48–50, 56, 91–92, 96, 121, 139, 140, 149, 162
   "charmed circle" 110, 121
   character 49–50, 99
   death of 118
   faith 48–49
   grasp of topography 54
   habits 49, 59, 94, 98
   secretiveness 60, 77, 94
   staff 55–59, 101, 106, 108, 110, 121 166
   wounded 113

James River 45
Jefferson County, Virginia 54
Jefferson Medical College, Philadelphia 57
Johnson, Edward "Allegheny" 63–64, 66, 124, 131
Johnston, Joseph E. 154
Jordan, Macon 62–63, 92, 165
"Judge not the Lord by feeble sense" 123
Junkin, Rev. Dr. George 17, 47
Junkin, George 84, 165

K
Keith, James 103, 105
Kernstown, Virginia 11, 50–51, 52, 60, 69, 71, 84, 92
Kershaw, Joseph B. 145, 150, 151

L
Lacy, Rev. Dr. Beverly Tucker 112, 115, 116, 131, 157
Laurel Hill, Virginia 24, 33, 36
Lee, Fitzhugh 159
Lee, Robert E. 7, 8, 9, 24, 41–43, 76, 77, 78, 79, 81, 82, 83, 87, 88, 89, 91, 92, 93, 94, 98, 99, 106, 107, 109, 110, 111, 112, 114, 115, 116, 118, 121–122, 123, 124, 126, 129, 131, 132, 133, 134, 139, 140, 142, 143, 145, 146, 152, 153, 154, 158, 159, 160, 166
Letcher, John 21, 36, 46, 49
Leviticus, verses from 75
Lexington, Virginia 17, 35, 47, 48, 49, 52, 77, 132, 134, 160
"Light Shining out of Darkness" 123, 167
Lilley, Robert Doak 35–36, 40, 163
Lincoln, Abraham 19, 21, 45, 46, 73, 79, 92, 93, 94, 109, 142, 152
Little North Mountain 144
Loch Willow Academy 17, 18, 19, 21, 94, 100, 134, 154;
    sold 107
Longstreet, James 81, 94, 97, 122, 124, 126, 160
Loring, William W. 23, 40–43, 49
Louisiana Troops
    Infantry 7th 130; 8th 71
Luray, Virginia 62, 92
Lynchburg, Virginia 134, 139, 140, 153, 154

M
Manassas Junction, Virginia 81, 91
Mapping 16, 27, 52, 54, 59, 92, 130, 131, 149
Maps 7, 29–30, 37, 40, 41, 42, 142;
    shortage of before 1861 38
Martinsburg, Virginia 83, 84, 124
Maryland Campaign 91, 140–142, 158, 159
Massachusetts Institute of Technology 156
Massanutten Mountain 52, 63, 69, 74, 144, 146, 147, 149, 161

McClellan, George B. 33, 34, 41, 45, 46, 50, 51, 60, 77, 78, 79, 87, 89, 91, 92, 93, 146, 167
McDowell, Irvin 73
McDowell, Virginia (see also Battle of McDowell) 40, 41, 42, 67, 68, 69
McGuire, Dr. Hunter Holmes 56, 57, 98, 114, 131, 159, 160, 161, 167, 168
McLaws, Lafayette 159
Meade, George G. 97, 125, 126, 131
Mechum's River Station, Virginia 66
Medical College of Virginia, Richmond 57
Menagerie 14
Mexican War 41, 48, 58
Middletown, Virginia 71, 84, 146, 151, 152
Milroy, Robert 124
Monocacy River 140
Monongalia County, Virginia 26
Monterey, Virginia 36, 37, 40
Morrison, J. G. 56
"Moss Neck" 98, 99, 100, 101, 105, 106, 145, 156
Mossy Creek Academy 16, 92
Mossy Creek Ironworks 15
Mossy Creek, Virginia 15, 17, 69, 162
Mt. Jackson, Virginia 51
Mt. Meridian, Virginia 75
Munford, Thomas 159, 160, 161

N
Napoleon 37, 57, 60
Narrow Passage Creek, Virginia 52, 53
Natural Bridge, Rockbridge County, Virginia 14
New Market Gap, Virginia 69
New Market, Virginia 69, 144
Nine-Sheet Map of Virginia 37, 38
North Fork of the Shenandoah River 52, 53
North Mountain 52
North River 69
North River Gap, Virginia 68

O
Oltmanns, C. W. 131, 132
Orange and Alexandria Railroad 134

P
Page Valley, Virginia 64, 69, 71, 74, 92
Parkersburg-Staunton Turnpike 24
Pegram, John 33–36, 149, 150, 151, 163;
    Hotchkiss's opinion of 149
Pendleton, Alexander Swift "Sandie" 52, 55, 56, 57, 58, 74, 101, 106, 113, 126, 131, 145, 157, 167
Peninsula Campaign 45
Pennsylvania Railroad 83
Pennsylvania, invasion of 123–126

Petersburg, Virginia 33, 133, 134, 142, 143, 145, 146, 152, 154
Philadelphia, Pennsylvania 123, 129
Pickett, George 126
Pope, John 79, 81, 91
Port Republic, Virginia 14, 65, 66, 74, 77, 82, 145
Potomac River 13, 46, 72, 73, 82, 84, 88, 89, 91, 124, 126, 129, 140, 142

R
Ramseur, Stephen Dodson 150
Rapidan River 109, 130, 132
Rappahannock River 94, 109, 118
Rawley Springs, Virginia 68
Rich Mountain, Virginia 24, 26, 27, 29, 33–37, 41, 45, 163
Richmond, Virginia 19, 38, 41, 45, 49, 50, 57, 60, 77, 78, 79, 94, 133, 142, 146, 152, 154
Robinson, Sampson, B. 130, 131, 132
Rockfish Gap, Virginia 153
Rodes, Robert E. 124, 131, 144, 150
Rogers, William B. 156
Romney, Virginia 49
Rosecrans, William S. 34, 41
Rude's Hill, Virginia 61

S
Salem Church, Virginia 109
Scarlet fever 52, 59, 106
Schenck, Robert C. 67–68, 69
Secession 19, 21
Second Corps of the Army of Northern Virginia (see also Ewell's Corps) 91, 93, 121, 122, 123, 126, 130, 134, 139, 140, 154, 157
Second Manassas Campaign (see also Battle of Second Manassas) 81–82, 122
Shakespeare 58, 116
Sharpsburg, Maryland 88, 89, 94, 143, 158
Shenandoah River (See also North Fork and South Fork) 52, 53, 62, 69, 74, 75, 84, 149, 150
Shenandoah Valley 9, 18, 45, 83, 92, 123–124, 132, 134, 142, 147, 163;
    beauty of 14, 46;
    strategic importance of 45–46
Shepherdstown, Virginia 89
Sheridan, Philip S. 142, 143, 144, 145, 146, 147, 148, 149, 151, 153
Sherman, William T. 146
Shields, James 74, 75
Shippensburg, Pennsylvania 125
Signal Knob (see also Massanutten Mountain) 69, 147
Sketchbook 28
Slavery 19, 63

Smith, James Power 56, 96, 98, 99, 112, 113, 159, 161, 162, 166
South Fork, Shenandoah River 52, 62, 69, 74, 75, 149, 150
South Mountain, Maryland 83
South Side Railroad, Virginia 134
St. Paul 123, 153
States' rights 19, 43
Staunton, Virginia 11, 14, 18, 19, 38, 47, 66, 77, 78, 92, 94, 100, 131, 132, 134, 144, 145, 153, 155, 160, 162
Stephenson's Depot, Virginia 124
Sterrett, Franklin F. 24, 26, 68, 73
Stonewall Brigade 67, 73, 75, 100
Strasburg, Virginia 61, 69, 71, 73, 144, 147, 149
Stribling Springs, Virginia 17
Stuart, Jeb 8, 81, 89, 90, 96, 99, 100, 102–103, 115, 133
Sunday school 18, 48, 75, 119
Surveying 16, 23, 27–30, 41, 52, 53, 54, 59, 94, 129, 131, 149, 155
  determining directions 29;
  difficulties of 27;
  measuring altitudes 29;
  measuring distances 27;
  tools and equipment 27–30
Swift Run Gap, Virginia 61, 62, 63, 66, 145

T
Talcott, T. M. R. 110
Taliaferro, William B. 37, 67
Taylor, Richard S. 75

"The Oaks" 155
The Peak (see also Massanutten Mountain) 64, 66, 74
The Wilderness (see also Battle of the Wilderness) 111, 132, 134–135
Three Top Mountain (see Massanutten Mountain and Signal Knob)
Tinkling Spring, Virginia 63
Tom's Brook, Virginia 11, 51, 166
Tygart Valley, Virginia 41

U
Union Presbyterian Church, Churchville, Virginia 18
Union Theological Seminary 63
United Confederate Veterans 160
United States Ford, Rappahannock River 107
United States Military Academy (West Point) 24, 48, 139
University of Pennsylvania 57
University of Virginia 47

V
Valley Turnpike 50–51, 92, 163
Virginia and Tennessee Railroad 134
Virginia Central Railroad 109, 144, 153
Virginia Military Institute 17, 47, 48, 49, 134
Virginia Troops, Cavalry 1st 105; 9th 99; Infantry 2nd 57, 73; 5th 47, 71, 82; 10th 64, 82; 20th 33; 23rd 37; 25th 26, 35, 37, 41; 33rd 57; Militia 46; 160th Regiment 47

Von Borcke, Heros 100
von Bucholtz, Ludwig 38

W
Walker, John G. 85
Washington College, Lexington, Virginia 17, 35, 47, 55, 84
Washington, D.C. 21, 41, 45, 46, 50, 69, 79, 81, 82, 83, 87, 93, 98, 123, 140, 142, 146, 151, 158, 160
Waynesboro, Virginia 153
Weather and Flower Table 13
Wellford, Charles B. 111
Wellington, Duke of 57
Weyer's Cave, Virginia 14, 15, 74
Wilderness Tavern 111, 114, 115
Williamsport, Maryland 84, 129
Winchester Medical College 57
Winchester, Virginia 32, 46, 49, 50, 57, 69, 71, 72, 73, 91, 92, 124, 143–144, 146, 151, 163
Winder, Charles 73
Windsor, New York 12
Wood, John 37, 163
Woodstock, Virginia 53, 60, 69
World's Fair of 1884 156

Y
Yancey, William B. 64
Yerby's 106, 107
York River 45

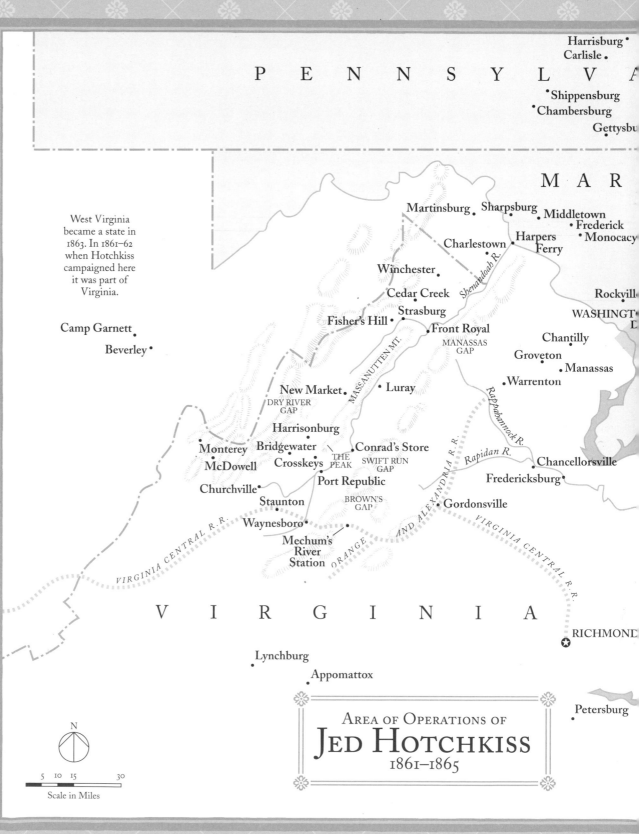

PENNSYLVA

Harrisburg •
Carlisle •

• Shippensburg
• Chambersburg

Gettysbu

MAR

West Virginia
became a state in
1863. In 1861–62
when Hotchkiss
campaigned here
it was part of
Virginia.

Martinsburg • Sharpsburg • Middletown
• Frederick
• Monocacy

Charlestown • Harpers
Ferry

Winchester •

Rockvill

Cedar Creek • *Shenandoah R.*

WASHINGT
D

Camp Garnett •

Beverley •

Fisher's Hill • Strasburg

• Front Royal

Chantilly

MANASSAS
GAP

Groveton •
• Manassas

New Market •

MASSANUTTEN MT.

• Luray

• Warrenton

DRY RIVER
GAP

Harrisonburg •

Rappahannock R.

Monterey •
McDowell •

Bridgewater •

Crosskeys •

• Conrad's Store

THE
PEAK

SWIFT RUN
GAP

Rapidan R.

• Chancellorsville

Churchville •

Port Republic •

ORANGE AND ALEXANDRIA R.R.

Fredericksburg •

Staunton •

BROWN'S
GAP

• Gordonsville

VIRGINIA CENTRAL R.R.

Waynesboro •

VIRGINIA CENTRAL R.R.

Mechum's
River
Station

ORANGE

VIRGINIA

⊛ RICHMOND

Lynchburg •

• Appomattox

AREA OF OPERATIONS OF

JED HOTCHKISS
1861–1865

• Petersburg

N

5 10 15   30

Scale in Miles